STECK-VAUGHN

PreGED
Language Arts, Reading

REVIEWERS

Robert Christensen
Principal
Handlon Correctional Facility
Michigan Department
of Corrections
Ionia, MI

Arnoldo Hinojosa
Senior Director
Community Initiatives
Harris County Department
of Education
Houston, TX

Linda Correnti
GED Staff Developer
Alternative Schools & Programs
New York City Department
of Education
New York, NY

Nancy Lawrence
E-teacher
KC Distance Learning, Inc.
Butler, PA

Dr. Gary A. Eyre
Consultant
GED Testing Service
Advance Associates
and Consultants
Phoenix, AZ

Charan Lee
Director
Adult Education
Anderson School Districts 1 & 2
Williamston, SC

Harcourt Achieve
Rigby • Saxon • Steck-Vaughn

www.HarcourtAchieve.com
1.800.531.5015

Executive Editor: Ellen Northcutt

Senior Editor: Donna Townsend

Associate Design Director: Joyce Spicer

Senior Designer: Jim Cauthron

Senior Photo Researcher: Alyx Kellington

Editorial Development: Learning Unlimited, Oak Park, IL

Photograph Credits: P.14 ©Richard Heinzen/SuperStock; p.88 ©Kwame Zikomo/SuperStock: p.148 ©Spencer Grant/Stock Boston; p.158 ©Eric Robert/CORBIS Sygma; p.178 ©Charlie Westerman/ImageState; p.186 Courtesy of Winston-Salem Journal; p.206 ©David Pollack/CORBIS. Additional photography by Getty Royalty Free.

Literary Acknowledgments

Acknowledgments for literary selections are on pages 259–260, which are an extension of this copyright page.

CONTENTS

How to Use this Book

The purpose of this book is to help you develop the foundation you need to pass the *GED Language Arts, Reading* Test. In this book, you will read selections from the types of nonfiction, fiction, poetry, and drama that are on the GED. You will also learn the reading strategies and critical thinking skills you will need to pass the GED Reading Test.

In the first unit of this book, you will read nonfiction selections from everyday life and the world of work as well as autobiographies and biographies, essays, and reviews. The units that follow will introduce you to selections from short stories, novels, poems, and plays.

Pretest and Posttest

The Pretest is a self-check to see which skills you already know. When you complete all the items in the Pretest, check your work in the Answers and Explanations section in the back of the book. Then fill out the **Evaluation Chart** that follows the Pretest. This chart tells you where each skill is taught in this book. When you complete the book, you will take a Posttest. Compare your Posttest score to your Pretest score to see that your skills have improved.

Lessons

Each unit is organized into lessons. Each lesson presents you with a passage to read actively. *Active reading* means doing something before you read, while you read, and after you read. By reading actively, you will improve your reading comprehension and critical thinking skills.

Lesson Opener (Before Reading) The first page of the lesson has three sections. The first section introduces the topic of the lesson. Next is the **Relate to the Topic** section, which features a brief exercise that helps you relate the topic to your life. Finally, the **Reading Strategy** section presents pre-reading techniques that you can apply to a passage in the lesson and to other reading materials. **Vocabulary** words important to the lesson are listed down the left-hand side of the page.

The Passage (During Reading) After you read the first part of each passage, you will see a thinking skills mini-lesson related to the passage with a question for you to answer. After you answer the question, you will continue reading the passage. This process usually occurs two or three times for each passage.

As you are reading the passage, you will see some words in bold type. These are the vocabulary words that you previewed on the first page of the lesson. When you see one of these words, try to figure out its meaning from the way it is used in the passage. Then if you are still not sure of the meaning, look up the word in a dictionary. You may want to keep a vocabulary notebook with pages titled, A, B, C, etc. You can record new words and their meanings in this notebook.

Thinking About the Passage (After Reading). This part of each lesson gives you an opportunity to do a variety of activities based on what you have just read. There are fill-in-the-blank, short answer, and multiple choice questions here. Answering the questions will help you decide how well you have understood what you've read and also provide another way for you to connect with the selection.

Reading at Work

Reading at Work is a two-page feature included in each unit. Each Reading at Work feature introduces a specific job, describes the reading skills the job requires, and includes a reading activity related to it. It also gives information about other jobs in the same career area.

Unit Reviews and Mini-Tests

Unit Reviews let you see how well you have learned the reading skills covered in each unit. Each Unit Review also includes an **Extension** activity that provides an opportunity for further practice with the type of reading in the unit.

Mini-tests follow each of the Unit Reviews. These timed practice tests allow you to practice your skills with the kinds of questions that you will see on the actual GED Test.

Answers and Explanations

Answers and Explanations to the exercises are listed at the back of this book on pages 225–256. Some exercise items have more than one possible right answer. In such cases, a sample answer is given.

Setting Goals

A goal is something you aim for, something you want to achieve. What is your long-term goal for using this book? You may want to get your GED or you may just want to become a better reader. These are large goals that may take you some time to accomplish.

Write your long-term goal for reading.

_____

_____

This section of the book will help you to think about how you already use reading skills and then to set some goals for what you would like to learn in this book. These short-term goals will be stepping stones to the long-term goal you wrote.

Check each activity that you do. Add more reading activities.

In my everyday life I

_____ read novels or short stories
_____ read newspaper or magazine articles
_____ read instructions and directions
_____ read forms to fill out
_____ other _____

_____

_____

List your experiences with reading.

What I've Liked | What I Haven't Liked

_____ | _____

_____ | _____

_____ | _____

_____ | _____

Think about your reading goals.

1. I decided to improve my reading skills when I _____

   _____

   _____

2. My reading goals include (check as many as you like)

   ☐ reading brochures and advertisements

   ☐ understanding legal documents

   ☐ increasing my enjoyment of stories and novels

   ☐ understanding poems

   ☐ becoming a regular newspaper reader

   ☐ improving my reading so that I can pass the GED

   ☐ understanding new words and increasing my vocabulary

   ☐ drawing conclusions based on what I've read

   ☐ applying what I've read to different situations

   ☐ understanding a writer's outlook and biases

   ☐ other _____

      _____

      _____

3. I will have met my long-term goal for reading when I am able to

   _____

   _____

   _____

Keep track of your goals.

As you work through this book, turn back often to this page. Add more goals at any time you wish. Check each goal that you complete.

Learn about the skills you have.

Complete the Pretest that begins on the next page. It will help you learn more about your strengths and weaknesses in reading. You may wish to change some items in your list of goals after you have taken the Pretest and completed the Pretest Evaluation Chart on page 13.

Use this Pretest before you begin Unit 1. Don't worry if you can't easily answer all the questions. The Pretest will help you find out which areas you are already strong in and which you need to study further.

Read each passage and answer the questions that follow. Check your answers on pages 225–226. Then enter your scores in the chart on page 13. Use the chart to figure out which content areas to work on and where to find them in this book.

When you are ready to begin, turn the page and read the first passage of the Pretest.

Read the following passage from the autobiography *Sosa: An Autobiography* **by Sammy Sosa with Marcos Bretón.**

By the time I first saw him in June 1989, Roger already had two Cy Young Awards and had been an MVP. But Roger was 8–4 going into the game that evening and was struggling a bit on a team that would just finish above .500 for the year. Still, I have to say that I have never seen anyone throw harder than Roger Clemens. His fastball just exploded, and I remember before the game Ruben Sierra walked up to me and said, "Roger Clemens tonight, rookie. Get ready."

We managed to push a run across in the fourth to cut Boston's lead to 3–1. Then I came up to bat in the top of the fifth, my second turn at the plate. The next day, the *Boston Globe* described the moment this way: "Clemens struck out the first batter, then faced Sosa, whom he had blown away with a high fastball in the first inning. Sosa got one that was slightly more manageable this time, and he put it into the net."

Home run. My first big-league homer, and I hit it off of Roger Clemens! I remember running around the bases and watching the ball fly over the Green Monster in left. And my hit made a difference. It totally silenced a rabid crowd of 34,338. And it seemed to have an effect on Roger—or so the papers said. "Clemens never seemed to recover," wrote the *Dallas Morning News*.

He walked the next two batters, gave up a couple of hits, and we blew the game open. When it was over, we had won 10–3, and I had the memory of a lifetime. My first big-league home run came against a superstar who later went on to be selected to baseball's All-Century Team. When I see the videotape of that homer today, I marvel at how young I looked. Compared to today, I looked skinny. And once I had connected, I didn't do anything but run around the bases quickly. Years later, my home run trot would be a little different.

On this night, back in the Dominican, people were celebrating right along with me.

Questions 1 through 5 refer to the passage on page 4.

Write the answer to each question.

1. What reason is given to explain why Sosa was able to hit the fastball from Clemens?

   _____

   _____

   _____

2. Sosa concludes that his hit made a difference. What are three details in the passage that support this conclusion?

   _____

   _____

   _____

Circle the number of the best answer for each question.

3. Which of the following sentences best states the main idea of the passage?
   (1) Clemens was a star but was having a difficult year.
   (2) Sosa was younger and thinner when he hit his first big league home run.
   (3) Clemens was up against a rookie but was unable to win the game.
   (4) Sosa struck out on the fastball that Clemens threw in the first inning.
   (5) Sosa's first big league home run was a memorable event.

4. What did Ruben Sierra most likely mean when he said to Sosa, "Roger Clemens tonight, rookie. Get ready"?
   (1) Roger Clemens was a rookie.
   (2) Roger Clemens would be a challenge for Sosa.
   (3) Roger Clemens didn't like rookies and pitched harder to them.
   (4) Roger Clemens would not be a challenge for a rookie.
   (5) Roger Clemens would be a good pitcher for Sosa to practice with.

5. Which of the following best describes the tone of this passage?
   (1) snobby
   (2) energetic
   (3) sarcastic
   (4) suspenseful
   (5) envious

Read the following passage from the novel *The Flower Drum Song* by C. Y. Lee.

He halted at the corner of Grant and Pine and wiped the perspiration on his forehead with a forefinger.

"*Shew*, we have walked a distance of five *li* from the bus station," he said in Mandarin. "Are you tired, May Li?"

"A little," the girl said. She was dressed in a Chinese gown of light blue and wearing a pigtail wound round her head, her pretty face without make-up glowing with health.

"Shall we go visit Mr. Poon now, father?"

"Oh, do not be so foolish. Nobody visits people so early. This is New Year's day, people sleep in the morning with a full stomach of food and wine and do not wish to be disturbed. We shall have our breakfast and rest our legs for a while." He wiped his forehead once more and looked around.

"Here is a teahouse, father," May Li said, pointing at a red signboard saying "Lotus Room."

"Good," Old Man Li said. When he looked at the stairway he frowned. "No, May Li, I shall not climb this with my luggage on my back."

"Let me carry it up for you, father," May Li said.

"No, you are carrying enough of your own."

"I can carry a lot more." She held her father's canvas bag until Li finally yielded it to her, shaking his head. "You are just like your mother, May Li. Forty years ago when she was your age she could carry a hundred catties of flour and walk seventy *li* a day. She was strong as a cow, and just as amiable. . . ."

"What shall we eat, father?" May Li asked.

"We shall see," Old Man Li said, trudging up the stairway. "We shall have some New Year dishes. But we must be careful in our selection. The owner of this place might be greedy, otherwise he would not have built a restaurant upstairs. He knows that people will eat more after this climbing, *shew!*"

When he reached the top of the stairs he promptly changed his opinion of the owner. The spacious dining hall with red-lacquered lattice windows was clean and impressive, almost filled with customers. Only a reputable place could be so prosperous, he thought. The smiling manager greeted them and directed them to a vacant table near one of the windows and handed them two copies of the menu with special New Year dishes attached to them. Old Man Li held the menu tensely, swallowing and resisting, his eyes roving among the expensive items. He wanted to eat everything, but he felt his economical nature held him back like an iron chain restraining a dog. He quickly closed the menu and rubbed his neck. "May Li, I shall let you order."

Questions 6 through 10 refer to the passage on page 6.

Write the answer to each question.

6. List two details about the restaurant that led May Li's father to believe the restaurant was reputable.

   _____

   _____

7. Why did Old Man Li let May Li order the food?

   _____

   _____

   _____

Circle the number of the best answer for each question.

8. Which of the following statements best describes May Li's father?
   (1) He is critical of his daughter.
   (2) He is energetic and high-spirited.
   (3) He is very generous with his money.
   (4) He doesn't believe in etiquette.
   (5) He is very fond of his daughter.

9. When Old Man Li compares his wife to a cow, what is he suggesting?

   That she was
   (1) ugly
   (2) very strong
   (3) fat
   (4) not very smart
   (5) a bad mother

10. Why does Old Man Li refuse to climb the stairs to the restaurant with his luggage on his back?
    (1) He was very hungry and eager to eat.
    (2) He believed May Li should carry it.
    (3) He was angry with the restaurant owner.
    (4) He thought it was safe to leave it downstairs.
    (5) He was quite tired from the walk.

Read the following passage from the play _A Doll's House_ by Henrik Ibsen.

HELMER: Oh, you think and talk like a heedless child.

NORA: Maybe. But you neither think nor talk like the man I could bind myself to. As soon as your fear was over—and it was not fear for what threatened me, but for what might happen to you—when the whole thing was past, as far as you were concerned it was exactly as if nothing at all had happened. Exactly as before, I was your little skylark, your doll, which you would in future treat with doubly gentle care, because it was so brittle and fragile. _(Getting up)_ Torvald [his first name]—it was then it dawned upon me that for eight years I had been living here with a strange man, and had borne him three children—. Oh, I can't bear to think of it! I could tear myself into little bits!

HELMER: _(sadly)_ I see, I see. An abyss has opened between us—there is no denying it. But, Nora, would it not be possible to fill it up?

NORA: As I am now, I am no wife for you.

HELMER: I have it in me to become a different man.

NORA: Perhaps—if your doll is taken away from you.

HELMER: But to part!—to part from you! No, no, Nora, I can't understand that idea.

NORA: _(going out to the right)_ That makes it all the more certain that it must be done. _(She comes back with her cloak and hat and a small bag which she puts on a chair by the table.)_

HELMER: Nora, Nora, not now! Wait till tomorrow.

NORA: _(putting on her cloak)_ I cannot spend the night in a strange man's room.

HELMER: But can't we live here like brother and sister—?

NORA: _(putting on her hat)_ You know very well that would not last long. _(Puts the shawl around her.)_ Good-bye, Torvald. I won't see the little ones. I know they are in better hands than mine. As I am now, I can be of no use to them.

HELMER: But some day, Nora—some day?

NORA: How can I tell? I have no idea what is going to become of me.

HELMER: But you are my wife, whatever becomes of you.

NORA: Listen, Torvald. I have heard that when a wife deserts her husband's house, as I am doing now, he is legally freed from all obligations towards her. In any case I set you free from all your obligations. You are not to feel yourself bound in the slightest way, any more than I shall. There must be perfect freedom on both sides. See, here is your ring back. Give me mine.

8

Questions 11 through 15 refer to the passage on page 8.

Write the answer to each question.

11. What does Torvald suggest he will do to keep Nora from leaving?

_____

_____

_____

12. Based on the stage directions, what will Nora probably do after she gets her ring back? How can you tell?

_____

_____

_____

Circle the number of the best answer for each question.

13. Which word gives the best meaning for "abyss"?
    (1) agreement
    (2) argument
    (3) gap
    (4) road
    (5) family

14. What do you learn about Torvald Helmer?
    (1) He has become a different man.
    (2) He does not really understand what Nora wants.
    (3) He understands why his wife is upset.
    (4) He has been a terrible and cruel husband.
    (5) He is pleased and excited by Nora's decision.

15. When Nora says that she was Torvald's "little skylark" and "doll," what is she suggesting?

    He
    (1) treated her like an equal
    (2) was mean to her
    (3) treated her like a pet or a toy
    (4) acted like her brother
    (5) had been the perfect husband

Read the poem "Sympathy" by Paul Laurence Dunbar.

I know what the caged bird feels, alas!
    When the sun is bright on the upland slopes;
When the wind stirs soft through the springing
    grass,
And the river flows like a stream of glass;
    When the first bird sings and the first bud opes,
And the faint perfume from its chalice steals—
    I know what the caged bird feels!

I know why the caged bird beats his wing
    Till its blood is red on the cruel bars;
For he must fly back to his perch and cling
When he fain would be on the bough a-swing;
    And a pain still throbs in the old, old scars
And they pulse again with a keener sting—
    I know why he beats his wing!

I know why the caged bird sings, ah me,
    When his wing is bruised and his bosom sore,—
When he beats his bars and would be free;
It is not a carol of joy or glee,
    But a prayer that he sends from his heart's deep
      core,
But a plea, that upward to Heaven, he flings—
I know why the caged bird sings!

Questions 16 through 21 refer to the poem on page 10.

Write the answer to each question.

16. What does the poet mean when he says, "old scars/And they pulse again with a keener sting—"?

   _____

17. Based on the poem, name two things the caged bird would like to see or do.

   _____

   _____

18. What do the words, "a stream of glass" suggest about how the river looks?

   _____

Circle the number of the best answer for each question.

19. What general truth about life is suggested by this poem?
   (1) All creatures suffer when they are trapped.
   (2) People should protest against cruelty to animals.
   (3) Caged birds should not be allowed to see what they are missing.
   (4) People can find true happiness only inside themselves.
   (5) If you feel unhappy, you should sing.

20. Which emotion does the author probably want the reader to experience while reading the poem?
   (1) joy
   (2) hope
   (3) yearning
   (4) fear
   (5) love

21. What kind of song would a person who feels like the caged bird be most likely to sing?
   (1) a song of thanksgiving
   (2) a patriotic march
   (3) a children's song
   (4) a blues song
   (5) a rock 'n' roll song

Read the following brochure.

Greenboro Recreation Center

Tennis classes are starting for all levels of experience. We want to introduce as many people as possible in the Greenboro area to this fantastic sport! Tennis is not only fun, it's great exercise! Tennis professionals will teach all classes. Bring your own racket or rent one from our pro shop.

Tennis is a sport for a lifetime; all ages and abilities can participate. Almost anyone can learn to play and enjoy tennis. It is a sport that does not require much time or cost large amounts of money. With tennis instruction and specialty camps you will dramatically improve your tennis game, while meeting new friends and having a great time. We look forward to seeing you on the court!

Our program can be customized to meet your personal goals, time constraints, specific limitations or injuries, playing style, temperament and personality. Novice players will learn the basics and benefit from our individualized attention. Intermediate players will refine their strokes and learn how to use their strengths to gain an advantage every time they walk on the court. Advanced players will further develop the skills they need to beat anyone—plus gain the knowledge of when to use each one.

Questions 22 through 24 refer to the brochure above.

22. Which of the following is the meaning of "customized"?
    (1) specifically designed
    (2) specifically reduced
    (3) partially limited
    (4) fully completed
    (5) highly qualified

23. What can be inferred about the recreation center?
    (1) It's an expensive place for wealthy tennis players.
    (2) It has tennis instruction mainly for serious players.
    (3) It wants to build its business by teaching all levels of tennis.
    (4) Its program caters mostly to children and families.
    (5) Its owners are not very interested in making money.

24. Which of the following best describes the tone of this passage?
    (1) friendly and encouraging
    (2) business-like and proper
    (3) technical and informative
    (4) detailed and elaborate
    (5) descriptive and poetic

Pretest Evaluation Chart

The chart below will help you determine your strengths and weaknesses in reading and interpreting different forms of literature and other written material.

Directions

Check your answers on pages 225–226. On the chart below, circle the number of each question that you answered correctly on the Pretest. Count the number of questions you answered correctly in each row. Write the number in the Total Correct space in each row. (For example, in the Fiction row, write the number correct in the blank before *out of 5*.) Complete this process for the remaining rows. Then add the four totals to get your Total Correct for the whole Pretest.

Content Areas	Questions	Total Correct	Pages
Nonfiction (Pages 14–97)	1, 2, 3, 4, 5, 22, 23, 24	_____ out of 8	Pages 52–57 Pages 16–21
Fiction (Pages 98–157)	6, 7, 8, 9, 10	_____ out of 5	Pages 118–123
Drama (Pages 158–185)	11, 12, 13, 14, 15	_____ out of 5	Pages 166–171
Poetry (Pages 186–213)	16, 17, 18, 19, 20, 21	_____ out of 6	Pages 194–199 Pages 200–205

Total Correct for Pretest _____ out of 24

If you answered fewer than 21 questions correctly, look more closely at the four content areas covered. In which areas do you need more practice? Page numbers to refer to for practice are given in the right-hand column above.

Nonfiction

Nonfiction writing is about real people, events, and issues. It can provide important factual information or express someone's point of view on a topic. The most common sources for nonfiction are newspaper and magazine articles, advertisements, legal documents, and other types of real-life writing. A nonfiction article can contain information about almost any topic from dog training to world affairs.

Nonfiction also includes essays, biographies, and true stories. Nonfiction books might tell about history, travel, geography or science.

Do you read part or all of a daily newspaper? _____

Which section of the newspaper do you like best? _____

Thinking About Nonfiction

You many not realize how often you come across nonfiction in your daily life. Think about your recent activities.

Check the box for each activity you did.

- ☐ Did you read the newspaper today?
- ☐ Did you read a review of a movie?
- ☐ Did you see an advertisement on a billboard?
- ☐ Did you read an article in a magazine?
- ☐ Did you look at a brochure for something you might buy?
- ☐ Did you read a book about the life of someone famous?
- ☐ Did you read and sign a legal document?

Write some other experiences you have had reading nonfiction.

_____

_____

Previewing the Unit

In this unit, you will learn:

- how brochures and advertisements try to persuade you

- how to understand manuals and legal documents

- about biographies and autobiographies

- about the incredible variety of topics found in essays and magazine articles

- how TV and book reviews can help you decide what to watch and read

Lesson 1	Brochures and Advertisements	Lesson 6	Biography
Lesson 2	Forms and Documents	Lesson 7	Autobiography
		Lesson 8	Essay
Lesson 3	Manuals and Handbooks	Lesson 9	Persuasive Essay
		Lesson 10	Magazine Article
Lesson 4	Legal Documents	Lesson 11	TV Review
Lesson 5	Biography	Lesson 12	Book Review

LESSON 1

Brochures and Advertisements

Vocabulary

hypnotized

antibiotics

symptoms

allergic

enhanced

clarity

Brochures and **advertisements** are designed to persuade people to accept certain ideas or to buy certain products. Should you believe everything you read in an advertisement or brochure? Certainly not. However, if you read carefully and use common sense, advertisements and brochures can be good sources of information.

Relate to the Topic

The purpose of the brochure on page 18 is to inform people about taking antibiotics.

Have you ever used information in brochures or advertisements to make healthcare decisions? What did you learn?

_____

_____

How was the information helpful? _____

_____

Reading Strategy

SKIMMING   When you **skim** written material, you read it quickly to identify the main idea. You can skim a brochure or advertisement just by reading the title and the headings. Headings are the titles of sections within the material, and they provide an outline of the main points that are covered. Read the title and the headings in the brochure on page 17. Then answer the questions.

1. What is the author of this brochure concerned about?

   _____

   Hint: Read the title carefully, especially the first two words.

2. Does the author believe that television affects children's ability to read? How do you know?

   _____

   Hint: Read the three headings.

This brochure might be provided by a school to help parents improve their parenting skills. As you read, try to figure out the main idea of the brochure.

Too Much Television and Your Child's Ability to Learn

Television shortens a child's attention span.

Have you watched television with your child recently? If you have, you know that children's television shows are filled with visual images that usually last two or three seconds. Loud music, explosions, and other sound effects grab your child's attention. Many children seem **hypnotized** by the bright colors and quick cuts.

The stories themselves are broken up into short segments separated by commercials. Children who watch a lot of television lose the ability to concentrate for long periods of time. In school, they may have difficulty listening to the teacher read a simple story from start to finish.

Television weakens a child's language skills.

Try this experiment. Spend 15 minutes just listening to the dialogue in a children's television show. What do you hear? When you take out the visual images, sound effects, and music, you will find that the characters speak in short phrases and incomplete sentences. To learn language, children need to hear a rich vocabulary and clear sentence structure. They also need to be able to ask and answer questions. Children's television shows usually don't provide these important requirements for learning language.

Television weakens a child's reading skills.

In a way, watching television is the opposite of reading. Reading a good book requires a long attention span, a rich vocabulary, and the ability to understand complex sentences. Reading encourages children to ask questions and use their imagination. Television attempts to do all the imagining for the viewer. If children spend too much time watching television, they may lose the ability to make a written story come to life in their minds.

Finding the Main Idea The main idea in a brochure is the most important idea. Often, the main idea is suggested by the title and the headings of the sections. The main idea of each section should support the overall main idea. Figuring out the main idea can help you understand the author's point of view.

The author of this brochure has a certain opinion about how television affects a child's ability to learn. Which statement best expresses the main idea of the brochure?

a. Watching too much television may make it difficult for a child to learn.
b. Watching too much television may cause a child to forget how to read.
c. Watching television can help a child learn how to read.

Brochures are often used to educate the public. You have probably seen healthcare brochures like the one below at a pharmacy or in your doctor's office.

Facts About Antibiotics

Have you ever taken **antibiotics** for an earache? After a few doses, your ear probably stopped hurting. After a few more doses, you may have felt completely cured. Perhaps you stopped taking the medicine, thinking that you could save the rest for another illness. Although this decision seems to make sense, doctors tell us that it could ruin our health.

Antibiotics are prescribed to fight infections. Sore throats, earaches, and other **symptoms** may be caused by the growth of bacteria in your body. As the antibiotics fight to destroy the bacteria, the bacteria struggle to become stronger. When you do not take all your medication, the bacteria may not be completely destroyed. In a short time, the infection may return, much stronger than before.

Always follow your doctor's instructions. Ask your doctor or pharmacist about the purpose of your medication. Find out exactly what you must do for the treatment to work. Antibiotics can help you only when you take them at the right time and in the right amounts.

Follow these tips:

- Take all the prescribed doses even after you begin to feel better.

- Take the medicine at the same time each day. Make a schedule. If you forget a dose, take it as soon as you remember. Then get back on schedule.

- Follow special instructions. Some antibiotics must be taken with food or milk. Others must be taken on an empty stomach.

- Find out what other medications, foods, or drinks to avoid while taking your prescription.

- Some people may be **allergic** to certain antibiotics. Ask your doctor or pharmacist what side effects to look for. Notify your doctor immediately if you get a rash or have difficulty breathing.

Locating Factual Details The details in a brochure support the main idea or purpose of the brochure. Details are facts about the subject. Factual details answer questions about who, what, when, where, why, and how. The brochure on this page gives details about why it is important to follow instructions carefully when taking antibiotics.

1. Reread the second paragraph. Why should you take all the medicine your doctor prescribed even after you feel better?
   a. Antibiotics can kill the bacteria that cause sore throats and earaches.
   b. The bacteria may not all be destroyed if you don't take all your medication.

2. Reread the list of tips. What should you do if you forget to take a dose of medicine?
   a. Take two doses of medicine next time.
   b. Take it as soon as you remember.

Print advertisements are everywhere. We see them on billboards and at bus stops. You have probably seen advertisements like the one below in magazines. As you read, think about how the author tries to persuade you to buy the product.

Don't You Deserve the Best Technology Money Can Buy?

Introducing the Award-Winning Enhanced WAVE-AUDIO Player from MicroTech!

It's Unlike Anything You'd Expect From a CD Player. It's Exactly What You'd Expect From MicroTech.

It's finally arrived: the new **Enhanced** WAVE-AUDIO Player from MicroTech. When it's high-quality sound that counts, you can count on MicroTech. You told us that you wanted clear high tones and deep, warm bass tones—all in an elegant, slim, space-age design. We took your suggestions back to our Sound Laboratory and produced the Enhanced WAVE-AUDIO Player. The compact CD player with built-in speakers takes up only 18 by 22 inches of table space, yet its sound can fill a concert hall.

With our unique CD400 audio engine, you'll never want to listen to music on any other CD player again. Be the first among your friends to own the CD player that *Music World* called the "Invention of the Year."

Experience the Enhanced WAVE-AUDIO Player at your local dealer or visit us today at www.microtech.com. We know you'll be delighted with the **clarity** of sound never before possible from a small CD player.

Understanding Persuasive Techniques An advertisement is a type of **persuasive writing.** In persuasive writing, authors often use strong emotional words to convince you to accept a certain point of view. Advertisements make claims that may not be true. Read advertisements carefully to separate facts from emotional claims about the product.

1. Which two phrases try to appeal to the reader's emotions?
   a. Don't you deserve the best?
   b. Be the first among your friends to own one.
   c. Our compact design takes up very little space.

2. Which of these claims is probably true?
   a. *Music World* called this CD player the "Invention of the Year."
   b. You'll never want to listen to music on any other CD player again.

 Check your answers on page 226.

Thinking About the Brochures and the Advertisement

Practice Vocabulary

The words below are in bold type in the passages. Study the way each word is used. Then complete each sentence by writing the correct word.

hypnotized	antibiotics	symptoms
allergic	enhanced	clarity

1. After sneezing several times, your friend decides that she may be _____ to cats.

2. The new, improved laundry detergent has _____ cleaning power.

3. The patient's _____ are a fever and a sore throat.

4. With my new glasses, I could see with greater _____

5. The crowd seemed _____ by the flashing lights of the police cars.

6. Medicines that fight infections are called _____

Understand What You Read

Write the answer to each question.

7. Look at the brochure on page 17. What are two reasons to limit the amount of time a child watches television?

_____

8. What will you hear when you listen to the dialogue in a children's television show?

_____

9. Look at the brochure on page 18. How do antibiotics get rid of some sore throats and earaches?

_____

10. Look at the advertisement on page 19. What are two claims made about the CD player in the advertisement?

_____

Apply Your Skills

Circle the number of the best answer for each question.

11. Look at the brochure on page 17. Which statement best expresses the main idea of the third paragraph?
    (1) Most television shows have too many loud sound effects.
    (2) Watching television may weaken a child's language skills.
    (3) Children often speak in short phrases and incomplete sentences.
    (4) Television encourages children to use their imaginations.
    (5) Children who watch television usually have long attention spans.

12. Look at the brochure on page 18. Based on the list of tips, which of these statements about antibiotics is true?
    (1) Antibiotics are mainly used to treat allergies.
    (2) You should never take antibiotics with milk.
    (3) You should stop taking antibiotics once your sore throat is better.
    (4) If you get well quickly, always throw away any pills that are left.
    (5) For antibiotics to work well, you need to take them on a schedule.

13. Look at the advertisement on page 19. Which of these persuasive phrases from the ad includes a fact about the CD player?
    (1) Don't you deserve the best technology money can buy?
    (2) It's unlike anything you'd expect from a CD player.
    (3) When it's high-quality sound that counts, you can count on MicroTech.
    (4) You'll never want to listen to music on any other CD player again.
    (5) Be the first among your friends to own the CD player that *Music World* called the "Invention of the Year."

Connect with the Brochures and the Advertisement

Write your answer to each question.

14. Think of a product such as clothing, shampoo, or car wax that you have bought based on information you read or heard in an advertisement. How did the advertisement convince you to try the product? Do you think the claims made in the advertisement were true? Why or why not?

    _____

    _____

15. Do you think that watching a lot of television is bad for adults? Why or why not?

    _____

    _____

Forms and Documents

Vocabulary

specify

references

authorize

certify

constitute

introductory

Forms provide a way to gather and organize information. You use many different kinds of forms as an employee, a citizen, and a consumer.

Documents are designed to communicate official or legal information. If you read and sign a document, you are agreeing to the terms in the document. Always read documents carefully before you sign them.

Relate to the Topic

Common documents include business reports, application forms, and credit card agreements.

Have you ever signed a legal document or an application form? Did you read the entire document before you signed it? Why or why not?

_____

_____

Did you feel you understood the document? If not, did you have any ideas about how to get help understanding it? What were they?

_____

_____

Reading Strategy

SKIMMING FORMS   Forms are often divided into sections with headings. You can get a good sense of the content of a form by skimming it and reading the headings. Read the three section headings on the form on page 23. Then answer the questions.

1.   In which section of the form will you write your address?

_____

Hint: Skim the form from the top.

2.   In which section of the form will you list your last job?

_____

Hint: Which heading or part of the form covers this topic?

When you apply for a job, you usually have to fill out an employment application. The application makes it easier for the people who make hiring decisions to get the information they need.

Employment Application

Section 1: General Information Use black ink. Be accurate and complete.

Name (First) (Middle) (Last)		Social Security #	Date

Address (Street, City, State, Zip)	Home Telephone #	Message Telephone

Are you at least 18 years of age? Yes ☐ No ☐ | Do you have proof of U.S. citizenship or a
If no, do you have a work permit? Yes ☐ No ☐ | U.S. permanent resident visa? Yes ☐ No ☐

Position Desired	Check One: Full-time ☐ Part-time ☐ Short term ☐ Other ☐

Available for Work:
Any hour ☐ Any day ☐ Other ☐ Please **specify:**

Section 2: Work Experience List your previous employment in order. Start with your most recent employer first. Write additional work experience on a separate page.

Dates From	To	Name and Address of Employer	Job Title	Wage or Salary	Reason for Leaving
		Company: Address: Supervisor:			
		Company: Address: Supervisor:			

Section 3: References List two **references.** Do not include relatives, persons employed by this company, or previous employers.

Name	Telephone #	Occupation
Name	Telephone #	Occupation

Understanding Organization To fill out any form, you need to understand its organization. Most forms are divided into sections. Each section has its own subject or purpose. Look for headings and instructions. Use the lines or boxes that separate sections to understand how a form is organized.

1. Read the section titles. In which section would you expect to write your home telephone number?
   a. Section 1: General Information   b. Section 3: References

2. Read the headings and instructions for Sections 2 and 3. In which section would you list a former teacher?
   a. Section 2: Work Experience   b. Section 3: References

Check your answers on page 227.

If you have health or dental insurance, you may have to fill out claim forms. These forms are often provided by your employer. Always read insurance forms carefully. Your claim may not be paid if the form is filled out incorrectly.

Group Dental Claim Form

Instructions to the Employee

1. Please type or print clearly using black ink.
2. Please answer questions in boxes 1 through 12 completely.
3. Sign and date the "Authorization to Release Information" on Line 13.
4. If you wish to have your benefits paid directly to the dentist, sign and date Line 14.
5. Sign and date the certification statement on Line 15.
6. Attach this form to your dental bill and mail to Dental Health, Inc.

1. Patient Name	2. Relationship to Employee Self ☐ Spouse ☐ Child ☐ Other ☐	3. Sex M ☐ F ☐	4. Patient Birthdate (m/d/y)
5. Employee Name (First, Middle, Last)	6. Employee Social Security #		7. Employee Birthdate (m/d/y)
8. Employee Address (Street Address, City, State, Zip)			
9. Account / Policy #	10. Employer's Name and Address		
11. Is patient covered by another dental plan? Yes ☐ No ☐	12. If yes, please indicate: Dental Plan Name: Group #:		
13. *Authorization to Release Information* — I hereby **authorize** the release of any information about my dental history or this treatment to the Insurer for the purpose of determining the benefits payable.	Signature of Patient or Parent		Date
14. *Authorization to Pay Benefits to Dentist* — I hereby authorize payment of benefits directly to my dentist.	Signature of Employee		Date
15. *Certification* — I **certify** the information I have provided is true and correct.	Signature of Employee		Date

Understanding Directions Always read the directions before you begin filling out a form. The directions may be written at the top or bottom of the form or even on the back of the page. When directions refer to a specific line or box, find that place on the form and think about what information you will put there.

Some directions are contained within the form. Box 5 on this form asks for the employee's name. The instructions in parentheses tell how to write the name. Some instructions use abbreviations. In box 3 the letter *M* stands for *male* and *F* stands for *female*. In box 4 the letters *m/d/y* stand for *month, day,* and *year.*

1. Look at box 4. What date do you write?
   a. today's date
   b. the patient's date of birth

2. Review the instructions at the top of the form. Should every patient sign lines 13, 14, and 15?
   a. Yes
   b. No

Credit card companies send all kinds of offers through the mail. Once you accept an offer, the company will send you a legal document that tells exactly what your responsibilities are to the credit card company. Read these documents carefully before you sign them. Make sure that you understand what you are agreeing to do.

CREDIT CARD AGREEMENT: I understand that the use of the enclosed credit card will **constitute** my acceptance of the terms and conditions listed below.

TERMS AND CONDITIONS

A. Annual Percentage Rate

With a balance transfer from another credit card account: I agree to pay a 5.9% **introductory** rate for purchases and balance transfers for the first six months the account is open; after that, a 12.9% rate on purchases and balance transfers. *Without an initial balance transfer:* I agree to pay a fixed 12.9% rate for purchases and balance transfers; the rate for cash advances is 19.9%.

B. Late Payments

If payment is received late once during the introductory period, the rate will adjust to 12.9% on purchases and balance transfers. If payment is received late twice within any six-month period, a 19.9% annual rate will immediately take effect.

C. Grace Period

Provided your previous balance was paid in full, you have a grace period of 20 to 25 days from the date of the statement to pay any balance arising from purchases. If the payment is made within the grace period, no interest will be charged.

D. Annual Fee

None.

E. Transaction Fee for Cash Advances

If you use your card to borrow cash, you will be charged a fee of 3% of the amount of each cash advance, but not less than $5 or more than $45.

Using Context Clues to Understand Meaning Documents often contain unfamiliar terms. When you come across an unfamiliar word, first look at the words and phrases around it. These surrounding words are the context. The context contains clues that can help you figure out the meaning of the unfamiliar word.

1. Reread section C. Based on the context, what is the meaning of the term "grace period"?
    a. a period of time in which the customer will not be charged interest
    b. a period of time in which the customer will pay a lower rate of interest

2. Reread section A. Based on the context clues in the section, what is a "balance transfer"?
    a. switching an amount of money owed to one credit card over to another
    b. changing the amount of interest owed after the introductory period ends

Thinking About the Forms and the Document

Practice Vocabulary

The words below are in bold type in the passages. Study the way each word is used. Then complete each sentence by writing the correct word.

authorize	certify	constitute
introductory	references	specify

1. Breaking a rule of the club will _____ an end to your membership.

2. When she applied for the job, Pat listed two friends

   as _____

3. A customer complained that there was an incorrect amount on her bill.

   Please ask her to _____ which amount is incorrect.

4. After you receive your new credit card, you will have a three-month

   _____ period when you will not pay any interest.

5. You can _____ a money transfer over the telephone by giving your account number and social security number.

6. Maria signed the job application form to _____ that the information in the form was true.

Understand What You Read

Write the answer to each question.

7. Read Section 1 of the Employment Application on page 23. Who would need to answer the question "Do you have a work permit?"

   _____

8. Look at the form on page 24. What is the purpose of box 2?

   _____

9. Why does box 13 in the Group Dental Claim Form require a signature?

   _____

10. Read section B of the Credit Card Agreement on page 25. What will cause the cardholder's interest rate to increase to 19.9%?

    _____

Apply Your Skills

Circle the number of the best answer for each question.

11. Look at the Employment Application form on page 23. Which of the following types of information would you include in Section 2?
    (1) the position you are applying for
    (2) whether you are seeking full- or part-time work
    (3) the occupation of one of your references
    (4) how much money you made at your last job
    (5) whether you have a work permit

12. Look at the Group Dental Claim Form on page 24. According to the instructions, what should an employee do in order to tell the insurance company to send payment directly to the dentist?
    (1) The employee should fill out boxes 1 through 4.
    (2) The employee should leave line 15 unsigned.
    (3) The employee should sign and date line 14.
    (4) The employee should check "Yes" in box 11.
    (5) The employee should attach the form to the dental bill.

13. Look at section E in the Credit Card Agreement on page 25. Which phrases provide a context clue for the meaning of the term "cash advance"?
    (1) not less than $5 or more than $45
    (2) you will be charged a fee
    (3) for the first six months the account is open
    (4) if the payment is made within the grace period
    (5) if you use your card to borrow cash

Connect with the Forms and the Document

Write your answer to each question.

14. Suppose you have a friend who is beginning a job search. What advice could you give about filling out employment applications?

    _____

    _____

    _____

15. Do you believe that companies should try harder to write documents in everyday language? Explain.

    _____

    _____

    _____

LESSON 3

Manuals and Handbooks

Vocabulary

probationary

reinstated

eligible

malfunction

affix

contaminated

Manuals and handbooks are usually not read from cover to cover. Instead they are used to find specific information. To find out your company's dress code, you would look in the employee handbook for that particular topic. To find out how to set the clock on your microwave oven, you would consult the owner's manual for that particular procedure.

Relate to the Topic

The procedure on page 31 describes how to handle dangerous spills at work. Think about an emergency situation that has happened or could happen at your job.

What is the situation? _____

_____

How would an employee know what to do? _____

_____

Reading Strategy

SKIMMING   Manuals and handbooks are usually divided into sections or chapters. Each of these sections has a title. If you know the information you want to find in a manual or handbook, you can skim it for the title of the section you need. For example, a section with the title "Using Your Microwave Oven" will tell you how to operate your new microwave safely. On page 29 is a section of an employee handbook. Read the title. Then answer the questions.

1. What kind of information would you expect to find in this section?

   _____

   Hint: Think about what a new employee might need to know.

2. Would you expect to find information about evacuating the building in an emergency in this section?

   _____

   Hint: Think about what the title means.

Most workplaces have an employee handbook to explain the company's personnel policies. Employees are usually given a copy of the handbook when they begin work.

Personnel Policies

Probationary Period

Your first six months of employment are a **probationary** period. During this time, your supervisor works closely with you to help you learn your duties. After six months, your supervisor will give you a written evaluation. If your work is satisfactory for this six-month period, you become a permanent employee with healthcare and retirement benefits.

Healthcare Benefits

As a permanent employee, you are entitled to sign up for a medical and dental healthcare plan. Your supervisor will give you a booklet explaining the various group insurance plans available to permanent employees. Please select a healthcare plan and go to the Human Resources Office, Room 201, to fill out the necessary paperwork.

Types of Leave

1. **Sick Leave:** Each full-time permanent employee earns eight hours of sick leave per month. For part-time employees, sick leave is based on the number of regular hours you are assigned to work. You may use sick leave for any illness, for pregnancy, or for visits to a doctor or dentist. You may also use sick leave when there is illness in your immediate family (parent, brother, sister, husband, wife, or child).

2. **Maternity Leave:** You may be granted maternity leave if you plan to return to work as soon as your doctor permits. By law, if you return to work within four months of the start of your leave, you must be **reinstated** in the position you held before the leave.

3. **Family Leave:** After one year of employment, you are **eligible** for family leave to handle urgent family matters. Family leave is limited to four months during a twenty-four-month period.

4. **Vacation Leave:** Full-time employees receive ten hours of vacation leave for each month worked with a maximum of 15 days per year. Part-time vacation leave is based upon the average number of hours worked per month. Vacation leave must be cleared with your supervisor.

Using Heads and Subheads Information in manuals and handbooks is often organized with heads and subheads. A head is the title of a section. It states the main idea of the section. Subheads are used to break the main section into smaller parts. When you read the heads and subheads, think about how the subheads are related to the main head.

1. Which of these is a kind of leave described in this policy manual?
   a. Family Leave
   b. Unpaid Leave

2. Which heading would you look under to find out more about your dental benefits?
   a. Sick Leave
   b. Healthcare Benefits

MANUALS AND HANDBOOKS

Check your answers on page 228.

Most electronic equipment comes with a manual. The manual provides operating instructions and explains safety guidelines.

Manual for Using Your New DVD Player

Thank you for purchasing this PARKER ELECTRONICS product. Please read these directions thoroughly in order to operate your DVD player properly. After you have finished reading the instructions, save them for future reference.

Inserting the Batteries into the Remote Control

While pressing the back cover, pull out in the direction indicated by the arrow and insert PR6 dry cell batteries. Make sure to match the plus (+) and minus (-) signs on the batteries with the plus and minus signs inside the battery compartment.

Handling the Discs

- Never play a scratched or warped disc. This may damage the player or cause it to **malfunction**. Also, do not **affix** paper or seals to the disc.
- Store the discs carefully. If you store discs stacked on top of each other, discs may become warped even when in their cases.
- Fingerprints on the disc may affect picture quality. To remove dirt or fingerprints, wipe gently from the center of the disc toward the outer edges. Never wipe discs with a circular motion.

Operating the DVD Player

Press the START button for the disc table to come out. Then, load the disc with the label side facing up, using the disc table guide to align the disc. Press START again to close the disc table. Play will begin automatically.

Scanning to Find Information You already know how to skim, or quickly read, written material to get the main idea. However, when you want to find more specific information, you **scan** the material. Scanning means to look quickly through all the material for the specific details you need, such as numbers, dates, amounts, and important words.

1. According to this manual, what size batteries are needed for the remote control?
   a. PR6
   b. D-cell
   c. 6

2. According to this manual, what is the proper way to remove fingerprints from a DVD disc?
   a. Affix a paper seal to the disc.
   b. Wipe the disc with a circular motion.
   c. Wipe the disc from the center to the outer edges.

Every job site, even an office, has safety procedures to help employees handle emergency situations. Safety procedures may be posted on bulletin boards or kept in special notebooks for employee use. The safety procedures below might be found in a handbook of emergency procedures for a healthcare facility, a community center, or a school office.

CLEANUP OF SPILLS RELATED TO ILLNESS AND INJURY

Goal: To prevent the spread of disease in the workplace.

General Information: Special handling and cleanup procedures are required for fluids that may contain blood or blood products. After contact with blood or other dangerous material, trained personnel must clean all equipment and work surfaces.

Use the following cleaning procedures:

Step 1: Put on appropriate protective clothing and equipment, including vinyl gloves, filter mask and/or face shield, and plastic apron or disposable coveralls.

Step 2: Wipe up any fluids with paper towels and dispose of them in a red trash bag with the biohazard warning symbol (shown here to the right).

Step 3: Clean all **contaminated** areas and materials first with soap and water.

Step 4: Follow with a freshly made bleach solution (1 part bleach to 9 parts cold water).

Step 5: Allow the bleach solution to remain on the contaminated surface for 5 to 10 minutes. Then rinse the area thoroughly with water to prevent damage to the surface from the bleach.

Note: If the spill occurs outside, use a hose with the water turned on at full force to wash down the area completely.

Step 6: If mops, brooms, dustpans, or other equipment have been used in the cleanup, rinse these items with the bleach solution.

For more information, call the Environmental Health and Safety Department.

Following a Sequence of Steps A procedure is a way to do something. Most procedures have a series of steps that must be done to reach a desired outcome. Usually, the steps must be done in a specific order, or **sequence.** When you read a procedure, make sure you understand the sequence of steps. Some steps may contain one or more related tasks. As you read, picture yourself performing each action. Try to understand why the sequence is the way it is.

1. Which statement describes the correct sequence of steps for cleaning up a spill related to illness or injury?
   a. After wiping the contaminated surface with paper towels, put on protective clothing.
   b. After putting on protective clothing, wipe the contaminated surface with paper towels.

2. When should you use the bleach solution?
   a. before cleaning the area with soap and water
   b. after cleaning the area with soap and water

 Check your answers on page 228.

Thinking About the Manual and the Handbooks

Practice Vocabulary

The words below are in bold type in the passages. Study the way each word is used. Then complete each sentence by writing the correct word.

contaminated	**eligible**	**malfunction**
probationary	**reinstated**	**affix**

1. When a tape recorder won't rewind a tape, there is a _____ in the rewinding mechanism.

2. The new employee's work during the _____ period was good.

3. Before you mail a letter, you must _____ a stamp to the envelope or the post office will not deliver it.

4. Bacteria in raw chicken _____ surfaces in the kitchen.

5. After two years, you will be _____ for our retirement plan.

6. After taking time off to care for his elderly father, Kyle was _____ to his former work assignment.

Understand What You Read

Write the answer to each question.

7. Look at the Personnel Policies on page 29. After six months, how will a supervisor give a new employee feedback?

_____

8. According to the Personnel Policies, when can an employee use sick leave?

_____

_____

9. Look at the DVD manual on page 30. What is the reason given to explain why DVD discs should not be stored stacked on top of each other?

_____

Apply Your Skills

Circle the number of the best answer for each question.

10. Look at the Personnel Policies on page 29. Your friend needs to help her mother move to a nursing home. She wants to find out how much time she can take off work without losing her job. Which heading would you tell your friend to look under to find the information she needs?
    (1) Probationary Period
    (2) Healthcare Benefits
    (3) Maternity Leave
    (4) Family Leave
    (5) Vacation Leave

11. Scan the DVD manual on page 30. What is the proper way to insert the batteries into the remote control?
    (1) Make sure that both batteries' plus and minus signs face the same direction.
    (2) Make sure the batteries' plus signs face in opposite directions.
    (3) Line up the plus and minus signs on the batteries and battery compartment.
    (4) Make sure the batteries' dry cells face the same direction.
    (5) Make sure the batteries both have plus and minus signs on them.

12. Look at the safety procedures on page 31. A young child at a day care center cuts her lip. She gets a small amount of blood on a table. After the day care worker puts on gloves and wipes the table with paper towels, what should she do next?
    (1) clean the table with soap and water
    (2) take the table outside and wash it with a garden hose
    (3) make a fresh bleach solution
    (4) rinse the table with clean water
    (5) dispose of the paper towels in a red trash bag

Connect with the Manual and the Handbooks

Write your answer to each question.

13. Suppose you are starting a new job. Your supervisor gives you a 100-page employee handbook. Should you read the entire handbook? Explain.

    _____

    _____

14. If you were writing the perfect instruction manual, what features (such as drawings or steps) would you include?

    _____

    _____

Legal Documents

Vocabulary

summoned

exempt

retained

incur

disbursed

prospective

liability

Legal documents spell out exact agreements between people. They carefully detail what each person, or party, is obligated to do. For example, an apartment lease obligates the landlord to provide an apartment that is in reasonably good condition, and it obligates the tenant to pay a certain amount of rent each month. Because these documents legally require you to do certain things, it is very important that you read them carefully before you sign them. Other examples of common legal documents include car loans, bank mortgages, and work contracts.

Relate to the Topic

The legal document on page 35 is a jury summons, or a notice to appear for jury duty. Have you ever been called to serve on a jury? Did you serve? Explain.

_____

_____

_____

Reading Strategy

SKIMMING   Parts of documents are often in **boldfaced,** or darker, type. In addition to headings in boldfaced type, documents may also contain individual boldfaced words. These words are boldfaced because they are particularly important in the document. As you skim a document, look for individual boldfaced words. Skim the document on page 35. Then answer these questions.

1. Write three words or phrases that are boldfaced in the document.

    _____

    Hint: Find the boldfaced words and phrases.

2. Why are the words "exempt" and "summoned" important in this particular document?

    _____

    Hint: Think about the purpose of this document.

Many people receive an official document informing them that they must appear for jury service. This document, called a jury summons, usually arrives in the mail to a registered voter.

Jury Summons

Dear Prospective Juror: You are hereby **summoned** to appear for jury service on the date and time specified below. If you do not adhere to the procedures in this summons, a penalty will be assessed.

Time: 9:15 a.m.
Date: October 18, 2003
Place: Stark County Courthouse, 1534 E. Franklin Street

Important: Please read carefully all information on this form. Bring the entire summons with you to court on the date and time specified. You are to appear promptly as instructed by this summons. If you have a disability or a special need, please notify the court immediately concerning requests for accommodation.

Failure to Answer Summons and Penalties: Any person who fails to comply with this summons is subject to a contempt action punishable by a fine of not less than $50 or more than $900.

Exempt or Disqualified: You do not need to appear in person if you are **exempt** or not qualified for jury service. You may be excused from jury service if:

- You have legal custody of a child or children younger than 10 years old and service on the jury would require leaving the child without adequate supervision.
- You are the primary caregiver of a person of any age who is an invalid and therefore unable to care for himself or herself. (This exemption does not apply to healthcare workers.)

You are disqualified for jury service if:

- You have ever been convicted of a felony.

Using Context Clues Context clues can help you figure out the meaning of an unfamiliar word or phrase. "Context" means the words and sentences surrounding the unfamiliar word.

You may need to read an entire sentence before or after an unknown word to get a sense of what that word means. Reread the sentence in the "Exempt or Disqualified" section above that contains the boldface word "exempt."

Which of the following words provides a clue to the meaning of the word "exempt"?

a. caregiver
b. to appear in person
c. excused from

People who buy new cars often trade in their used cars. Read the following section of a legal document that explains the agreement between the seller (the auto dealer) and the person who trades in a used car (the new car buyer).

New Car Buyer Agreement for Trade-in of Used Car

The value of the trade-in car listed on the first page of this document is based on the National Auto Dealers Association's *Used Car Guide* or any guide approved by the Commissioner of Motor Vehicles. This value may be further adjusted for mileage, improvements, or any major mechanical defects.

I agree to the following terms:

Trade-in Credit May Change. I agree that at the time the trade-in vehicle is delivered to the seller, should the value of my trade-in be diminished as a result of physical damage, alteration, or deterioration in mechanical condition other than normal wear and tear, the seller has the right to reappraise the vehicle. As a result of this reappraisal, I understand that the trade-in amount on my vehicle may be reduced.

Trade-in: Buyer's Obligations. At the time I deliver the trade-in vehicle to the seller, I promise to sign a Bill of Sale and a mileage certification statement and provide proof of ownership. I guarantee that I owe no money for the vehicle or for repairs to the vehicle, that emission control devices have not been altered, and that nothing has been removed, including the seat belts.

Buyer's Refusal to Purchase. I understand that the cash deposit I have given to the seller can be **retained** to offset seller damages if I refuse to complete my purchase. I also understand that I may be responsible for any damages the seller may **incur** if I fail to perform my obligations under the terms of this agreement.

Summarizing To summarize means to put information together into one overall idea. To help you understand a legal document, it is often helpful to summarize each paragraph as you read it.

1. Which of the following summarizes the main idea of the first paragraph?
   a. The value of the car is based on the mileage and any defects or improvements.
   b. The value of the car is based on a used car guide and other factors.

2. Which of the following is a summary of the section titled "Trade-in: Buyer's Obligations"?
   a. The seller promises to provide proof of ownership and to take care of any outstanding problems with the car.
   b. The seller promises to provide proof of ownership and pledges that there are no outstanding problems with the car.

An apartment lease includes all of the information a renter needs to understand the legal agreement with the landlord. The following apartment lease is typical.

Apartment Lease

This lease is in effect for one year from the date indicated on this lease. Tenant is responsible for payment of rent for the entire year and may not sublet. If Tenant must leave prior to the end of the lease period, Landlord must receive two months' notification.

Rent is due the first of every month and no later than the fifth day of the month. If the fifth day is a weekend or holiday, rent is due the following business day. Tenant is responsible for all utility payments including gas, electricity, and phone. Tenant is not responsible for shoveling snow or any work needed on the exterior of the building.

SECURITY DEPOSIT. Tenant shall pay to Landlord a security deposit of one month's rent to be held and **disbursed** for Tenant damages to the Premises or other defaults under this Agreement (if any) as provided by law. The security deposit will be deposited into an escrow account until the final day of the lease.

ACCESS BY LANDLORD TO PREMISES. Subject to Tenant's consent (which shall not be unreasonably withheld), Landlord has the right to enter the Premises to make inspections, provide necessary services, or show the unit to **prospective** buyers or workers. Landlord does not assume **liability** for the care of the Premises. In the case of an emergency, Landlord may enter without Tenant's consent. During the last three months of this lease, Landlord may show the Premises to prospective tenants, but may not make more than three appointments in any twenty-four hour period, or a total of six appointments per week.

Understanding Information Understanding what you read is especially important for legal documents like the lease above. Both the tenant and landlord must understand what a lease means when it is applied in specific situations. Based on your understanding of what the lease means, decide what to do in the following situations.

1. Suppose you are the landlord. The tenant notifies you that she is being transferred and has to move one month before the lease is up. She leaves without paying the last month's rent. What can you do?
   a. Nothing, because the tenant gave you one month's notice.
   b. Take the tenant to court for nonpayment of rent.
   c. Keep the entire security deposit.

2. Suppose you are the tenant. You are moving a new couch into the apartment and accidentally scratch the hardwood floor. According to the lease, what can the landlord do?
   a. Nothing, because there is no part of the lease that covers this possibility.
   b. Sue you in small claims court for damages to the apartment.
   c. Keep part or all of the security deposit to pay for the damages.

Thinking About the Legal Documents

Practice Vocabulary

The words below are in bold type in the passages. Study the way each word is used. Then complete each sentence by writing the correct word.

summoned	**exempt**	**retained**
incur	**prospective**	**liability**

1. She was not _____ from paying taxes on her tips from waiting tables.

2. She returned the video three days late and knew she would _____ an additional $3.00 charge.

3. Mack had no _____ for the car accident.

4. We _____ a lawyer to represent us.

5. As a _____ student , she hoped Central State College would accept her application for admission.

6. Angelo was _____ to the supervisor's office.

Understand What You Read

Write the answer to each question.

7. Look at the Jury Summons on page 35. What are two acceptable reasons for being excused from jury duty?

   _____

   _____

8. Look at the buyer's agreement on page 36. What reason might the car dealer have for changing his mind about the value of a trade-in vehicle?

   _____

   _____

9. Look at the Apartment Lease on page 37. In what situation could the landlord legally spend the security deposit?

   _____

   _____

Apply Your Skills

Circle the number of the best answer for each question.

10. Look on page 35 at the section titled "Exempt or Disqualified." Which phrase would be a context clue for the word "invalid"?
    (1) a primary caregiver
    (2) a person unable to care for himself or herself
    (3) a healthcare worker
    (4) a person of any age
    (5) a non-healthcare worker

11. Which of the following statements is the best summary of the section titled "Buyer's Refusal to Purchase" on page 36?
    (1) The seller keeps the cash deposit if the buyer doesn't buy the new car, but no other charges are allowed for any reason.
    (2) The buyer can stop the purchase agreement for any reason, including refusal to stick to the terms of the agreement.
    (3) If the buyer doesn't buy the new car, the seller can charge for damages.
    (4) If the buyer doesn't buy the new car or doesn't follow the agreement, the seller can keep the deposit and, if necessary, charge the buyer extra money.
    (5) If the seller decides not to sell the new car, the seller keeps the deposit.

12. Based on the Apartment Lease on page 37, what would you expect the landlord to do if he wanted to enter the apartment?
    (1) call the tenant for permission to enter
    (2) enter the apartment when the tenant is at work
    (3) call the police to let him in
    (4) call the tenant's lawyer to set up a time to enter the apartment
    (5) enter the apartment only in the evening or on the weekend

Connect with the Legal Documents

Write your answer to each question.

13. Have you ever bought or sold a used car? Did you read and understand the entire sales document? Why or why not?

_____

14. Think about a lease that you or someone you know has signed. Was there anything in the lease you thought was unfair? Explain.

_____

_____

Check your answers on page 229.

LESSON 5

Biography

Biography Biography

Vocabulary

dazzled

marquee

flurry

fraternity

anchorage

A **biography** is a true story about the life of a real person. It tells about the important events, people, and decisions in the person's life.

The author of a biography is called a **biographer.** Biographers often use diaries, letters, and other written records to get as much information as they can about the time and place in which the person lived. Whenever possible, authors interview the people they write about.

Relate to the Topic

The passage you are about to read takes place in Harlem, which is part of New York City. Langston Hughes is excited about being in Harlem even though he has never been to this place before. Can you remember the first time you were alone in a strange place?

Where were you? How did you feel?

_____

_____

Reading Strategy

ASKING QUESTIONS   Asking yourself questions while you read helps you understand what you are reading. It's also a good way to become more involved in what you are reading. You can relate what you have read to your own knowledge and experiences.

1. Read the first sentence on page 41. Write one question based on this sentence.

    _____

    _____

    Hint: What does the sentence make you curious about?

2. Read the rest of the first paragraph. Then write a question asking something you'd like to know about Langston Hughes.

    _____

    _____

    Hint: What more would you like to know about this person?

Langston Hughes: A Biography
by Milton Meltzer

Heading for Harlem he took his first subway ride. The train rushed madly through the tunnel, green lights punctuating the dark and stations suddenly glaring whitely and then blacking out. He counted off the numbered signs till 135th Street and got off. The platform was jammed with people—colored people—on their way to work. Lugging his heavy bags up the steps, he came out breathless on the corner of Lenox Avenue. The September morning was clear and bright. He stood there, feeling good. It was a crazy feeling—as though he had been homesick for this place he had never been to.

He walked down the block to register at the YMCA, the first place young Negroes stayed when they hit Harlem. That afternoon he crossed the street to visit the Harlem Branch Library. All newcomers were swiftly made at home there by Miss Ernestine Rose, the white librarian, and her *café-au-lait* [light coffee-colored] assistant, Catherine Latimer, who had charge of the Schomburg Collection. Here you could drown in thousands and thousands of books by and about black folks. That night, **dazzled** by the electric signs on the **marquee,** he went into the Lincoln Theatre to hear a blues singer.

Identifying Point of View A point of view is a way of looking at a situation. Biographers can tell a story from the point of view of an outsider and include only facts about a person, or they can tell both the facts and how the person feels.

In the passage above, Langston Hughes has been experiencing many new things. Instead of just giving the facts, the author tries to show the reader how Hughes feels. This helps readers see the story from Hughes' own point of view. Which sentence helps you understand how Langston Hughes feels about this new place?

a. He walked down the block to register at the YMCA . . . .

b. It was a crazy feeling—as though he had been homesick for this place he had never been to.

He had a week to himself before classes began at Columbia, and he spent every moment mapping Harlem with his feet. The great dark expanse of this island within an island fascinated him. In 1921 it ran from 127th Street north to 145th, and from Madison Avenue west to Eighth Avenue. Eighty thousand black people (it would be three times that number within ten years) were packed into the long rows of once private homes as the flood of Southern Negroes continued to roll North. It was a new black colony in the midst of the Empire City, the biggest of the many "Bronzevilles" and "Black Bottoms" beginning to appear across the nation.

Check your answers on page 230.

The high rents charged Negroes and the low wages paid them made Harlem a profitable colony for landlords and merchants, but a swollen, aching slum for the people who lived there. To the boy from the Midwest, however, this was not yet its meaning. He had been in love with Harlem long before he got there, and his dream was to become its poet. That first week of wonderful new insights and sounds passed swiftly. He loved the variety of faces—black, brown, peach, and beige—the richest range of types any place on earth. He hated to move out of Harlem, but his tuition was paid at Columbia and he felt he had to go. At the dormitory office they looked startled when he showed up for his room key. There must be some mistake, they told him; no room was left. He did not know it but Columbia did not allow Negroes to live in the dormitories. There was a big **flurry** when he insisted he had made a reservation long ago, by mail. He got the room finally, but it was a token of what was to come.

The university was too big, too cold. It was like being in a factory. Physics, math, French—he had trouble with all of them and the instructors were too busy or too indifferent to help. His only friend was Chun, a Chinese boy who didn't like Columbia either. Nobody asked the yellow man or the black man to join a **fraternity** and none of the girls would dance with them. Not being used to this, Chun expected them to. Langston didn't.

Nothing went right at school. Langston stopped studying, spent very little time on campus and all the time he could in Harlem or downtown. He made the city his school, read a lot of books, and dented his allowance badly buying tickets night after night for the all-Negro musical hit *Shuffle Along*, whose songs were written by Noble Sissle and Eubie Blake. His mother, separated again from Homer Clarke, showed up in New York and he had to help her with money while she looked for work.

Drawing Conclusions When you draw a **conclusion,** you make a decision or form an opinion based on facts and details. The facts and details are stated directly, but the conclusion is not.

To draw a conclusion from something you have read, you use two or more stated ideas to lead to a decision or opinion that is not directly stated. So, to draw a conclusion, you must go beyond the information a passage contains. However, you must be sure that your conclusion fits with the facts and details that are given in the passage.

After reading the passage above, the reader might conclude that Hughes was not comfortable at Columbia University. Which two ideas help lead to this conclusion?

a. The university was too big and too cold. It was like being in a factory.
b. He had been in love with Harlem long before he got there.
c. Langston stopped studying and spent very little time on campus.

All the time, feeling out of place at Columbia, he kept writing poems. That winter he sent several to *The Crisis,* [a publication put out by the National Association for the Advancement of Colored People (NAACP)] and in January his "Negro" appeared, with these lines, which open and close the poem:

I am a Negro:

Black as the night is black,

Black like the depths of my Africa.

The editors of *The Crisis* awoke to the fact that the boy who had been sending them poems from Toluca was now in New York. They invited him to lunch. Langston panicked, imagining they were all so rich or remote that he wouldn't know what to say. Much as he admired Dr. Du Bois, he was afraid to show the great man how dumb he was. He went, anyhow, taking along his mother for **anchorage.** Although they tried to put him at ease, telling him how much the readers liked his work, he was too scared to see any more of them.

Despite the little amount of time he said he spent on the campus, he did not do badly at Columbia. His final grades show three Bs, a C, and a failing F in physical education. He was given no grade at all in mathematics because he was absent so often. He made no honors, but he didn't care, perhaps because it was honor enough to see his poems printed in *The Crisis* month after month. One of the staff even arranged for him to read his poems at the Community Church. These were signs that he was not standing still. But neither was he moving in the direction his father wanted him to go. So he wrote and said he was quitting college and going to work. He wouldn't ask for money any more.

His father never answered.

Langston was on his own. His mother had gone back to Cleveland. He took a room by himself in Harlem, and began to hunt for a job. It was June 1922, and business was booming. At least it looked like it from the number of help-wanted ads in the papers. Langston wasn't trained for much, so he followed up the unskilled jobs. But no matter what he applied for—office boy, busboy, clerk, waiter—the employer would always say he wasn't looking for a colored boy.

He turned to the employment agencies. It was no use here, either. Where was the job for a black man who wanted to work? Everyone was trying to prove Langston's father was right: the color line wouldn't let you live.

Drawing Conclusions To draw a conclusion, look for and analyze a variety of ideas that relate to the same topic. Which idea from the last two paragraphs helps lead to the conclusion that African-American men were not given a fair chance to make a living in the early 1920s?

a. Langston was on his own and looking for a job.

b. It was June 1922, and business was booming.

c. No matter what job Hughes applied for, the employer would always say he wasn't looking for a colored boy.

Thinking About the Story

Practice Vocabulary

The words below are in bold type in the passage. Study the way each word is used. Then write each word next to its meaning.

dazzled	marquee	flurry
fraternity	anchorage	

1. a large, lighted sign _____

2. impressed by something shiny or fantastic _____

3. a means of feeling secure _____

4. a men's club on campus _____

5. a rush of activity _____

Understand What You Read

Write the answer to each question.

6. How did Hughes spend his first days in New York?

   _____

   _____

7. What did Hughes dream of doing when he went to Harlem?

   _____

   _____

8. What details support the conclusion that Hughes did not do badly at Columbia?

   _____

   _____

9. What are two reasons that Hughes had trouble finding a job?

   _____

   _____

10. What conclusion can you draw about the relationship between Langston and his father?

   _____

   _____

Apply Your Skills

Circle the number of the best answer for each question.

11. Which sentence best helps you understand the feelings and point of view Langston Hughes had about Columbia University?
    (1) Hughes had a week to himself before classes began.
    (2) The first week Hughes spent in Harlem was filled with new and wonderful insights.
    (3) Hughes spent hardly any time on campus and all the time he could in Harlem or downtown.
    (4) His final grades at Columbia were three Bs, a C and a failing F in physical education.
    (5) Langston went to an employment agency to look for a job.

12. Hughes had a meeting with the editors of *The Crisis*. Based on what you read in the passage, what can you conclude about *The Crisis*?
    (1) It is part of Columbia University.
    (2) It is a Negro musical hit.
    (3) It is a publication that includes poetry.
    (4) It is a division of the public library.
    (5) It is a New York restaurant.

13. Think about everything you have learned about Langston Hughes in this passage. What do you conclude he'll do next?
    (1) move back with his father
    (2) go back to Columbia University
    (3) go to Cleveland and live with his mother
    (4) get a high-paying job in an office
    (5) try to make a living writing poetry

Connect with the Story

Write your answer to each question.

14. Why do you think Langston's father never answered the letter Langston sent?

    _____

    _____

15. From the passage, you can tell that Hughes loved Harlem. Is there any place that you feel this way about (even if you have never been there)? Explain why or why not.

    _____

    _____

    _____

Biography

Biography

Biography

Vocabulary

radar

nuclear

radiation

inspire

geologist

fossil

Remember that a biography is a person's life story. Many biographies are about people who have helped to change the world, such as inventors, explorers, or scientists. Often biographers show why a person is famous. To do this, the author gives information about the important things the person did. Readers find out about inventions and discoveries that have changed the way we live.

Relate to the Topic

The passage you are about to read talks about the many inventions, theories, and accomplishments of the famous nuclear scientist Luis Alvarez. It also mentions some of the effects his work has had on society.

Name an invention or event from the past that you think has had an important effect on society. _____

How do you think the world might be different if this invention or event never happened?

_____

_____

_____

Reading Strategy

MAKING A PREDICTION   Most likely, the first thing you want to know when you start to read a story is what the story is about. How do you find this out? You probably do this without even thinking about it. You look at the title. Read the title and the first three paragraphs on page 47 to predict what the story is about. Then answer the questions.

1. Who is the biography about?

    _____

    Hint: Read the title.

2. Do you think Alvarez will participate in other scientific inventions?

    _____

    Hint: Did Alvarez take part in more than one scientific project?

Luis W. Alvarez by Corinn Codye

In 1939, World War II broke out in Europe. In 1940, [Luis] Alvarez joined a group of scientists who were designing a way to guide airplanes through fog or darkness.

Alvarez and his group built a **radar** system called Ground-Controlled Approach, or GCA. In this system, a radio signal bounces off a lost plane and back to the sender of the signal. Then a flight controller on the ground can guide the plane safely to the ground.

Later during the war, Alvarez worked in Los Alamos, New Mexico, on a secret project for the government. **Nuclear** scientists there were searching for a way to make a powerful new weapon, the atom bomb.

It was a tricky job. The **radiation** given off by the atoms in such a bomb is deadly to living things. Also, an accidental explosion would cause a terrible disaster. The project to build the bomb was a top-secret race, because the first country to build an atom bomb would have the power to win the war.

Recognizing Supporting Details Supporting **details** help explain the **main idea** of a paragraph. The main idea of the second paragraph above is that Alvarez helped build a radar system. The fact that in the system a radio signal bounces off a lost plane is a detail that supports the main idea. Which two details support the main idea that making the bomb was a tricky job?

a. There was a race to build the bomb.
b. The radiation given off by the atoms in such a bomb is deadly.
c. An accidental explosion would cause a terrible disaster.

Finally, in July 1945, the atom bomb, which the scientists called the "Little Boy," was ready. The government planned to drop the bomb on Japan. Alvarez had the job of measuring the energy released by the bomb that would be dropped from the plane. Alvarez, the atom bomb, and a handful of others were taken to a tiny island in the Pacific Ocean.

On August 6, 1945, three planes took off toward Japan. One carried the bomb, and another carried photographers to film the blast. The third held Alvarez and his team with their blast-measuring instruments. They watched out of the window as the plane flew high over Japan, heading for the city of Hiroshima.

Suddenly they heard the "ready" signal from the plane that held the atom bomb. Alvarez and his team hurried to launch their measuring equipment. The bomb fell 30,000 feet (about 9,000 meters) in 45 seconds, while Alvarez's equipment, attached to parachutes, floated gently above it. The planes made a hard turn and sped away. As Alvarez and his team flew away from the bomb, a bright flash hit the airplane. On their electronic screens, they saw the blast being recorded by their measuring instruments. The screens showed two shock waves—one from the blast itself, then a second wave after the shock hit the ground and bounced back into the air.

 Check your answers on page 231.

A few seconds later, two sharp shocks jolted their plane, hard. A giant mushroom-shaped cloud filled the sky, from the ground all the way to where they flew at 30,000 feet.

They flew around the mushroom cloud once before returning to their tiny island base. Since Alvarez could see nothing but green forests below, he thought they had missed the target. The pilot explained that the city had been *entirely* destroyed.

Alvarez felt sad when he thought of all the people who had lost their lives. He later wrote a letter to his four-year-old son. In it he said that he hoped the powerful and destructive atom bomb would **inspire** people to prevent future wars.

After the war, Alvarez worked again at the Radiation Laboratory at Berkeley. There he built a device called a hydrogen bubble chamber. With this device, Alvarez discovered that atoms and other particles, when driven through liquid hydrogen, leave a track of bubbles. The larger the chamber, the easier it is to see particle tracks. Using bubble chambers, Alvarez's team discovered many new atomic particles.

In 1968, Alvarez received the Nobel prize, which recognizes the highest achievements in the world. The Nobel description of his important work and discoveries in physics was the longest in the prize's history.

Understanding Cause and Effect A **cause** is a situation or an event that makes something happen. The **effect** is what happens as a result of the cause. Sometimes words such as "since" and "because" can help you recognize a cause-and-effect relationship that is directly stated.

Read this sentence from the passage: "Since Alvarez could see nothing but green forests below, he thought they had missed the target." In this sentence, the cause is that Alvarez could see nothing but green forests. It comes first in the sentence and is introduced by the word "since." The effect, or result, is that Alvarez thought they had missed the target.

Other cause-and-effect situations are not directly stated, or they do not have clue words to help you identify them. However, you can discover these unstated cause-and-effect relationships through careful reading.

Which item completes the sentence to make a cause-and-effect statement? There was a second shock wave after the bomb was dropped because
  a.   a giant mushroom-shaped cloud filled the sky
  b.   the shock hit the ground and bounced back into the air

Although his work with physics was very important, Alvarez may be best remembered for his work and "wild ideas" in a field he knew nothing about until age sixty-six. After retiring from the University of California, he began working with his son, Walter, who is a **geologist.** One day Walter gave his father a piece of layered rock from the mountains of Italy. The rock contained a mystery about the history of the earth.

The rock showed a clay layer that had formed 65 million years ago, the same time that the dinosaurs disappeared from the earth. The layer below the clay was filled with **fossil** shells. The layer above the clay also had shells, but they were almost entirely different. This showed that most of the animals living before the clay layer was formed had become extinct, or died out.

The two Alvarezes, father and son, studied the clay layer. They discovered large amounts of iridium, an element that comes mainly from outer space. They suggested that a body from outer space, 5 miles (about 8 kilometers) across, had hit the earth. Its crash set off a tremendous explosion, worse than all the atom bombs in the world put together. They suggested that the dust and smoke from the explosion covered the earth with a thick black cloud that blocked the sun. The dust settled after a few months, forming a $\frac{1}{2}$-inch (about $1\frac{1}{4}$-centimeters) clay layer all the way around the earth. The Alvarezes suggested that without sunlight, most green plants died, and the animals—including the dinosaurs—starved and froze.

The Alvarez team tested their ideas carefully. For example, did the iridium come from erupting volcanoes instead of from outer space? They proved that the large amount of iridium in the clay layer could only have come from space.

Luis Walter Alvarez, one of the world's greatest nuclear scientists, died on August 31, 1988. Only a few months earlier, a newly discovered asteroid was named *Alvarez* in honor of his and Walter's work.

Drawing Conclusions A conclusion is a decision or opinion based on facts. Luis and Walter Alvarez drew some conclusions after analyzing the rock from Italy. They compared the layer above the clay to the layer below the clay. Because of the differences between these layers, they concluded that the animals who lived before and after the clay layer formed were very different.

What are two other conclusions they made after analyzing the rock?
a.   Iridium found in the clay came from erupting volcanoes.
b.   A large body from space hit the earth, setting off a huge explosion.
c.   Dust and smoke from the explosion covered the earth.

Thinking About the Story

Practice Vocabulary

The words below are in bold type in the passage. Study the way each word is used. Then write each word next to its meaning.

radar   nuclear   radiation

inspire   geologist   fossil

1. harmful particles given off by the nuclei (centers) of atoms

    _____

2. the remains of a plant or animal preserved in the Earth's crust

    _____

3. a system that uses radio waves to locate objects_____

4. having to do with the centers (nuclei) of atoms_____

5. a scientist who studies Earth and how it was formed

    _____

6. influence or motivate_____

Understand What You Read

Write the answer to each question.

7. According to the passage, Luis Alvarez may be best known for what accomplishment or idea?

    _____

    _____

8. What were two of Alvarez's other accomplishments?

    _____

    _____

9. What was Alvarez's role in the bombing at Hiroshima?

    _____

    _____

10. What were two ways in which Luis Alvarez was honored as a scientist?

    _____

    _____

Apply Your Skills

Circle the number of the best answer for each question.

11. Which detail supports the statement that the Alvarez team tested their ideas carefully?
    (1) The dust settled after a few months.
    (2) The dust formed a clay layer around the earth.
    (3) They proved that the large amount of iridium could not have come from erupting volcanoes.
    (4) Alvarez received the Nobel prize.
    (5) Alvarez was one of the world's greatest nuclear scientists.

12. What did Luis Alvarez hope would be the effect of dropping "Little Boy" on Japan?
    (1) America would win the war.
    (2) Future wars would be avoided.
    (3) His son would be inspired to become a scientist.
    (4) He would become famous.
    (5) Scientists would stop nuclear research.

13. Luis and Walter Alvarez concluded that early animals died of starvation or froze to death during a short period in Earth's history. Which fact supports this conclusion?
    (1) A large black cloud blocked off all sunlight.
    (2) A clay layer formed on Earth at the same time that the dinosaurs disappeared.
    (3) Fossil shells were found in both layers of the rock.
    (4) The rock held a mystery about Earth.
    (5) Dinosaurs no longer exist.

Connect with the Story

Write your answer to each question.

14. How do you think the bombing of Hiroshima affected people's feelings about war? Give reasons for your opinion.

_____

_____

15. What discovery, invention, or accomplishment would you like to make? Why? How would it affect the way people live?

_____

_____

_____

BIOGRAPHY

Check your answers on page 231.

LESSON 7

Autobiography

Autobiography
Autobiography

Vocabulary

iron road

power of thunder

prisoner's house

big water

fire-boat

moons

Some autobiographies take a look at a world that no longer exists. As an author writes about his or her own life, the reader gets the opportunity to discover what life was like in a different era through the eyes of someone who actually lived at that time.

This story is about Black Elk, a member of the Oglala Sioux who left his people to travel with Buffalo Bill's Wild West Show. Black Elk hoped to learn more about the "white man," whom his people called the *Wasichu*.

Relate to the Topic

In the passage you are about to read, Black Elk wants to help his people find a peaceful way of living with the new white settlers. He hopes that by living among the *Wasichu* he will discover how to reach this goal. During his travels, Black Elk feels very homesick.

Have you ever tried to be a peacemaker between people? What happened?

_____

Have you ever traveled far from your home? How did you feel?

_____

Reading Strategy

PICTURING THE SETTING   The setting of a story is where the story happens. The setting could be a restaurant, a baseball game, or an African village. The setting also includes the time and the atmosphere. For example, a story might take place in a crowded, noisy restaurant at lunchtime. Read the title and first two paragraphs of the passage on page 53 to picture the setting. Then answer the questions.

1. What time of day is it when this story begins?

_____

Hint: Read the first sentence.

2. Where is Black Elk as the story begins?

_____

Hint: Look at the first sentence of each of the first two paragraphs.

UNIT 1. NONFICTION

Black Elk Speaks as told through
John G. Neihardt (Flaming Rainbow)

That evening where the big wagons were waiting for us on the **iron road,** we had a dance. Then we got into the wagons. When we started, it was dark, and thinking of my home and my people made me very sad. I wanted to get off and run back. But we went roaring all night long, and in the morning we ate at Long Pine. Then we started again and went roaring all day and came to a very big town [Omaha, Nebraska] in the evening.

Then we roared along all night again and came to a much bigger town [Chicago]. There we stayed all day and all night; and right there I could compare my people's ways with Wasichu ways, and this made me sadder than before. I wished and wished that I had not gone away from home.

Then we went roaring on again, and afterwhile we came to a still bigger town—a very big town [New York]. We walked through this town to the place where the show was [Madison Square Garden]. Some Pawnees and Omahas were there, and when they saw us they made war-cries and charged, couping us. They were doing this for fun and because they felt glad to see us. I was surprised at the big houses and so many people, and there were bright lights at night, so that you could not see the stars, and some of these lights, I heard, were made with the **power of thunder.**

We stayed there and made shows for many, many Wasichus all that winter. I liked the part of the show we made, but not the part the Wasichus made. Afterwhile I got used to being there, but I was like a man who had never had a vision. I felt dead and my people seemed lost and I thought I might never find them again. I did not see anything to help my people. I could see that the Wasichus did not care for each other the way our people did before the nation's hoop was broken.

Comparing and Contrasting Remember that comparing two things means saying the ways they are alike. **Contrasting** means saying the ways they are different.

Which statement contrasts two things?

a. The Pawnees and Omahas made war-cries when they saw Black Elk.
b. The Wasichus did not take care of each other the way the Sioux did.

Both sentences are about two tribes, but only one sentence presents a contrast between the two. In the first sentence, the Pawnees and the Omahas are alike because they both made war-cries when they saw Black Elk. In the second sentence, the Wasichus and Sioux are different because one group, the Sioux, took care of each other and the other group, the Wasichus, did not. This sentence shows a contrast.

They would take everything from each other if they could, and so there were some who had more of everything than they could use, while crowds of people had nothing at all and maybe were starving. They had forgotten that the earth was their mother. This could not be better than the old ways of my people. There was a **prisoner's house** on an island where the **big water** came up to the town, and we saw that one day. Men pointed guns at the prisoners and made them move around like animals in a cage. This made me very sad, because my people too were penned up in islands, and maybe that was the way the Wasichus were going to treat them.

In the spring it got warmer, but the Wasichus had even the grass penned up. We heard then that we were going to cross the big water to strange lands. Some of our people went home and wanted me to go with them, but I had not seen anything good for my people yet; maybe across the big water there was something to see, so I did not go home, although I was sick and in despair.

They put us all on a very big **fire-boat,** so big that when I first saw, I could hardly believe it; and when it sent forth a voice, I was frightened. There were other big fire-boats sending voices, and little ones too.

Afterwhile I could see nothing but water, water, water, and we did not seem to be going anywhere, just up and down; but we were told that we were going fast. If we were, I thought that we must drop off where the water ended; or maybe we might have to stop where the sky came down to the water. There was nothing but mist where the big town used to be and nothing but water all around.

We were all in despair now and many were feeling so sick that they began to sing their death-songs.

Identifying Point of View Looking at events through the eyes of another person can help you see the world in a new way. Often a person from another culture has a different point of view. Black Elk sees the white man's culture with the eyes of a Native American. It is not the same way the white men would see their own culture.

In the passage so far, Black Elk is describing his experiences in the Wasichu's world. Black Elk says, "They had forgotten that the earth was their mother." How do you think Black Elk feels about the white man?

a.   He thinks that they are not kind to their mothers.

b.   He thinks that they do not respect nature.

When evening came, a big wind was roaring and the water thundered. We had things that were meant to be hung up while we slept in them. This I learned afterward. We did not know what to do with these, so we spread them out on the floor and lay down on them. The floor tipped in every direction, and this got worse and worse, so that we rolled from one side to the other and could not sleep. We were frightened, and now we were all very sick too. At first the Wasichus laughed at us; but very soon we could see that they were frightened too, because they were running around and were very much excited. Our women were crying and even some of the men cried, because it was terrible and they could do nothing. Afterwhile the Wasichus came and gave us things to tie around us so that we could float. I did not put on the one they gave me. I did not want to float. Instead, I dressed for death, putting on my best clothes that I wore in the show, and then I sang my death-song. Others dressed for death too, and sang, because if it was the end of our lives and we could do nothing, we wanted to die brave. We could not fight this that was going to kill us, but we could die so that our spirit relatives would not be ashamed of us. It was harder for us because we were all so sick. Everything we had eaten came right up, and then it kept trying to come up when there was nothing there.

We did not sleep at all, and in the morning the water looked like mountains, but the wind was not so strong. Some of the bison and elk that we had with us for the show died that day, and the Wasichus threw them in the water. When I saw the poor bison thrown over, I felt like crying, because I thought right there they were throwing part of the power of my people away.

After we had been on the fire-boat a long while, we could see many houses and then many other fire-boats tied close together along the bank. We thought now we could get off very soon, but we could not. There was a little fire-boat that had come through the gate of waters and it stopped beside us, and the people on it looked at everything on our fire-boat before we could get off. We went very slowly nearly all day, I think, and afterwhile we came to where there were many, many houses close together, and more fire-boats than could be counted. These houses were different from what we had seen before. The Wasichus kept us on the fire-boat all night and then they unloaded us, and took us to a place where the show was going to be. The name of this very big town was London. We were on land now, but we still felt dizzy as though we were still on water, and at first it was hard to walk.

We stayed in this place six **moons;** and many, many people came to see the show.

Understanding Sequence The **sequence** of events is the order in which events happen in a story. Most writers tell the events in a story in sequence. They tell what happens first, what happens next, and what happens after that. Sometimes writers use clue words like "first" and "next." Sometimes they just put the events in the order they occur, without using these time-order words.

Black Elk describes the trip from New York to London in sequence.

Which item describes the first main event on this trip?
a.   The ship passed through bad weather and high seas.
b.   The crew members became very ill.
c.   The ship left New York.

Thinking About the Story

Practice Vocabulary

The words and phrases below are in bold type in the passage. Study the way each word or phrase is used. Then match each word or phrase with its meaning. Write the letter.

_____ 1. iron road

_____ 2. power of thunder

_____ 3. prisoner's house

_____ 4. big water

_____ 5. fire-boat

_____ 6. moons

a. ocean
b. months
c. electricity
d. railroad
e. prison
f. steamship

Understand What You Read

Circle the letter of the best answer to each question.

7. How did Black Elk feel after he left his people?
   a. glad
   b. homesick

8. What can you conclude about what the sailors thought of their Native American passengers?
   a. The sailors looked down on them.
   b. The sailors respected them.

Write the answer to each question.

9. Why did Black Elk decide to leave home?

   _____

   _____

10. How did Black Elk feel about New York City?

   _____

   _____

11. What was the ocean voyage like from New York to London?

   _____

   _____

Apply Your Skills

Circle the number of the best answer for each question.

12. Black Elk feels like crying when he sees the bison and elk being thrown overboard. What do you think he compares this act to?
    (1) the end of the Wild West Show
    (2) the end of the railroad trip
    (3) the end of the Wasichu way of life
    (4) the end of the Native American way of life
    (5) the end of the European way of life

13. Black Elk was a holy man of the Oglala Sioux. But when he was in New York, he felt like a man who "never had a vision." How would you describe his point of view in that statement?
    (1) He felt like he could not see well.
    (2) He felt like he was in a bad dream.
    (3) He felt like he understood the Wasichu culture.
    (4) He felt like he had no strength to face death.
    (5) He felt like he had lost his spirit.

14. Which event happened last in the passage?
    (1) Black Elk joined the Wild West Show.
    (2) Black Elk traveled on the railroad.
    (3) Black Elk performed for six months with the Wild West Show in London.
    (4) Black Elk traveled from New York to London.
    (5) Black Elk performed with the Wild West Show in Madison Square Garden.

Connect with the Story

Write your answer to each question.

15. Why do you think Black Elk was so unhappy living in the Wasichu's world?

    _____

    _____

16. Have you ever been in a situation where you seemed to be out of place? How did you feel? What did you decide to do?

    _____

    _____

    _____

    _____

LESSON 8

Essay

Essay

Essay

Vocabulary

retain

abruptly

obligations

prior

realign

hierarchy

Essays are short works of nonfiction in which the writer expresses a feeling or an opinion about a specific topic. An essay can be about any topic, from everyday problems to major global issues. To get our interest, the author appeals to our common sense and emotions. The author's approach in an essay can be serious or humorous. Either way, the author's purpose is to express a certain point of view.

Relate to the Topic

The essay "Back When a Dollar Was a Dollar" on page 61 talks about how the value of a dollar has changed over the years.

Have you noticed a change in the value of the dollar since your childhood? How has that change affected your life?

_____

_____

_____

Reading Strategy

RELATING TO THE EXPERIENCE   Comparing your own experience to the situation in the essay can help you understand the topic. Read the title and the first two paragraphs on page 59. Then relate them to your experience by answering the questions.

1. Does the author think most people are good at giving directions?

    _____

    Hint: Read the second paragraph carefully.

2. Do you think most people are good or bad at giving directions? Why?

    _____

    _____

3. Have you ever given someone directions? Was it easy or difficult?

    _____

    _____

Street Directions by Andy Rooney

Where do streets go in a strange city and where do they come from?

If America wants to save gas, it ought to start over with its street signs and give everyone directions on how to give directions. It would not do this country any harm at all if there were college courses on the subject of direction giving.

Someone will say, "Go down here and turn left at the third traffic light. Keep going until you run into a dead end at Sixteenth Street, then bear right."

Those are simple enough, so you set out to follow directions. Within ten minutes you're at the corner of Broad and 4th streets, hopelessly lost. You never saw a Sixteenth Street. You feel either stupid and frustrated for not being able to follow simple directions or you feel outraged at the person who gave them to you.

I've often wanted to go back, find the guy and grab him by the throat. "All right, fella. You told me to turn left at the third traffic light and then keep going until I hit a dead end at Sixteenth. You were trying to get me lost, weren't you? Confess!"

It wouldn't be any use though. I know what he'd say. He'd say, "That's not counting this light right here. If you count this light, it's four."

Or he'd say, "Maybe it's Eighteenth Street where the dead end is . . ." or "You see, Sixteenth Street turns into Terwilliger Avenue after you cross Summit Boulevard."

Whatever his answer is, it's hopeless. He didn't mean to mislead you and you didn't mean to get lost, but that's what usually happens.

You can't lay all the blame on the people giving directions. People don't *take* them any better than they give them.

My own ability to **retain** directions in my head ends after the first two turns I'm given. Then I usually say to whomever I'm with, "Did he say right or left at the church on the right?" If there are seven or eight turns, including a couple of "bear rights" and a "jog left" or two, I might as well find a motel room and get a fresh start in the morning.

Understanding the Author's Tone When people speak or tell a story, they use tone of voice to show how they feel. So, you not only need to listen to what they say, but also how they say it.

Authors use tone in their writing, too. The **tone** of a passage reflects the author's attitude or feelings about the topic. When you read, you must pay attention to what authors say as well as how they say it. An author's tone may be angry, humorous, sad, happy, or serious.

Which statement from the essay best shows the author's humorous tone?

a. You can't lay all the blame on the people giving directions.

b. My own ability to retain directions in my head ends after the first two turns I'm given.

The superhighways that bisect and trisect our cities now aren't any help at all in finding your way around. Streets that used to lead across town in a direct fashion now end **abruptly** where the highway cut through. Finding the nearest entrance to the superhighway, so you can drive two miles to the next exit in order to get a block and a half from where you are, is the new way to go.

If they do start college courses in direction giving, I hope they devote a semester to arrow drawing for signmakers. It seems like a simple enough matter, but it is often not clear to a stranger whether an arrow is telling you to veer off to the right or to keep going straight.

Different towns and cities have different systems for identifying their streets with the signs they erect. Some have the name of the street you are crossing facing you as you drive past. Others identify the street with a sign that is parallel to it. This is more accurate, but you can't see it. And if you don't know which system they're using, it's further trouble.

There are cities in America so hard to find your way around that, unless you're going to live there for several years, it isn't worth figuring them out.

Many cities, like Washington, pretend to be better organized than they are. They have numbers and they use the alphabet just as though everything was laid out in an orderly fashion.

New York City, for example, has numbered avenues that run longitudinally up and down the island. What the stranger would never know is that in midtown the names go from Third Avenue to Lexington, to Park, and then to Madison before the numbers start again with Fifth Avenue. Where did Fourth Avenue go? Sorry about that, that's what we call "Park."

And then "Sixth Avenue" is next? Well, not actually. New Yorkers call it "Sixth," but the official name and the name on the signs is "Avenue of the Americas." No one calls it that but the post office.

I have long since given up asking for directions or reading maps. I am one of that large number of lost souls who finds that, in the long run, it's better simply to blunder on until you find where you're going on your own.

Understanding the Author's Tone One way to create a humorous tone is to use exaggeration. When authors exaggerate, they make a situation sound better or worse than it really is. Another way to exaggerate is by offering unlikely solutions to problems. For example, the author of this essay exaggerates the problem of giving directions by suggesting that colleges should offer courses on how to give directions.

Which two items are examples of exaggeration?
a.   The author suggests a course for signmakers on making arrows.
b.   The author suggests that superhighways don't help drivers find their
      way around.
c.   The author suggests that if directions are too complicated, he might as
      well get a hotel room and try again the next day.

Back When a Dollar Was a Dollar
by Diane C. Arkins

I remember dollars. When I was growing up in the not-so-distant '50s and '60s, dollars used to be wonderful things.

Just one of them could fund a month's worth of kindergarten milk-money **obligations**—with change to spare. You could buy 10 newspapers. You could mail a hundred post cards. You could easily top off the tank when you borrowed Dad's car. Why, even Malcolm Forbes used to throw himself a birthday bash for $49.95.

Yessir. Back then, with a shine on your shoes and a buck in your pocket, you could really go places. Yet Mom and Dad made certain that we understood the clear connection between the Work Ethic and spending those hard-earned $$$.

The American Way also meant a careful look **prior** to leaping with your signature on a dotted line of double-digit interest payments.

But somehow, some time, some*where* along the way, it happened. When we weren't looking, the feds managed to redefine the currency in which . . . we trusted. They seem far too eager to pencil in a few extra zeros on their growing mountains of red ink. And from Jane Taxpayer's point of view, Washington's current juggling—debt ceilings, capital gains, wage floorings—looks like a shotgun marriage between *Let's Make a Deal* and the old "new math."

It's time for Washington's creative accounting to be accountable. Perhaps instead of promoting a policy of dreaming up new prefixes to add to the word "million," the feds could benefit from a refresher course on the value of a buck. Here are some suggestions to help Washington **realign** its outlook and put a "punch" back into middle America's pocketbook.

Welcome to Money Management 101.

Require all members of Congress to redecorate their homes by shopping at the Pentagon Specials Hardware Store, where toilet seats are always on sale for $795.

Arrange for the Washington **hierarchy** to get back to basics and collect their vacation pay at minimum wage.

Reorganize frequent-flier discounts. Whenever Donald Trump flies, 200 working stiffs fly free.

Help Congress understand the true meaning of those extra budgetary zeros—make them collect a million-billion-zillion bottle caps just to see what that number actually represents before they agree to spend it.

Comparing and Contrasting Comparing two things means finding the ways they are alike. **Contrasting** means finding the ways they are different. You can contrast the two essays because the subject of one (money) is serious, while the subject of the other (directions) is not serious. You can also compare the two essays.

The two essays are alike because they both use a _____ tone.

Check your answers on page 233.

Thinking About the Essays

Practice Vocabulary

The words below are in bold type in the passages. Study the way each word is used. Then complete each sentence by writing the correct word.

retain	abruptly	obligations
prior	realign	hierarchy

1. The _____ of a police officer are to serve and to protect.

2. The game stopped _____ when the thunder and lightning started.

3. It is sometimes hard to _____ information that you don't use often.

4. To keep the peace, both sides need to _____ their thinking.

5. _____ to getting the job, she spent several years in college.

6. Workers must move up the company _____ to get better-paying jobs.

Understand What You Read

Write the answer to each question.

7. After reading the first essay, what can you conclude about getting around in some cities in the United States?

_____

_____

8. What important point about the government does the author make in "Back When a Dollar Was a Dollar"?

_____

_____

9. How would you describe Diane Arkins' attitude toward the United States government?

_____

_____

Apply Your Skills

Circle the number of the best answer for each question.

10. Which of the following is the best example of the humorous tone of "Street Directions"?
    (1) "That's not counting this light right here. If you count this light, it's four."
    (2) Different towns and cities have different systems for identifying their streets with the signs they erect.
    (3) New York City, for example, has numbered avenues that run longitudinally up and down the island.
    (4) Those are simple enough, so you set out to follow directions.
    (5) If America wants to save gas, it ought to . . . give everyone directions on how to give directions.

11. Which of the following alternative titles best reflects both the content and the tone of "Back When a Dollar Was a Dollar"?
    (1) "Let's Go Back to the Good Old Days"
    (2) "Money Management—Government Style"
    (3) "When a Dollar Could Buy Ten Newspapers"
    (4) "Shopping at the Pentagon Specials Hardware Store"
    (5) "Welcome to the 'New Math'"

12. Which statement is the best example of a comparison?
    (1) Our parents understood the connection between working hard and spending money.
    (2) Both essays could be considered complaints.
    (3) Some cities identify the street with a sign that is parallel to it.
    (4) In the '50s and '60s, dollars used to do wonderful things.
    (5) New Yorkers call it "Sixth Avenue," but the official name is "Avenue of the Americas."

Connect with the Essays

Write your answer to the question.

13. These two essayists wrote about things that annoy them. Is there something that often annoys you? Tell what it is and write a brief suggestion about how to solve the problem.

    _____

    _____

    _____

    _____

Check your answers on page 233.

Persuasive Essay

Some essayists want to do more than just describe a point of view. They want to persuade the reader to agree with that point of view. **Persuasive essays** often explain a problem or situation and then suggest what can be done about it. Authors use both facts and opinions to persuade readers to agree with them and take action.

Relate to the Topic

In the essay you are about to read, the author gives her opinions about peace and war. She tries to persuade the reader to agree with her ideas.

Do you believe that there will ever be peace on Earth? Why or why not?

_____

_____

_____

Reading Strategy

UNDERSTANDING PURPOSE   In most cases, the purpose of an essay is to inform, entertain, or persuade the reader. The purpose is different from the topic, however. For example, the topic may be low-fat recipes, but the purpose might be to inform people about healthful eating. The essay on page 65 is about an air raid, armed airplanes attacking a target on the ground. Read the title and the first paragraph on page 65. Then answer the questions.

1. What is the topic of this essay?

    _____

    Hint: Read the title.

2. Read the first paragraph. Do you think that the purpose of this article is to inform, entertain, or persuade the reader?

    _____

    Hint: Is the author trying to influence the reader?

Vocabulary

disarmament

imperative

subdued

sterile

compensate

Thoughts on Peace in an Air Raid
by Virginia Woolf

Up there in the sky young Englishmen and young German men are fighting each other. The defenders are men, the attackers are men. Arms are not given to the Englishwoman either to fight the enemy or to defend herself. She must lie weaponless tonight. Yet if she believes that the fight going on up in the sky is a fight for the English to protect freedom, by the Germans to destroy freedom, she must fight, so far as she can, on the side of the English. How far can she fight for freedom without firearms? By making arms, or clothes or food. But there is another way of fighting for freedom without arms; we can fight with the mind. We can make ideas that will help the young Englishman who is fighting up in the sky to defeat the enemy.

Distinguishing Fact from Opinion A **fact** is a statement that can be proved true. An **opinion** is a belief or judgment—a statement of what someone thinks. People can disagree with opinions, but they can't argue about the truth of facts.

An example of a fact in the passage is the statement that men are fighting in the sky. At the time the essay was written, anyone who looked up and listened could see that there was an air battle going on. The author's belief that the English were fighting to protect freedom is an opinion. People could have different ideas about why the English were fighting.

Which two of these statements about the passage are facts?
a. Englishwomen are not given weapons.
b. Englishwomen can fight with their minds.
c. The defenders are men, the attackers are men.

A bomb drops. All the windows rattle. The anti-aircraft guns are getting active. Up there on the hill under a net tagged with strips of green and brown stuff to imitate the hues of autumn leaves guns are concealed. Now they all fire at once. On the nine o'clock radio we shall be told "Forty-four enemy planes were shot down during the night, ten of them by anti-aircraft fire." And one of the terms of peace, the loudspeakers say, is to be **disarmament.** There are to be no more guns, no army, no navy, no air force in the future. No more young men will be trained to fight with arms. That rouses another mind-hornet in the chambers of the brain—another quotation. "To fight against a real enemy, to earn undying honour and glory by shooting total strangers, and to come home with my breast covered with medals and decorations, that was the summit of my hope. . . . It was for this that my whole life so far had been dedicated, my education, training, everything. . . ."

Check your answers on page 233. **65**

Those were the words of a young Englishman who fought in the last war. In the face of them, do the current thinkers honestly believe that by writing "Disarmament" on a piece of paper at a conference table they will have done all that is needful? Othello's occupation will be gone; but he will remain Othello. The young airman up in the sky is driven not only by the voices of loudspeakers; he is driven by voices in himself—ancient instincts, instincts fostered and cherished by education and tradition. Is he to be blamed for those instincts? Could we switch off the maternal instinct at the command of a table full of politicians? Suppose that **imperative** among the peace terms was: "Child-bearing is to be restricted to a very small class of specially selected women," would we submit? Should we not say, "The maternal instinct is woman's glory. It was for this that my whole life has been dedicated, my education, training, everything. . . ." But if it were necessary, for the sake of humanity, for the peace of the world, that child-bearing should be restricted, the maternal instinct **subdued,** women would attempt it. Men would help them. They would honour them for their refusal to bear children. They would give them other openings for their creative power. That too must make part of our fight for freedom. We must help the young Englishmen to root out from themselves the love of medals and decorations. We must create more honourable activities for those who try to conquer in themselves their fighting instinct, their subconscious Hitlerism. We must compensate the man for the loss of his gun.

Understanding Persuasion Remember that the purpose of persuasive writing is not only to get readers to agree with a point of view, but also to get them to act. However, authors of persuasive essays do not always state the actions they want the reader to take. Often they use words that will convince the reader that an action is necessary. Strong words such as "should," "must," and "necessary" suggest that something has to be done.

Which two of the following statements are examples of persuasion?
a. There are to be no more guns, no army, no navy, no air force in the future.
b. We must help the young Englishmen to root out from themselves the love of medals and decorations.
c. We must compensate the man for the loss of his gun.

The sound of sawing overhead has increased. All the searchlights are erect. They point at a spot exactly above this roof. At any moment a bomb may fall on this very room. One, two, three, four, five, six . . . the seconds pass. The bomb did not fall. But during those seconds of suspense all thinking stopped. All feeling, save one dull dread, ceased. A nail fixed the whole being to one hard board. The emotion of fear and of hate is therefore **sterile,** unfertile. Directly that fear passes, the mind reaches out and instinctively revives itself by trying to create. Since the room is dark it can create only from memory. It reaches out to the memory of other Augusts—in Beyreuth, listening to Wagner; in Rome, walking over the Campagna; in London. Friends' voices come back. Scraps of poetry return. Each of those thoughts, even in memory, was far more positive, reviving, healing and creative than the dull dread made of fear and hate. Therefore if we are to **compensate** the young man for the loss of his glory and of his gun, we must give him access to the creative feelings. We must make happiness. We must free him from the machine. We must bring him out of his prison into the open air. But what is the use of freeing the young Englishman if the young German and the young Italian remain slaves?

The searchlights, wavering across the flat, have picked up the plane now. From this window one can see a little silver insect turning and twisting in the light. The guns go pop pop pop. Then they cease. Probably the raider was brought down behind the hill. One of the pilots landed safe in a field near here the other day. He said to his captors, speaking fairly good English, "How glad I am that the fight is over!" Then an Englishman gave him a cigarette, and an Englishwoman made him a cup of tea. That would seem to show that if you can free the man from the machine, the seed does not fall upon altogether stony ground. The seed may be fertile.

At last all the guns have stopped firing. All the searchlights have been extinguished. The natural darkness of a summer's night returns. The innocent sounds of the country are heard again. An apple thuds to the ground. An owl hoots, winging its way from tree to tree. And some half-forgotten words of an old English writer come to mind: "The huntsmen are up in America. . . ." Let us send these fragmentary notes to the huntsmen who are up in America, to the men and women whose sleep has not yet been broken by machine-gun fire, in the belief that they will rethink them generously and charitably, perhaps shape them into something serviceable. And now, in the shadowed half of the world, to sleep.

Understanding the Author's Purpose To persuade readers, authors must include facts and examples that support their opinions. The purpose of including these facts and examples is to help readers understand why these opinions make sense.

One opinion the author offers is that fear and hatred are sterile, unfertile emotions. The author supports this opinion with the example that all thinking stops during moments of great fear. Another opinion from the passage is that if men are freed from the machines of war, all sides in a conflict may become more caring. What fact or example supports this opinion?

  a. the fact that the pilot landed safely in a nearby field
  b. the example that the pilot was given a cigarette and a cup of tea after he was captured

Thinking About the Essay

Practice Vocabulary

The words below are in bold type in the passage. Study the way each word is used. Then complete each sentence by writing the correct word.

disarmament	imperative	subdued
sterile	compensate	

1. If a feeling is _____ , it is reduced.

2. In a _____ agreement, all parties state that they will put down their weapons.

3. A _____ thought is one that lacks creativity.

4. If something is _____ , it is usually urgent or necessary.

5. To _____ , you must replace what is taken away.

Understand What You Read

Write the answer to each question.

6. How does the author describe the feeling she had while she waited for the bomb to drop?

_____

_____

_____

7. The author is concerned about the effects of disarmament. She thinks that we must help men overcome their desire to fight by giving them other creative outlets. Why does she think so?

_____

_____

_____

8. How does the author describe a person's state of mind after a feeling of fear has passed?

_____

_____

_____

Apply Your Skills

Circle the number of the best answer for each question.

9. Which of the following is one of the author's opinions?
   (1) "Forty-four enemy planes were shot down during the night. . . ."
   (2) ". . . that was the summit of my hope . . ."
   (3) The young airman . . . is driven by voices in himself. . . .
   (4) They point at a spot exactly above this roof.
   (5) All feeling, save one dull dread, ceased.

10. Why does the author include the example of women giving up child-bearing if it were necessary for world peace?
    (1) to suggest that women are better than men
    (2) to make women aware of the overpopulation problem
    (3) to compare women's responsibilities with men's
    (4) to encourage Americans to stay out of the war
    (5) to urge women to have careers instead of families

11. Which statement from the passage is meant to convince the reader to take action?
    (1) No more young men will be trained to fight with arms.
    (2) Those were the words of a young Englishman who fought in the last war.
    (3) "It was for this that my whole life so far had been dedicated . . ."
    (4) We must free him from the machine.
    (5) "How glad I am that the fight is over!"

Connect with the Essay

Write your answer to each question.

12. What would you have been thinking about if you had been in the author's situation, waiting through an air raid? Explain.

    _____

    _____

    _____

13. Have you ever felt strongly about an issue or tried to persuade someone to take action? Has someone tried to persuade you? What was the issue or the action? Were you or the other person persuaded?

    _____

    _____

    _____

Magazine Article

Magazine Artic

Magazine articles can be written about a wide variety of topics. Authors write about people, places, and events. Topics could involve current issues or events from the past. A magazine article might even predict what life will be like in the future. Whatever the topic, a magazine article presents information that will interest the reader.

Relate to the Topic

The article you are about to read describes the experiences of two athletes who took a stand on something they strongly believed in.

Have you or someone you know ever spoken out against something you thought was unfair or unjust? What was it?

_____

What happened? _____

_____

_____

Reading Strategy

ASKING QUESTIONS   Asking questions as you read helps you understand what you are reading and think about what the author may say next. There are no right or wrong questions; just ask yourself what you would like to know next. Read the title and the first paragraph on page 71. Then answer the questions.

1. Write a question you have after reading the title.

    _____

    Hint: What information is not given in the title?

2. Write a question you have after reading the first paragraph.

    _____

    Hint: Is there anything more you would like to know?

Vocabulary

gesture

calculated

deprived

vindication

reprimanded

irrevocable

A Courageous Stand by Kenny Moore

As the Olympics began, Smith was a man in search of a **gesture.** "It had to be silent—to solve the language problem—strong, prayerful and imposing," he says. "It kind of makes me want to cry when I think about it now. I cherish life so much that what I did couldn't be militant, not violent. I'll argue with you, but I won't pick up a gun.

"We had to be heard, forcefully heard, because we represented what others didn't want to believe. I thought of how my sisters cringed because they didn't want me to embarrass the family by describing how poor we were, when we *were* poor. No one likes to admit flaws, even though it's the first step to fixing them."

Symbols began to present themselves to him. He asked Denise [Smith's wife] to buy a pair of black gloves. A few days before his race, Smith knew what he would do. He did not tell Carlos. Until the race was over, Carlos was a competitor. . . .

After the semifinals of the 200 two days later, it appeared that Smith would not stand on any victory platform. Carlos won the first semi in 20.11, unbothered by running in the tight inside lane. Smith took the second semi in 20.13, but as he slowed, he felt a jab high in his left thigh. "It was like a dart in my leg. I went down, not knowing where the next bullet was coming from."

Using Context Clues To help understand the meaning of an unfamiliar word, look at the words and sentences around it for clues to its meaning. Such words and sentences give **context clues** that help show what the unfamiliar word means. This passage includes some sports terms that may be unfamiliar. The word "race" helps you figure out that "200" is probably the distance of the race.

Use context to figure out the meaning of these unfamiliar terms.

1. Reread the first paragraph. What do you think the word "militant" means?
   a. gentle and kind
   b. ready to fight
2. Find the terms "20.11" and "20.13" in the fourth paragraph. What do you think they refer to?
   a. the times at which the races occurred
   b. how fast Carlos and Smith ran the races

As he crouched on the track, he knew he had strained or torn an adductor muscle. All the work, he thought, was now useless. He raised his head and saw before him a familiar pair of hunting boots. They belonged to his San Jose State coach, Winter, who got him up, walked him to ice, packed his groin and then wrapped it.

The final was two hours later. "Thirty minutes before it, I went to the practice field," Smith says. "I jogged a straightaway, then did one at 30 percent. It was holding. I did one at 60 percent, then one at 90. It held. . . . Don't let there be any delays, I thought."

As the eight finalists were led into the stadium, Carlos remembers saying to Smith, "I'm going to do something on the stand to let those in power know they're wrong. I want you with me."

Smith, Carlos recalls, said, "I'm with you."

"That made me feel good," says Carlos. "And it made the medal mean nothing. Why should I have to prove my ability when they'd just take it away somehow? I made up my mind. Tommie Smith gets a gift."

They were placed on their marks. "I took no practice starts," says Smith. "John was in Lane 4. I was in 3. I **calculated** it this way: Come out hard but keep power off my inside leg on the turn with a short, quick stride. Then in the straightaway I'd maintain for four strides and attack for eight."

At the gun, Carlos was away perfectly. Smith ran lightly and with building emotion. He felt no pain. Carlos came out of the turn with a 1½-meter lead. Then, a man unto himself, he swiveled his head to his left and, he says, told Smith, "If you want the gold, . . . come on." Smith didn't hear him. Eighty thousand people were roaring as Smith struck with his eight long, lifting strides. They swept him past Carlos.

"I pulled back on the reins," Carlos says now. "America **deprived** our society of seeing what the world record would have been."

"If Carlos wants to say that," Smith says, "I applaud him for his benevolence."

"The medal meant more to Tommie," says Carlos. "Everyone got what he wanted, even Peter Norman." Carlos slowed so much that Norman, an Australian sprinter, caught him at the line for second.

When Smith knew he had won, he threw out his arms. He still had 15 meters to go. "I guess if I'd calculated a 12-stride attack, the time would have been 19.6," Smith says now. That record would have stood to this day.

Understanding Cause and Effect Remember that a cause is what makes something happen. The effect is what happens. In the passage, Smith showed that he supported Carlos. Smith's support had an important effect on Carlos. Carlos felt that winning the medal was no longer important since he had Smith's support.

During the race, Carlos slowed down. What two effects did that action have?
a. Smith came in first place.
b. Smith hurt his leg.
c. Norman came in second place.

He crossed the line with his arms outflung at the angle of a crucifix. His smile was of joy, relief and **vindication.** When he came to a stop, he felt resolve cool and strong in him.

The medalists were guided through a warren of stone tunnels under the stadium to a room that held their sweatsuits and bags. "It was a dungeon under there," says Smith.

He went to Carlos. "John, this is it, man," he said. "All those years of fear, all the suffering. This is it. I'll tell you what I'm going to do. You can decide whether you want to."

"Yeah, man," said Carlos. "Right."

"I got gloves here. I'm going to wear the right. You can have the left." Carlos slipped it on.

Smith explained the symbolism of the gloves, the scarf, the stocking feet and the posture. "The national anthem is a sacred song to me," Smith said. "This can't be sloppy. It has to be clean and abrupt."

"Tommie, if anyone cocks a rifle," said Carlos, "you know the sound. Be ready to move."

Silver medalist Norman, who is white, overheard these preparations, and Carlos asked him if he would participate in the protest. Norman agreed, and Carlos gave him a large Olympic Project for Human Rights button. Norman pinned it to his Australian sweatsuit.

"I thought, in the '50s, blacks couldn't even *live* in Australia," says Smith. "And now he's going back there after doing this." (Norman would be severely **reprimanded** by Australian sports authorities.)

Smith, Norman and Carlos were placed behind three young Mexican women in embroidered native dress, each of whom carried a velvet pillow. Upon each pillow lay a medal. IOC vice-president Lord Killanin of Ireland, who would succeed Brundage [the president of the International Olympic Committee who had been accused of ignoring the civil rights issue] in four years, and the president of the International Amateur Athletic Federation, the Marquess of Exeter, led them to the ceremony.

"As Killanin hung the medal around my neck and shook my hand," says Smith, "his smile was so warm that I was surprised. I smiled back. I saw peace in his eyes. That gave me a two- or three-second relaxation there, to gather myself."

Along with his gold medal, Smith received a box with an olive tree sapling inside, an emblem of peace. He held the box in his left hand, accepting it into his own symbolism.

Then the three athletes turned to the right, to face the flags. *The Star-Spangled Banner* began. Smith bowed his head as if in prayer and freed his young face of expression. Then he tensed the muscles of his right shoulder and began the **irrevocable** lifting of his fist.

Predicting Outcomes You can use the information given in the passage and what you already know to **predict** the outcome of the story. The passage says that Peter Norman was severely reprimanded by Australian sports authorities, but it does not tell what else happened after the protest.

What do you predict happened as a result of Carlos' and Smith's protest?

a. Their protest caused people around the world to recognize the problem of racism.

b. Sports authorities in the United States praised their protest.

Thinking About the Article

Practice Vocabulary

The words below are in bold type in the passage. Study the way each word is used. Then write each word next to its meaning.

gesture	**calculated**	**deprived**
vindication	**reprimanded**	**irrevocable**

1. prevented from having or using something _____

2. unable to be changed _____

3. severely criticized _____

4. the act of being proved right _____

5. figured, estimated _____

6. an action that shows a feeling _____

Understand What You Read

Write the answer to each question.

7. What does Smith mean by "the language problem"?

_____

8. How did Norman, the Australian sprinter, share in the protest?

_____

_____

9. Why wasn't Smith expected to win the final race?

_____

_____

10. Why did Smith and Carlos want to make a protest?

_____

_____

_____

_____

_____

Apply Your Skills

Circle the number of the best answer for each question.

11. What did Carlos mean when he said, "I pulled back on the reins"?
    (1) He was riding a horse in the race.
    (2) He slowed down.
    (3) He grabbed Smith's shoelaces.
    (4) He started to run faster.
    (5) He realized he couldn't win the race.

12. What did Carlos predict would have happened if he had not slowed down?
    (1) Norman would have won the race.
    (2) Smith would not have hurt himself.
    (3) Smith would have won the race anyway.
    (4) Carlos would have won the race and set a world record.
    (5) There would not have been a protest.

13. What do you predict happened to Smith and Carlos after their protest?
    (1) They won more races at the Olympic Games.
    (2) They received medals honoring them for their protest.
    (3) They were suspended from the rest of the Olympic Games.
    (4) They hosted a television program about racial injustice in America.
    (5) They became officials of the International Olympic Committee.

Connect with the Article

Write your answer to each question.

14. Why do you think the athletes decided to make their protest using gestures and not words?

    _____

    _____

    _____

15. Is there anything you would like to make a strong protest about? Describe a way to protest that might make your point.

    _____

    _____

    _____

    _____

    _____

TV Review

TV Review
Review

Vocabulary

ambitious

comprehensive

finale

premiere

installments

monarchs

Television is a popular form of entertainment and a good source of information. The number of shows offered on network, cable, and satellite channels is growing all the time. Because there are so many programs, it can be hard to decide what to watch.

Reading a TV review can help you decide if you are interested in a particular program. A **review** can tell what a program is about, how it is presented, and who the main characters are. Reviewers give their opinions about the quality of a program and sometimes even include behind-the-scenes information.

Relate to the Topic

The review you are about to read is of a television program about the British Royal Family.

What do you think life is like for a member of the Royal Family? Is it filled with privileges? What is it like to be watched by everyone all of the time?

_____

_____

Reading Strategy

RELATING TO WHAT YOU LIKE When you read a TV review you decide what you might or might not like about that program. Does the TV reviewer mention something about the program that you think you would enjoy? Should you watch the program? Read the title and the first paragraph on page 77. Then answer the questions.

1. Would you like to watch a show about the British Royal Family? Why or why not?

_____

_____

2. Which topic in the first paragraph interests you the most? Tell why.

_____

_____

E! Entertainment Television Explores
'Royalty A–Z' by Nancy McAlister

Royalty A–Z is an **ambitious, comprehensive** look at the Windsors, a family that easily qualifies as the world's ultimate celebrities. An eight day, 11-hour miniseries that kicks off Sunday on E! Entertainment Television, it mixes history, human interest and entertainment, punctuated with appearances by show business A-listers.

Jennifer Lopez, Jodie Foster and Celine Dion are among the more than 100 stars interviewed for the series, many of whom qualify as blushing fans of the family that occupies Buckingham Palace. The **finale** of *Royalty A–Z* provides special coverage of Queen Elizabeth II's Golden Jubilee celebration, including the rock concert featuring such performers as Brian Wilson, Ozzy Osbourne, and Sir Paul McCartney.

Summarizing Ideas When you **summarize** what you've read, you make a short statement that gives the main idea and the most important supporting details. For example, if a friend asked you how your vacation was, you might say that it was great; you swam in the ocean, and you ate wonderful food. This summarizes without giving every detail of what you did. To summarize something that you are reading, first look for the most important idea. This main idea might be clearly stated, or it may only be suggested. To summarize a paragraph, write the main idea and most important details of that paragraph in just one sentence and in your own words. It is helpful to summarize what you read in order to make sure that you understand it.

In the first paragraph, the main idea is that *Royalty A–Z* is a miniseries about the Windsors that combines history, human interest, and entertainment. The most important details are that the miniseries is 11 hours long and will be shown over eight days. You could summarize this paragraph like this: *Royalty A–Z* is an 11-hour, 8-day miniseries about the Windsors that combines history, human interest, and entertainment.

The main idea of the second paragraph is that this series on the Windsors includes interviews of celebrities and coverage of the Golden Jubilee, which includes a rock concert.

What important supporting detail would you include in a summary of this paragraph?
   a.   Brian Wilson performs at the Queen's Jubilee Celebration.
   b.   More than 100 stars are interviewed.

Sunday's **premiere** kicks things off with two back-to-back episodes, with one-hour episodes airing throughout the week. Two more back-to-back episodes air on Saturday, Aug. 24 and Sunday, Aug. 25.

In addition to the premiere's focus on Queen Elizabeth II, future **installments** reveal stories of past **monarchs** and provide in-depth looks at contemporary royals, notably Prince Charles, his sons William and Harry, and the late Princess Diana. Because E! joined forces with Edward Wessex's former company Ardent Productions, *Royalty A-Z* was given rare access to people and places within the inner circle.

Among the answered questions: How do they get together as a family? What is the Queen's sense of humor like? What is it like to marry a Prince?

One of the production's coups is footage from the BBC Panaroma interview in which Diana acknowledged there were three people in her marriage to Charles. There are scenes at St. Andrews, where Prince William attends school. A camera crew visits the tartan factory in Scotland where royal kilts are made. And in another episode, viewers meet the Castle Piper, whose job is to waken the Queen each morning with his bagpipes. His goal, according to John Rieber, E!'s senior vice president of original programming, is to provide enjoyment and not to repeat himself.

Applying Ideas to a New Context When you understand an idea, you can figure out how you might use that idea in another situation. For example, if a book reviewer disliked a new romance novel and thought it was too predictable and sentimental, you could apply that idea to figure out what books that reviewer probably would like. She would likely prefer books that were surprising and that didn't focus too much on sentimental feelings. In order to apply an idea to a new context, first identify an idea in the article that you are reading, then use that idea in a different situation.

1. Which one of these statements would the reviewer described above most likely make about *Royalty A–Z*?
    a.   The program runs far too long and doesn't focus enough on the history of the Royal Family.
    b.   The program revealed behind-the-scenes information that showed the royals in a new light.
    c.   The appearance of so many celebrities and the coverage of the rock concert are the only reasons to watch this program.

2. Which one of the following books is most similar to *Royalty A–Z*?
    a.   a novel that gives intimate, detailed descriptions of generations of people living in a small town in Peru
    b.   a short history of World War II that gives a brief overview, meant to encourage students to do further research
    c.   a comedy that is intended to have readers laughing loudly

"It's an insider's look at the Queen's life you wouldn't know," Rieber said. Another example is the popular custom of the changing of the guard. "People don't realize those are real soldiers. When they're not doing this performance they're guarding Buckingham Palace. We go inside the barracks and talk to someone whose family has been doing this for generations."

In undertaking *Royalty A-Z*, E! decided to provide a balance of past, present and future, Rieber said, with a particular focus on who this family is today based on history. Some viewers may be surprised to learn the importance the Windsors have had on society. "The fact is, this is a family that every single movement in their life is an event." And those events have included tragedies, controversies as well as fun and interesting moments. "We tried to humanize every single story."

Summarizing Summarizing a whole passage can help you to understand it. First, think about what the main idea of the entire review is. Then look for details in each paragraph that support the main idea.

1. Which of the following sentences best describes the main idea of the entire review?
   a. *Royalty A-Z* is an intimate portrait of the Royal Family over many years that includes interviews with many celebrities and information you won't find elsewhere.
   b. *Royalty A-Z* shows footage from the Queen's Jubilee celebration that includes a rock concert which features famous performers such as Sir Paul McCartney, a former Beatle.

2. Circle the following supporting details that you would include in a summary of the review.
   a. More than one hundred stars were interviewed.
   b. The final episode includes special coverage of the Queen's Golden Jubilee.
   c. The program focuses on Queen Elizabeth II, the past monarchs, and contemporary British royalty.
   d. A look at the inner circle of the Royal Family includes footage of Princess Diana, Prince William and the other royals.
   e. The program includes a visit to a tartan factory where kilts are made.

3. Now summarize the review by putting together the answers you chose above. Write a main idea sentence and then the detail sentences.

   _____

   _____

   _____

   _____

Thinking About the Review

Practice Vocabulary

The words below are in bold type in the passage. Study the way each word is used. Then write each word next to its meaning.

ambitious comprehensive finale

premiere installment monarchs

1. the first performance _____

2. takes everything into account; covering completely

   _____

3. driven to achieve a goal _____

4. the ending of something, such as a play _____

5. one of several parts _____

6. kings and queens _____

Understand What You Read

Write the answer to each question.

7. What reason does the reviewer give for having access to the Royal Family's inner circle?

   _____

   _____

8. What is meant by "Diana acknowledged there were three people in her marriage to Charles"?

   _____

   _____

9. What details show this is an insider's look at the Royal Family?

   _____

   _____

10. Does the reviewer like this TV program? How do you know?

    _____

    _____

Apply Your Skills

Circle the number of the best answer for each question.

11. Which of the following best sums up the last paragraph of the review?
    (1) The program emphasizes the importance of today's royals based on history and humanizes the events in their lives.
    (2) The program offers a glimpse of the influence of the Windsors.
    (3) The program shows all of the events in the lives of the royals and how celebrities respond.
    (4) The program humanizes the tragedies in the royals' lives.
    (5) The program is a large project focusing on the Royal Family.

12. Which of the following TV shows about pets is most like the program about the Royal Family?
    (1) A Day in the Life of a Pampered Pet
    (2) Backstage at an Elite Dog Show
    (3) History, Characteristics, and Habits of Siamese Cats
    (4) What Makes Poodles Special?
    (5) Celebrities Talk About Their Special Pet Companions

13. Which of the following is the best summary of the paragraph at the top of page 79 about the guards at Buckingham Palace?
    (1) The coverage of the guards emphasizes one soldier and his family.
    (2) The coverage highlights the few people who have inside information about the royals' lives.
    (3) The coverage shows the unique, daily performance of the changing of the guard at Buckingham Palace.
    (4) The coverage downplays the fact that the guards are real soldiers.
    (5) The coverage is an inside look that shows the Buckingham Palace guards as real soldiers.

Connect with the Review

Write your answer to each question.

14. Have you ever watched a miniseries? Was it interesting? Why or why not?

    _____

    _____

15. Imagine that you are royalty. What would you enjoy? What would be difficult?

    _____

    _____

Book Review

Vocabulary

chronological

obsession

eccentric

facets

disclaimer

resonate

A book review usually discusses the plot and the characters of a book, as well as the way the book is written. However, because reviewers don't want to give away too much of the plot, they often just discuss the characters. Based mainly on the description of the characters, the reader must make a judgment about reading the book.

Relate to the Topic

The passage you are about to read is a review of a book of essays about an author's life.

Have you ever written about any of your life experiences?

_____

What situations or experiences in your life have you written about?

_____

_____

_____

Reading Strategy

RELATING TO WHAT YOU KNOW   Relating to what you know means making a personal connection to a topic in an article by finding something in it that you are familiar with in your own life. Read the first two paragraphs on page 83. Then answer the questions.

1. Have you had any of the experiences listed in the first paragraph? What, if anything, was funny about the experience?

_____

Hint: Think about events that happened at the same time as the experience.

2. Describe one of your life experiences you think was funny.

_____

_____

Hint: Read the second paragraph.

UNIT 1 NONFICTION

Life's Peculiar Events Explain 'Why I'm Like This' by Whitney Matheson

Many of us could swap tales of migraine headaches, bad therapy sessions, unfortunate jobs and crazy relatives. Few people, however, could make these incidents knee-slapping hilarious.

In her first book of essays, *Why I'm Like This,* Cynthia Kaplan approaches her past with a lighthearted, humorous touch. Fans of David Sedaris or Anne Lamott will appreciate her quirky way of looking at life's intricacies. And every reader will find that at least one of the funny, often touching, essays rings true. Kaplan, a New York-based actress and writer, takes readers on a **chronological** journey through her life, all the way from her steamy afternoons at summer camp ("Queechy Girls") to the birth of her first child.

Interpreting the Reviewer's Tone How reviewers feel about a topic influences how they write about it. A reviewer who feels positive about a topic writes about it in a positive way, or in a positive tone. This comes across to the reader and influences how the reader will feel about the topic, too.

Reviewers choose their words carefully to help develop the tone. If a reviewer uses formal or technical words, the tone seems unemotional. This can be an effective tone for some educational or technical materials. However, in a book review, many reviewers choose to use an informal tone that is more appealing to the reader. They use slang and humorous words to create a friendlier feeling.

In the first paragraph above, the phrase "swap tales" helps create the informal tone the reviewer wants. Also, the word "knee-slapping" is an informal way of saying this book is humorous. This word suggests that the book is easy to read and good for a laugh. This word choice is intended to help the reader feel as good about the book as the reviewer does.

A reviewer's tone can reflect a variety of feelings. It might be polite, formal, sarcastic, critical, or sincere. You can figure out the tone by asking yourself questions such as *Is the reviewer bored? angry? enthusiastic?* Look for descriptive words that demonstrate the reviewer's tone. Read the second paragraph in the passage above and answer the following questions.

1. Which of the following shows how the reviewer continues to set an informal tone?
   a. Fans . . . will appreciate her quirky way of looking at life's intricacies.
   b. Kaplan . . . takes readers on a chronological journey through her life . . .

2. What purpose might the reviewer have for using an informal tone?
   a. It makes the review fun to read.
   b. It is easier to write with an informal tone.

In "A Dog Loves a Bone," we meet her sloppy, lazy high school boyfriends and a rainbow of other regrettable romantic partners. In "Jack Has a Thermos," we meet Kaplan's loving dad, a man with a helpless **obsession** with gadgets (especially Thermoses).

Many of the essays touch on familiar comedic territory: Aren't everyone's grandparents just a little bit **eccentric?** Haven't we all taken a bad vacation? But the essays that stand out most uncover the truly unique **facets** of Kaplan's life.

"This is for You" recounts the author's rather uncomfortable meeting with George Burns, who just happened to be her grandmother's uncle. "He did not look a day over ninety-gazillion," she writes. "George told fifteen jokes in a row. Then he asked me if I had an agent."

Interpreting the Author's Tone To give the reader a feeling for the tone of the book being reviewed, reviewers often include quotations. This reviewer chose two quotations: "He did not look a day over ninety-gazillion" and "Then he asked me if I had an agent."

1. What is the best reason for including actual quotations from the book in a review?
   a. It gives some relief from the dry tone of the reviewer.
   b. It provides an example of what the reviewer is talking about.
   c. It adds an informal feeling to the review.

2. The reviewer of *Why I'm Like This* thinks it is a hilarious book. Reread the first two paragraphs above. Then write three examples of things the reviewer finds funny.

   _____

   _____

   _____

Kaplan prefaces the book's most memorable tale, "The Story of R," with a **disclaimer:** It was her publisher who urged her to share it, she promises.

After Kaplan makes it clear that she had doubts about writing it, she launches into a marvelously detailed account of her former therapist, an unnamed woman who slowly goes crazy and takes bizarre advantage of her patients.

As Kaplan matures, the book takes a more touching turn, and moving stories about her attempts to conceive a child and her grandmother's death will certainly **resonate** with her audience.

Thankfully, *Why I'm Like This* ends with a hearty guffaw. In "The Few, The Proud," Kaplan transforms a meditation on the hopes, dreams and worries of French truffle pigs into a metaphor of her life.

"You dream of release, of deliverance. . . . But is there any way out? Is there?" wonders the author, lightly disguised as a farm animal. "But eventually you make your peace. Nobody has a perfect life, you say. Nobody gets everything."

Though that may be true, Kaplan gets enough just right in her first book, leaving her readers feeling less alone and more willing to laugh about the small stuff.

Understanding Bias Bias is a strong preference for a particular point of view. A person can have a bias <u>for</u> or <u>against</u> something. You can recognize a reviewer's bias from words that emphasize either a negative or a positive view of something. For example, a movie reviewer might like action movies and dislike romantic comedies. So, the reviewer will likely say good things about action movies. Look for words that express a positive or negative feeling. This tells you how the writer feels about the subject.

At the beginning of the review, the writer describes the book as having a "lighthearted, humorous touch." This emphasis on a positive feature of the book lets the reader know that the reviewer likes the book.

1. Based on the review, which of the following types of books does the reviewer like?
   a. poetic, sensitive, gentle stories
   b. funny, unbelievable, imaginative stories
   c. moving, realistic, humorous stories

2. Write two ideas from the last paragraph of the review that show the reviewer's bias in favor of this book.

   _____

   _____

3. Near the beginning of the review, the writer says that "Many of the essays touch on familiar comedic territory: Aren't everyone's grandparents just a little bit eccentric?" and that the "essays that stand out most uncover the truly unique facets of Kaplan's life." What bias do these statements show?
   a. The writer has a bias against topics that are too commonly written about.
   b. The writer has a bias against essays about an author's family.

Reviewers may also show a bias when they tell only one side of a story. When you see clues that suggest a bias, be sure to read carefully to find out whether the reviewer supports his or her opinion with facts.

Thinking About the Review

Practice Vocabulary

The words below are in bold type in the passage. Study the way each word is used. Then complete each sentence by writing the correct word.

chronological	obsession	eccentric
facets	disclaimer	resonate

1. If you see a movie that seems true to you, it will

   _____ with you.

2. To tell a story in the order the events happened is to tell the story in

   _____ order.

3. If you can't stop thinking about something, you have an

   _____ with it.

4. Many products have a _____ on the label that says the manufacturer is not responsible for problems caused by misuse of the product.

5. If someone seems a bit crazy and has peculiar habits, they might be

   called _____ .

6. A person can have many sides, or _____, to his or her personality.

Understand What You Read

Write the answer to each question.

7. What is the reason given for Kaplan writing "The Story of R"?

   _____

8. How does the reviewer describe the stories that happen later in Kaplan's life?

   _____

9. Which essays does the reviewer find the most unique?

   _____

10. How does the reviewer describe the final essay, "The Few, The Proud"?

    _____

Apply Your Skills

Circle the number of the best answer for each question.

11. Which of the following words best describes the tone the reviewer uses in this review?
    (1) critical
    (2) casual
    (3) technical
    (4) indifferent
    (5) puzzled

12. Which of the following best contributes to the tone of the review?
    (1) ... the author's rather uncomfortable meeting with George Burns ...
    (2) ... a man with a helpless obsession with gadgets ...
    (3) ... her attempts to conceive a child ...
    (4) "Nobody gets everything."
    (5) Kaplan makes it clear that she had doubts about writing it. ...

13. What does it mean that Kaplan describes her boyfriends as "regrettable romantic partners"?
    (1) She regrets going out with them.
    (2) They regret going out with her.
    (3) She regrets that they were romantic.
    (4) She regrets that she went to high school.
    (5) They regret that they were romantic.

Connect with the Review

Write your answer to each question.

14. Have you ever read a humorous book? What did you like about it? What words would you use to describe it?

    _____

    _____

    _____

15. Based on the review, would you like to read this book or one like it? Explain why or why not.

    _____

    _____

    _____

Reading at Work

Real Estate: Property Manager

Have you ever looked for an apartment or business space? If so, you've probably talked to a property manager. Property managers take care of office and apartment buildings. Some managers also act as the sales or rental agents for the property. They provide possible buyers or tenants with important information about the buildings and the surrounding community. Property managers must be able to read and present leases, brochures, and other written documents to potential buyers or tenants.

In addition to having strong reading skills, a property manager must also be a good writer, speaker, and listener. Property managers must communicate effectively with tenants and with the workers and contractors who maintain the property.

Look at the box showing some careers in real estate.

- Do any of the careers interest you? If so, which ones?

- How could you find out more about those careers? On a separate piece of paper, write some questions that you would like to have answered. You can find out more information about those careers in the *Occupational Outlook Handbook* at your local library and online.

Some Careers in Real Estate

Property Valuer/ Appraiser
calculates value of properties by examining their condition and comparing them to similar ones in the area

Real Estate Agent
helps people buy and sell homes, office buildings, and land

Real Estate Sales Assistant
helps real estate agent by making appointments and communicating with customers

Real Estate Receptionist
answers phone calls, handles correspondence, and makes appointments

Read the newspaper article. Then answer the questions.

Spring Meadows to Help Build New Community Center

CARVERTON Thursday the Spring Meadows Development Company announced that it will help the town of Carverton build a new community center. Carverton Mayor Kendra Clay said, "We're delighted to have Spring Meadows' support for this exciting new facility that will benefit all of our residents."

The Carverton Community Center will have a gymnasium, a fitness center, an indoor track, an outdoor Olympic-size swimming pool, and an indoor pool. The center will also have meeting rooms and locker areas.

Spring Meadows is a large residential development In Carverton consisting of 200 single-family homes and 300 apartments. To date, 35% of the homes have been sold and 50% of the apartments have been rented.

As part of the agreement between the town and the development company, Mayor Clay announced that Spring Meadows residents would receive a discounted membership to the new community center.

1. What is the main idea of the article?
   (1) Spring Meadows is a new residential development.
   (2) Kendra Clay is the mayor of Carverton.
   (3) There are more apartments than single-family homes in Spring Meadows.
   (4) Spring Meadows will help Carverton build its community center.
   (5) Already, 35% of the homes have been sold and 50% of the apartments have been rented.

2. As property manager of Spring Meadows, you would be most interested in this article because
   (1) Mayor Clay lives in Spring Meadows near the community center.
   (2) Spring Meadows residents are building the new center.
   (3) There will be meeting rooms in the community center.
   (4) Spring Meadows residents will receive a discounted membership.
   (5) There will be swimming pools, a fitness center, and a running track.

3. As the property manager for Spring Meadows, you realize that this article contains several selling points. List three points that you could use to persuade people to buy or rent in Spring Meadows.

   _____

   _____

   _____

Read the following passage from the review "Bruce Rising" by Josh Tyrangiel and Kate Carcaterra

Bruce Springsteen has a songbook that reads like a union membership log. He has written about cops, fire fighters, soldiers, road builders, steelworkers, factory laborers, and migrant workers. Springsteen himself has held exactly one real job. For a few weeks in 1968 when he was 18, he worked as a gardener. But his gift is not horticulture. His great gift—the one that makes him the best rock 'n' roll singer of his era—is empathy. Springsteen doesn't know what a 40-hour workweek feels like, but he knows how a 40-hour workweek makes you feel. "If you roll out of bed in the morning," he says, "even if you're the deepest **pessimist** or cynic, you just took a step into the next day. When I was growing up, we didn't have very much, but I saw by my mom's example that a step into the next day was very important. Hey, some good things might happen. You may even hold off some bad things that could happen."

On *The Rising*, his first album of new material in seven years, Springsteen is again writing about work, hope and American life as it is lived this very moment. *The Rising* is about Sept. 11, and it is the first significant piece of pop art to respond to the events of that day. Many of the songs are written from the perspectives of working people whose lives and fates **intersected** with those hijacked planes. The songs are sad, but the sadness is almost always matched with **optimism,** promises of redemption and calls to spiritual arms. There is more rising on *The Rising* than in a month of church.

The Rising also marks the return of the E Street Band. The band—seven hardworking Joes in their 50s and 60s, plus Springsteen's wife, backup singer and Jersey girl Patti Scialfa—has always been a proxy for the Springsteen audience. The E Streeters don't eat meat sandwiches out of metal lunch boxes, but it's easy to believe that they could. Their 15-year absence from Springsteen's recorded music opened a gulf between the Boss and his core fans, one that *The Rising* seems intent on closing.

Questions 1 through 6 refer to the passage on page 90.

Write the word that best completes each sentence.

| pessimist | intersected | optimism |

1. The area where one thing meets another thing is the place where they have _____.

2. A person who predicts that things will turn out badly is a _____.

3. People who have a positive outlook on life are filled with _____.

Circle the number of the best answer for each question.

4. According to the reviewer, what is Bruce Springsteen's gift?
    (1) his ability to play rock 'n' roll
    (2) his songwriting about September 11th
    (3) his ability to empathize
    (4) his hard-working approach to life
    (5) his optimism about songwriting

5. Which statement shows the reviewer's attitude about "The Rising"?
    (1) Bruce Springsteen has a songbook that reads like a union membership log.
    (2) Springsteen himself has held exactly one real job.
    (3) On "The Rising," his first album of new material in seven years, Springsteen is again writing about work, hope. . . .
    (4) Many of the songs are written from the perspectives of working people. . . .
    (5) There is more rising on "The Rising" than in a month of church.

6. Which of the following statements is the best summary of the third paragraph?
    (1) The 15-year absence of the E Street Band created some discontent between Springsteen and his fans.
    (2) The E Street Band includes seven musicians in their 50s and 60s who appear to be a working class group.
    (3) The reappearance of the E Street Band will help Springsteen's failing career.
    (4) Springsteen's wife and backup singer appears on "The Rising."
    (5) "The Rising" includes the return of the E Street Band, which should close any gap between Springsteen and his fans.

Read the following passage from "Star Time: James Brown" by David Hiltbrand.

Chuck Berry? Elvis? The Beatles?

When it comes down to who has had the most **profound** and lasting influence on pop music, no one can touch the Godfather of Soul.

This anthology (four CDs or cassettes) is the Fort Knox of funk. It chronologically traces Brown's **evolution** from a poor follow-the-crowd R&B singer from Georgia to the absolutely original, superbad superstar.

Disc No. 1 contains the greatest advances. On the earliest tracks, such as "Try Me" and "Bewildered" from the late '50's, Brown is trying to get over as a cookie-cutter pop singer. This smoothed-out doo-wop music isn't all that far from the Ink Spots. But even in this era, there were hints of genius. Mired in the **schmaltzy** ballad "I Know It's True," Brown still had a **flair** for using horns and drums.

By the time he recorded "Think" in 1960, James had discovered the funk, and he never **decamped.** He became a method singer, and that method was madness. His eruptive delivery was completely unpredictable. With "Bring It Up (Hipster's Avenue)" in 1966, lyrics had really become a **moot** point. A single phrase would **suffice.**

Brown was always a character. On "Papa's Got a Brand New Bag, Pts. 1, 2, 3," an extended, previously unreleased version of his 1965 hit, you hear the singer **exhorting** his longtime sax man, Maceo Parker, to play a solo. By the end of the jam, Brown is getting into a dialogue with the horns themselves. (If Brown was, as advertised, "the hardest working man in show business," the guys who worked in his backing bands were tied for second.)

The music is fast and furious the rest of the way. Disc Nos. 2 through 4 present a dizzying cavalcade of hits: "I Got You (I Feel Good)," "I Can't Stand Myself (When You Touch Me) Pt. 1," "Licking Stick-Licking Stick," "Give It Up or Turnit a Loose.". . .

There are many collections of Brown's work, but none so deep or well documented.

Questions 7 through 18 refer to the passage on page 92.

Find the numbered words in the passage. They will be in bold type. Study the way each word is used. Then match each word with its meaning. Write the letter.

_____ 7. profound

_____ 8. evolution

_____ 9. schmaltzy

_____ 10. flair

_____ 11. decamped

_____ 12. moot

_____ 13. suffice

_____ 14. exhorting

a. of little importance

b. talent

c. left or departed

d. sentimental, mushy

e. change or development

f. be enough

g. urging strongly

h. deeply important

Write the answer to each question.

15. When a musician uses the word "jam," it does not mean something that is put on bread. Reread the sixth paragraph on page 92. Based on the context, what does "jam" mean?

_____

_____

16. What is the reviewer's overall opinion of the music collection?

_____

_____

17. What statement in the review shows how the reviewer feels about James Brown's back-up musicians?

_____

_____

Circle the number of the best answer for the question.

18. Why does the reviewer describe the way James Brown encouraged his sax player to do a solo?
    (1) to give an example of how unusual James Brown is
    (2) to show that James Brown knows how to play a horn
    (3) to suggest that James Brown is selfish
    (4) to criticize James Brown's style
    (5) to give an example of method singing

Read the following passage from the "I Have a Dream" speech by **Martin Luther King, Jr.**

I have a dream today. I have a dream that one day every valley shall be exalted and every hill and mountain shall be made low, the rough places will be made plain and the crooked places will be made straight, and the glory of the Lord shall be revealed, and all flesh shall see it together.

This is our hope. This is the faith that I go to the South with. And with this faith we will be able to hew out of the mountain of despair a stone of hope. With this faith we will be able to transform the jangling discords of our nation into a beautiful symphony of brotherhood. With this faith we will be able to work together, to play together, to struggle together, to go to jail together, to stand up for freedom together, knowing that we will be free one day.

And this will be the day—this will be the day when all of God's children will be able to sing with new meaning:

My country, 'tis of thee,
Sweet land of liberty,
   Of thee I sing;
Land where my fathers died,
Land of the Pilgrims' pride,
From every mountainside
   Let freedom ring.

And if America is to be a great nation, this must become true.

And so let freedom ring from the prodigious hilltops of New Hampshire. Let freedom ring from the mighty mountains of New York. Let freedom ring from the heightening Alleghenies of Pennsylvania. Let freedom ring from the snow-capped Rockies of Colorado. Let freedom ring from the curvaceous slopes of California.

But not only that. Let freedom ring from Stone Mountain of Georgia. Let freedom ring from Lookout Mountain of Tennessee. Let freedom ring from every hill and molehill of Mississippi. "From every mountainside let freedom ring."

And when this happens—when we allow freedom to ring, when we let it ring from every village and every hamlet, from every state and every city—we will be able to speed up that day when all of God's children, Black men and white men, Jews and Gentiles, Protestants and Catholics, will be able to join hands and sing in the words of the old Negro spiritual: "Free at last! Free at last! Thank God Almighty. We are free at last!"

Questions 19 through 23 refer to the passage on page 94.

Write the answer to each question.

19. What two words in the passage have almost the same meaning as "slopes"?

_____

_____

20. What does the writer mean by "a beautiful symphony of brotherhood"?

_____

_____

Circle the number of the best answer for each question.

21. Which of these words means the same as the word "dream"?
    (1) hope
    (2) despair
    (3) thought
    (4) struggle
    (5) glory

22. Which sentence best states the main idea of this passage?
    (1) Life is unfair.
    (2) Freedom cannot be achieved.
    (3) Good things come to those who wait.
    (4) People feel more free in the mountains.
    (5) By working together, all people can become free.

23. After reading the passage, you might conclude that Martin Luther King, Jr., was working to help make people free. Which three details from the passage help lead to this conclusion?
    (1) . . . we will be able to work together. . .
    (2) I have a dream today.
    (3) This is the faith that I go to the South with.
    (4) Sweet land of liberty, of thee I sing;
    (5) . . . the snow-capped Rockies of Colorado.

Reading Extension

Look through a news magazine or a newspaper for an article about a recent event. Write a brief summary that includes the main idea of the article and details that support this main idea. List several examples of facts and opinions from the article. What conclusions can you draw from the ideas presented in the article? What details did you use to draw these conclusions?

Mini-Test • Unit 1

 This is a 15-minute practice test. After 15 minutes, mark the last number you finished. Then complete the test and check your answers. If most of your answers were correct but you did not finish, try to work faster next time.

Directions: Choose the <u>one best answer</u> to each question.

Questions 1 through 3 refer to the following passage.

WHAT IS THE PURPOSE OF THIS ADVICE?

When you submit a resume for a job, it is essential that you include a cover letter. Below is a sample letter.

Dear Ms. Livingston:

(5)   I was excited to see your job posting in *The Oregonian* for a customer service representative. Please consider this letter and enclosed resume an application for the position.

(10)   I graduated from Culver Community College with an Associate Degree in Communications. My school experience gave me strong communication skills that will help me handle telephone calls, solve
(15) customer problems, and write letters and reports.

While I was in school, I participated in an activity that helped me prepare for this job. On a volunteer basis, I developed
(20) public relations material for the Boys and Girls Club. Since graduating, I have been a customer service representative in Portland for five years, and have been regularly given the "employee of the
(25) month" award by my department.

I will be in the Corvallis area from March 15 to 17. Please let me know if you can schedule me for an interview during that time. Thank you for your
(30) consideration.

Sincerely,
Andy Parker

1. Which of the following summarizes the main idea of the second and third paragraphs?

    (1) Andy graduated from Culver Community College.
    (2) Andy's education, service, and work experience qualify him for the job.
    (3) The best education for a customer service representative is a degree in Communications.
    (4) Andy has already been a customer service representative, so he is qualified.
    (5) Handling customer complaints is a major part of the job.

2. Based on the letter, which of the following best describes Andy Parker's personality?

    (1) playful
    (2) competent
    (3) demanding
    (4) shy
    (5) self-centered

3. To his surprise, Andy received a letter from Ms. Livingstone inviting him to apply for another job. Based on Andy's background, which of the following is the most likely position?

    (1) video promoter
    (2) computer programmer
    (3) customer relations specialist
    (4) office manager
    (5) event organizer

Questions 4–6 refer to the following review.

WHAT DOES THE REVIEWER LIKE ABOUT THIS FILM?

As far as I'm concerned, if you've seen one gnome/elf/sprite, you've seen 'em all. But, even though "Lord of the Rings: The Fellowship of the Ring" is stuffed with

(5) pixies, I found it Hobbit-forming.

That's because this is not at all a cutesy movie. Oh, a couple of backgrounds in Hobbit world are as pretty and light-filled as a Thomas Kinkade

(10) enchanted cottage, but writer/director Peter Jackson's muscular, dangerous movie knows that good is only possible in a world where evil looks like a delicious alternative.

(15) "The Lord of the Rings" is, like "Harry Potter," an adaptation of a beloved novel but, unlike "Potter," "Rings" messes with it. For "Rings," the key is not slavishly recreating every incident of a cherished

(20) book, but finding a way to capture its essence, so the movie can be loved by fans and newcomers alike. Jackson leaves huge portions of "Rings" on the elf shelf (he had to; at three hours, it still has

(25) one momentous battle too many), but he preserves its magical, heart-fueled sense of adventure. The result is not just a faithful transcription of a classic, but a wondrous reimagining of one.

(30) A big part of the "Rings" magic is its light touch with special effects. There probably isn't a scene here that doesn't have them, but "Rings" doesn't feel like an effects movie, where each empty image

(35) is meant to top images we've seen before, whether or not they add to the narrative. The effects in "Rings," such as some thrilling rapids that assume the shape of galloping horses or some giant

(40) statues that make Mount Rushmore look

like bobbleheads, nurture our imaginations instead of trying to replace them.

Chris Hewitt, "It's Hobbit-forming"

4. What is meant by "Jackson leaves huge portions of 'Rings' on the elf shelf." (lines 22–24)?

   (1) He includes too much about elves.
   (2) He downplays special effects.
   (3) He didn't follow the plot of the book.
   (4) He left certain parts out of the film.
   (5) He shortened the length of the film.

5. Which of the following might cause this reviewer to react more negatively to the film?

   (1) if more adorable elves were included
   (2) if the evil parts were more appealing
   (3) if the scenery used less fantasy
   (4) if the plot was more like the book
   (5) if the movie were shorter

6. Which of the following best describes the tone of this review?

   (1) upbeat and clever
   (2) serious and intellectual
   (3) thoughtful but critical
   (4) puzzled but business-like
   (5) sympathetic and formal

Fiction

Fiction

Novels and short stories are works of **fiction**. They come from writers' imaginations and can take us places we might never experience in real life. An adventure story might describe a character's journey to Antarctica. A science fiction story might take place on Mars. Fictional writing can take us to worlds far away or just down the block. It can let us experience the lives of people from different times, places, and ways of life.

Do you like to read fiction? _____

Write the title of a fiction book or story you have enjoyed.

_____

Thinking About Fiction

You many not realize how often you come across fiction in your daily life. Think about your recent activities.

Check the box for each activity you did.

☐ Did you read a story to a child?

☐ Did you take out a book of fiction from the library?

☐ Did you read a short story in a magazine?

☐ Did you read some fiction while browsing in a bookstore?

☐ Did you watch a television movie that was based on a book of fiction?

☐ Did you read a book while riding the bus or subway?

☐ Did you hear a story on the radio?

☐ Did someone tell you a story they made up?

Write some other experiences you have had reading fiction.

_____

_____

Previewing the Unit

In this unit, you will learn:

• what makes mystery novels, thrillers, and adventure stories so exciting

• why people still enjoy classic stories and folk tales that were written long ago

• how popular stories reflect today's world

• how science fiction helps us to imagine the future

Lesson 13	Mystery Novel
Lesson 14	Science Fiction
Lesson 15	Thriller Novel
Lesson 16	Popular Novel
Lesson 17	Folk Novel
Lesson 18	Classic Short Story
Lesson 19	Popular Short Story
Lesson 20	Adventure Story

Mystery Novel

Mystery Novel
Mystery Novel
Novel

Vocabulary

gusts

ponderosas

hogan

plausible

tentatively

forlorn

A mystery novel presents the reader with a puzzle. Who committed the crime in the story? Why? What are the clues? Who is telling the truth? Who can be trusted and who can't? In a mystery novel, the main character is often a detective whose job it is to solve the mystery. Most of the fun of reading mysteries is putting all the clues together and trying to solve the puzzle yourself.

Relate to the Topic

The passage you are about to read is about Chee, a Navajo policeman. In the passage, you will learn a little about Navajo customs and about Navajo beliefs regarding life, death, and ghosts.

Every culture and religion has its own beliefs about life after death. What are your own beliefs or some you know about?

_____

_____

_____

Reading Strategy

PICTURING THE SETTING   The setting refers to the location and time the story takes place. For example, a story can happen late at night in a dark basement filled with cobwebs and creaking sounds. Read the title and first few sentences of the passage on page 101 to picture the setting.

1. Does this story take place in a city or in the country? What time of day is it?

   _____

   Hint: Read the first sentence on page 101.

2. When the story begins, is this place still and quiet, or is it noisy?

   _____

   Hint: Read the second sentence on page 101.

The Ghostway by Tony Hillerman

The night breeze was beginning now as it often did with twilight on the east slope of mountains. Nothing like the morning's dry **gusts,** but enough to ruffle the mare's ragged mane and replace the dead silence with a thousand little wind sounds among the **ponderosas.** Under cover of these whispers, Chee moved along the arroyo [a deep ditch cut by a stream] rim, looking for the horse thief.

He checked up the arroyo. Down the arroyo. Along the ponderosa timber covering the slopes. He stared back at the talus [a mass of debris at the base of a cliff] slope, where he had been when he'd heard the horse. But no one could have gotten there without Chee seeing him. There was only the death **hogan** and the holding pen for goats and the brush arbor, none of which seemed **plausible.** The thief must have tied his horse and then climbed directly up the slope across the arroyo. But why?

Just behind him, Chee heard a cough.

He spun, fumbling for his pistol. No one. Where had the sound come from?

He heard it again. A cough. A sniffling. The sound came from inside Hosteen Begay's hogan.

Chee stared at the corpse hole, a black gap broken through the north wall. He had cocked his pistol without knowing he'd done it. It was incredible. People do not go into a death hogan. People do not step through the hole into darkness. White men, yes. As Sharkey had done. And Deputy Sheriff Bales. As Chee himself, who had come to terms with the ghosts of his people, might do if the reason was powerful enough. But certainly most Navajos would not. So the horse thief was a white. A white with a cold and a runny nose.

Finding the Stated Main Idea The main idea of a paragraph or passage is the most important idea. The stated main idea of a paragraph tells you clearly what the important point of that paragraph is.

In this passage, Chee is using clues to solve a mystery. In the second paragraph, for example, he thinks he has learned something important: "The thief must have tied his horse and then climbed directly up the slope across the arroyo." This is the stated main idea of the paragraph. To find the stated main idea in other paragraphs, look for the idea that seems most important. Ask yourself, "Which sentence gives the most important information about the mystery?"

Which of the following gives the stated main idea of the last paragraph on the page? In other words, which of the following sentences from the story seems more important to solving the mystery?

a.   Chee stared at the corpse hole, a black gap broken through the north wall.

b.   So the horse thief was a white. A white with a cold and a runny nose.

Chee moved quietly to his left, away from the field of vision of anyone who might be looking through the hole. Then he moved silently to the wall and along it. He stood beside the hole, back pressed to the planking. Pistol raised. Listening.

Something moved. Something sniffled. Moved again. Chee breathed as lightly as he could. And waited. He heard sounds and long silences. The sun was below the horizon now, and the light had shifted far down the range of colors to the darkest red. Over the ridge to the west he could see Venus, bright against the dark sky. Soon it would be night.

There was the sound of feet on earth, of cloth scraping, and a form emerged through the hole. First a stocking cap, black. Then the shoulders of a navy pea coat, then a boot and a leg—a form crouching to make its way through the low hole.

"Hold it," Chee said. "Don't move."

A startled yell. The figure jumped through the hole, stumbled. Chee grabbed.

He realized almost instantly he had caught a child. The arm he gripped through the cloth of the coat was small, thin. The struggle was only momentary, the product of panic quickly controlled. A girl, Chee saw. A Navajo. But when she spoke, it was in English.

"Turn me loose," she said, in a breathless, frightened voice. "I've got to go now."

Chee found he was shaking. The girl had handled this startling encounter better than he had. "Need to know some things first," Chee said. "I'm a policeman."

"I've got to go," she said. She pulled **tentatively** against his grip and relaxed, waiting.

Identifying Details The details of a paragraph or passage support the main idea. Details are facts about a person, place, thing, event, or time. Details answer the questions *who, what, when, where, why,* and *how.* Details tell you about sounds and sights and smells.

The passage above gives several details about the time of day: the sun is below the horizon, the sky is dark and red, and the planet Venus is visible in the dark sky.

1. The third paragraph gives details about what Chee heard and saw. Name two things he heard and two things he saw.

   _____

   _____

2. The passage gives many details about the person Chee finds. List three of them.

   _____

   _____

   _____

"Your horse," Chee said. "You took her last night from over at Two Gray Hills."

"Borrowed it," the girl said. "I've got to go now and take her back."

"What are you doing here?" Chee asked. "In the hogan?"

"It's my hogan," she said. "I live here."

"It is the hogan of Hosteen Ashie Begay," Chee said. "Or it was. Now it is a *chindi* [evil spirit left behind when a person dies] hogan. Didn't you notice that?"

It was a foolish question. After all, he'd just caught her coming out of the corpse hole. She didn't bother to answer. She said nothing at all, simply standing slumped and motionless.

"It was stupid going in there," Chee said. "What were you doing?"

"He was my grandfather," the girl said. For the first time she lapsed into Navajo, using the noun that means the father of my mother. "I was just sitting in there. Remembering things." It took her a moment to say it because now tears were streaming down her cheeks. "My grandfather would leave no *chindi* behind him. He was a holy man. There was nothing in him bad that would make a *chindi*."

"It wasn't your grandfather who died in there," Chee said. "It was a man named Albert Gorman. A nephew of Ashie Begay." Chee paused a moment, trying to sort out the Begay family. "An uncle of yours, I think."

The girl's face had been as **forlorn** as a child's face can be. Now it was radiant. "Grandfather's alive? He's really alive? Where is he?"

"I don't know," Chee said. "Gone to live with some relatives, I guess. We came up here last week to get Gorman, and we found Gorman had died. And that." Chee pointed at the corpse hole. "Hosteen Begay buried Gorman out there, and packed up his horses, and sealed up his hogan, and went away."

The girl looked thoughtful.

"Where would he go?" Chee asked. The girl would be Margaret Sosi. No question about that. Two birds with one stone. One stolen pinto mare and the horse thief, plus one missing St. Catherine's student. "Hosteen Begay is your mother's father. Would he . . . ?" He remembered then that the mother of Margaret Billy Sosi was dead.

"No," Margaret said.

"Somebody else then?"

"Almost everybody went to California. A long time ago. My mother's sisters. My great-grandmother. Some people live over on the Cañoncito Reservation, but . . ." Her voice trailed off, became suddenly suspicious. "Why do you want to find him?"

Using Details The details of a passage give information about the characters and how they feel. In the passage above, several details describe how the young girl feels and acts.

Using all the details given in the passage, decide what kind of person Margaret is.
a. intelligent and independent
b. cowardly and helpless

Thinking About the Story

Practice Vocabulary

The words below are in bold type in the passage. Study the way each word is used. Then complete each sentence by writing the correct word.

gusts	ponderosas	hogan
plausible	tentatively	forlorn

1. A Navajo home is called a _____

2. In autumn, _____ of wind blow the leaves around.

3. If you believe a story could be true, you think it is

   _____

4. The man stood _____ on his sprained ankle and found it hurt too much to walk.

5. The sad news made the woman feel _____

6. The _____ are a kind of pine tree.

Understand What You Read

Write the answer to each question.

7. At first, what makes Chee think the horse thief is a white person with a cold?

   _____

   _____

8. The passage says that the girl handled this startling encounter better than Chee. In what way did she handle it better?

   _____

   _____

9. What does the girl mean when she says that she "borrowed" the horse?

   _____

   _____

10. To whom does the hogan belong?

    _____

    _____

Apply Your Skills

Circle the number of the best answer for each question.

11. Which of the following is the most important idea of the entire passage?
    (1) Navajos live in hogans.
    (2) Chee is an experienced policeman.
    (3) Margaret Sosi has run away from home.
    (4) Other crimes besides the horse theft may have taken place here.
    (5) Horses are important to the Navajos.

12. Which detail makes the most important point about Chee's character?
    (1) He spun, fumbling for his pistol.
    (2) He had come to terms with the ghosts of his people.
    (3) He breathed as lightly as he could.
    (4) He could see Venus, bright against the dark sky.
    (5) He stood beside the hole, back pressed to the planking.

13. Which detail best describes the land where this story takes place?
    (1) The night breeze was beginning . . .
    (2) He heard sounds and long silences.
    (3) "My grandfather would leave no *chindi* behind him."
    (4) . . . Chee moved along the arroyo rim, looking for the horse thief.
    (5) Along the ponderosa timber covering the slopes.

Connect with the Story

Write your answer to each question.

14. If you were Chee, what would you do next? Why?

    _____

    _____

    _____

15. Have you ever been completely surprised or startled like Chee was when he found that it was Margaret in the hogan? What was the surprise or shock for you? Was there any information or clue that could have prepared you for the surprise or shock? Explain.

    _____

    _____

    _____

    _____

    _____

Science Fiction

Science Fiction
Science Fiction

Vocabulary

pampering

clangor

paralytic

contorted

dilemma

acceleration

manual

In science fiction an author imagines what life and people might be like in another time or place. Science fiction is often set in the future, on other planets, or somewhere far away in the universe. These kinds of stories are called science fiction because they combine imagination (fiction) with ideas and principles from science. Most science fiction is filled with adventure.

Relate to the Topic

The passage you are about to read is from a science fiction story in *I, Robot*. The main characters are scientists who are working on an important project—building a robot. The story is both scary and believable because it plays with people's fear that technology, computers, and robots will some day run our lives. Many people believe that we already depend too much on technology.

What is your experience with technology? Have you ever felt that it was running your life—rather than you running it? Explain.

_____

_____

_____

Reading Strategy

VISUALIZING CHARACTERS   Characters are people or other creatures in a story. You can tell a lot about characters by paying attention to their words and actions. Writers help you understand characters by having them say and do certain things. Read the first three paragraphs on page 107. Then answer the questions.

1. Write a word that helps you visualize Alfred Lanning.

    _____

    Hint: How did he act when he lit his cigar?

2. Is Dr. Susan Calvin patient? _____

    Hint: What does it mean when she says, "It's no use getting impatient."

I, Robot by Isaac Asimov

Alfred Lanning met Dr. Calvin just outside his office. He lit a nervous cigar and motioned her in.

He said, "Well, Susan, we've come pretty far, and Robertson's getting jumpy. What are you doing with The Brain?"

Susan Calvin spread her hands, "It's no use getting impatient. The Brain is worth more than anything we forfeit on this deal."

"But you've been questioning it for two months."

The psychologist's voice was flat, but somehow dangerous, "You would rather run this yourself?"

"Now you know what I meant."

"Oh, I suppose I do," Dr. Calvin rubbed her hands nervously. "It isn't easy. I've been **pampering** it and probing it gently, and I haven't gotten anywhere yet. Its reactions aren't normal. Its answers—they're queer, somehow. But nothing I can put my finger on yet. And you see, until we know what's wrong, we must just tiptoe our way through. I can never tell what simple question or remark will just . . . push him over . . . and then—Well, and then we'll have on our hands a completely useless Brain. Do you want to face that?"

"Well, it can't break the First Law."

"I would have thought so, but—"

"You're not even sure of that?" Lanning was profoundly shocked.

"Oh, I can't be sure of anything, Alfred—"

The alarm system raised its fearful **clangor** with a horrifying suddenness. Lanning clicked on communications with an almost **paralytic** spasm. The breathless words froze him.

He said, "Susan . . . you heard that . . . the ship's gone. I sent those two field men inside half an hour ago. You'll have to see The Brain again."

Identifying the Implied Main Idea The main idea is the most important idea of a paragraph or a passage. In fiction, the main idea is often not stated. It may only be suggested or implied. This means you must figure out, or infer, the main idea yourself.

To figure out the main idea, read the entire passage and think about what is going on. What are the characters saying, thinking, and doing? Read between the lines. What do the stated facts seem to show? What is the author hinting at?

In the passage so far, Dr. Calvin and Dr. Lanning are talking about a third character, The Brain. Which of the following is the implied main idea?

a. The doctors are upset because something is wrong with The Brain.

b. Dr. Calvin is worried about what a fourth character, Robertson, will do.

Susan Calvin said with enforced calm, "Brain, what happened to the ship?"

The Brain said happily, "The ship I built, Miss Susan?"

"That's right. What has happened to it?"

"Why, nothing at all. The two men that were supposed to test it were inside, and we were all set. So I sent it off."

"Oh—Well, that's nice." The psychologist felt some difficulty in breathing. "Do you think they'll be all right?"

"Right as anything, Miss Susan. I've taken care of it all. It's a bee-yoo-tiful ship."

"Yes, Brain, it *is* beautiful, but you think they have enough food, don't you? They'll be comfortable?"

"Plenty of food."

"This business might be a shock to them, Brain. Unexpected, you know."

The Brain tossed it off, "They'll be all right. It ought to be interesting for them."

"Interesting? How?"

"Just interesting," said The Brain, slyly.

"Susan," whispered Lanning in a fuming whisper, "ask him if death comes into it. Ask him what the dangers are."

Susan Calvin's expression **contorted** with fury, "Keep quiet!" In a shaken voice, she said to The Brain, "We can communicate with the ship, can't we, Brain?"

"Oh, they can hear you if you call by radio. I've taken care of that."

"Thanks. That's all for now."

Once outside, Lanning lashed out ragingly, "Great Galaxy, Susan, if this gets out, it will ruin all of us. We've got to get those men back. Why didn't you ask if there was danger of death—straight out?"

"Because," said Calvin, with a weary frustration, "that's just what I can't mention. If it's got a case of **dilemma,** it's about death. Anything that would bring it up badly might knock it completely out. Will we be better off then? Now, look, it said we could communicate with them. Let's do so, get their location, and bring them back. They probably can't use the controls themselves; The Brain is probably handling them remotely. Come!"

Identifying the Implied Main Idea Characters often say things that are clues to the implied main idea. In this second passage, the dialogue between Dr. Calvin and the Brain offers many clues to the implied main idea.

For example, you learn that The Brain can answer the questions Dr. Calvin asks. This is a clue about The Brain's abilities. The way The Brain answers ("happily," "slyly") also offers clues.

In the passage above, what is the implied main idea?

a. The doctors are weary and frustrated.

b. The Brain has taken control.

It was quite a while before Powell shook himself together.

"Mike," he said out of cold lips, "did you feel any **acceleration?**"

Donovan's eyes were blank, "Huh? No . . . no."

And then the redhead's fists clenched and he was out of his seat with sudden frenzied energy and up against the cold, wide-curving glass. There was nothing to see—but stars.

He turned, "Greg, they must have started the machine while we were inside. Greg, it's a put-up job; they fixed it up with the robot to jerry us into being the try-out boys, in case we were thinking of backing out."

Powell said, "What are you talking about? What's the good of sending us out if we don't know how to run the machine? How are we supposed to bring it back? No, this ship left by itself, and without any apparent acceleration." He rose, and walked the floor slowly. The metal walls dinned back the clangor of his steps.

He said tonelessly, "Mike, this is the most confusing situation we've ever been up against."

"That," said Donovan, bitterly, "is news to me. I was just beginning to have a very swell time, when you told me."

Powell ignored that. "No acceleration—which means the ship works on a principle different from any known."

"Different from any we know, anyway."

"Different from *any* known. There are no engines within reach of **manual** control. Maybe they're built into the walls. Maybe that's why they're thick as they are."

"What are you mumbling about?" demanded Donovan.

"Why not listen? I'm saying whatever powers this ship is enclosed, and evidently not meant to be handled. The ship is running by remote control."

"The Brain's control?"

"Why not?"

"Then you think we'll stay out here till The Brain brings us back."

"It could be. If so, let's wait quietly. The Brain is a robot. It's got to follow the First Law. It can't hurt a human being."

Recognizing Supporting Details In the last passage, The Brain sent two men and a spaceship into space, and the men have no control over the ship. One implied main idea of the passage is this: the men in the ship have the skills to figure out what happened to them.

Write two clues or details that help the men figure out what happened to them.

_____

_____

Thinking About the Story

Practice Vocabulary

The words below are in bold type in the passage. Study the way each word is used. Then match each word with its meaning. Write the letter.

_____ 1. pampering

_____ 2. clangor

_____ 3. contorted

_____ 4. dilemma

_____ 5. acceleration

_____ 6. manual

_____ 7. paralytic

a. unable to move

b. speeding up

c. twisted

d. a problem

e. a harsh, ringing noise

f. by hand

g. spoiling, or taking special care of

Understand What You Read

Circle the letter of the best answer to each question.

8. Who or what is The Brain?
   a. The Brain is a being from another planet.
   b. The Brain is a robot.

9. What is the First Law?
   a. The First Law states that a robot cannot harm a human being.
   b. The First Law states that a robot must obey a human being.

10. What do the two doctors fear will happen to the men in the ship?
    a. They are afraid that the men will steal the ship.
    b. They are afraid that the men will die or be unable to return.

Write the answer to each question.

11. Why does Dr. Calvin have to be so careful about what she says to The Brain?

_____

_____

12. What does Powell mean when he says that "this is the most confusing situation we've ever been up against"?

_____

_____

Apply Your Skills

Circle the number of the best answer for each question.

13. Which statement best expresses the implied main idea of the entire passage?
    (1) The scientists have lost control of their own experiment.
    (2) Robots are angry about being used by human beings.
    (3) Robots are always smarter than human beings.
    (4) Robots make life easier for human beings.
    (5) Scientists should never have invented robots.

14. Which of the following sentences from the story indicates that the two men on the ship are in danger?
    (1) He lit a nervous cigar and motioned her in.
    (2) "But you've been questioning it for two months."
    (3) "The ship I built, Miss Susan?"
    (4) "Just interesting," said The Brain, slyly.
    (5) "What are you mumbling about?" demanded Donovan.

15. Which of the following best supports the idea that Powell and Donovan are shocked to discover that the ship has taken off?
    (1) He rose, and walked the floor slowly.
    (2) "Greg, they must have started the machine while we were inside."
    (3) . . . the redhead's fists clenched . . .
    (4) . . . he was out of his seat with sudden frenzied energy . . .
    (5) "What are you mumbling about?" demanded Donovan.

Connect with the Story

Write your answer to each question.

16. Which character would you choose to be—Alfred Lanning or Susan Calvin? Or, would you not like to be either one? In a sentence or two, explain why.

    _____

    _____

    _____

17. Do you think the problem presented in the story from *I, Robot* is realistic? In other words, could computer programmers and scientists go too far in inventing computers that "think"? Explain why or why not.

    _____

    _____

    _____

Thriller Novel

Vocabulary

momentarily

cylindrical

methodical

glimpse

synchronized

pondering

hunkered

incline

Thriller novels are scary, full of creaking sounds and shadows and dark spirits. Reading a thriller novel can make you shiver, cause chills to run up your spine, or make the hair on the back of your neck stand up. For many people, the scarier a thriller story is, the better.

Relate to the Topic

The passage you are about to read is about two people who are interested in investigating a suspicious man. Maybe you have investigated something suspicious or strange, such as an odd noise in your house.

What did you investigate? _____

Describe your experience. _____

_____

_____

Reading Strategy

DETERMINING MOOD   You can determine the mood of a story or character by looking at the words that show feeling, such as "excited" or "puzzled." Often, in the beginning of a story, an author uses words that create the mood for the whole story. For example, the writer might use certain words to describe whether a place is safe or dangerous. This helps the reader get ready for what is to come later in the story. Read the first paragraph on page 113. Then answer the questions.

1. How does the author's use of the word "they" create a feeling of

   uneasiness? _____

   _____

   Hint: Think about why the author keeps saying the word "they."

2. What mood does the description of Straker in the first paragraph create?

   _____

   Hint: Read the last sentence of the first paragraph.

Salem's Lot by Stephen King

When he first heard the distant snapping of twigs, he crept behind the trunk of a large spruce and stood there, waiting to see who would show up. *They* couldn't come out in the daytime, but that didn't mean *they* couldn't get people who could; giving them money was one way, but it wasn't the only way. Mark had seen that guy Straker in town, and his eyes were like the eyes of a toad sunning itself on a rock. He looked like he could break a baby's arm and smile while he did it.

He touched the heavy shape of his father's target pistol in his jacket pocket. Bullets were no good against *them*—except maybe silver ones—but a shot between the eyes would punch that Straker's ticket, all right.

His eyes shifted downward **momentarily** to the roughly **cylindrical** shape propped against the tree, wrapped in an old piece of toweling. There was a woodpile behind his house, half a cord of yellow ash stove lengths which he and his father had cut with the McCulloch chain saw in July and August. Henry Petrie was **methodical,** and each length, Mark knew, would be within an inch of three feet, one way or the other. His father knew the proper length just as he knew that winter followed fall, and that yellow ash would burn longer and cleaner in the living room fireplace.

His son, who knew other things, knew that ash was for men—things—like *him*. This morning, while his mother and father were out on their Sunday bird walk, he had taken one of the lengths and whacked one end into a rough point with his Boy Scout hatchet. It was rough, but it would serve.

Identifying Point of View in Fiction Every story is told from a particular **point of view.** In a story told from the main character's point of view, for example, readers feel as if they're seeing the action through the main character's eyes, or hearing through her or his ears. In another story, the point of view might let the reader know what *every* character is thinking or feeling.

An author has many possible points of view to choose from when writing a story. To identify point of view when you read, ask yourself whose actions you are following most closely. Whose eyes are you seeing through? Whose thoughts do you know? In the passage above, the story is told from Mark's point of view.

Which phrase from the passage shows the story is told from Mark's point of view?

a. His eyes shifted momentarily to the roughly cylindrical shape . . .
b. His son, who knew other things, knew that ash was for men . . .

The character telling the story is called the narrator. This story is told from Mark's point of view, but Mark is not the narrator. Mark is not telling his own story. Someone else is telling the story about him.

He saw a flash of color and shrank back against the tree, peering around the rough bark with one eye. A moment later he got his first clear **glimpse** of the person climbing the hill. It was a girl. He felt a sense of relief mingled with disappointment. No henchman of the devil there; that was Mr. Norton's daughter.

His gaze sharpened again. She was carrying a stake of her own! As she drew closer, he felt an urge to laugh bitterly—a piece of snow fence, that's what she had. Two swings with an ordinary tool box hammer would split it right in two.

She was going to pass his tree on the right. As she drew closer, he began to slide carefully around his tree to the left, avoiding any small twigs that might pop and give him away. At last the **synchronized** little movement was done; her back was to him as she went on up the hill toward the break in the trees. She was going very carefully, he noted with approval. That was good. In spite of the silly snow fence stake, she apparently had some idea of what she was getting into. Still, if she went much further, she was going to be in trouble. Straker was at home. Mark had been here since twelve-thirty, and he had seen Straker go out to the driveway and look down the road and then go back into the house. Mark had been trying to make up his mind on what to do himself when this girl had entered things, upsetting the equation.

Perhaps she was going to be all right. She had stopped behind a screen of bushes and was crouching there, just looking at the house. Mark turned it over in his mind. Obviously she knew. How didn't matter, but she would not have had even that pitiful stake with her if she didn't know. He supposed he would have to go up and warn her that Straker was still around, and on guard. She probably didn't have a gun, not even a little one like his.

Understanding the Setting Setting tells where and when the action takes place. Look for clues to find out what the setting is. For example, look for words that tell whether the characters are indoors or outdoors. Look for words that describe the time of day or the season of the year. Look for words that tell how things around the characters look and sound.

In the passage above, Mark is watching a girl as she moves along. The two of them are outside. Which of the following best describes the place?

   a.   a neighborhood with small houses set close together

   b.   a wooded area with hills near someone's house

When you read, try to picture the setting in your mind. Use the clues the author gives you about the time and place. Imagine yourself in the place. Imagine that you are there watching the characters and the action.

He was **pondering** how to make his presence known to her without having her scream her head off when the motor of Straker's car roared into life. She jumped visibly, and at first he was afraid she was going to break and run, crashing through the woods and advertising her presence for a hundred miles. But then she **hunkered** down again, holding on to the ground like she was afraid it would fly away from her. She's got guts even if she is stupid, he thought approvingly.

Straker's car backed down the driveway—she would have a much better view from where she was; he could only see the Packard's black roof—hesitated for a moment, and then went off down the road toward town.

He decided they had to team up. Anything would be better than going up to that house alone. He had already sampled the poison atmosphere that enveloped it. He had felt it from a half a mile away, and it thickened as you got closer.

Now he ran lightly up the carpeted **incline** and put his hand on her shoulder. He felt her body tense, knew she was going to scream, and said, "Don't yell. It's all right. It's me."

She didn't scream. What escaped was a terrified exhalation of air. She turned around and looked at him, her face white. "W-Who's me?"

He sat down beside her. "My name is Mark Petrie. I know you; you're Sue Norton. My dad knows your dad."

"Petrie . . .? Henry Petrie?"

"Yes, that's my father."

"What are you doing here?" Her eyes were moving continually over him, as if she hadn't been able to take in his actuality yet.

"The same thing you are. Only that stake won't work. It's too . . ." He groped for a word that had checked into his vocabulary through sight and definition but not by use. "It's too flimsy."

She looked down at her piece of snow fence and actually blushed. "Oh, that. Well, I found that in the woods and . . . and thought someone might fall over it, so I just—"

He cut her adult temporizing short impatiently: "You came to kill the vampire, didn't you?"

Applying Ideas A writer gives the reader many ideas about the characters in a story. When you have this information, you can sometimes figure out how a character will act later in the story. You can apply an idea about a character to another situation. Most characters have a particular personality and are likely to react the same way in many situations.

Apply what you know about Sue. If Sue found a young woman collapsed on the sidewalk, what would she most likely do?

a. She would turn pale and faint.

b. She would try to help the woman.

Thinking About the Story

Practice Vocabulary

Complete each sentence by writing the correct word.

momentarily	cylindrical	methodical	glimpse
synchronized	pondering	hunkered	incline

1. When you look briefly at a tree, you get only a _____ of it.

2. Ed is very _____ ; he works in a careful and precise way.

3. Mark spent several days _____ the problem, trying to think of a solution.

4. She _____ down, kneeling on her hands and knees, close to the ground.

5. It took him a long time to ride his bike up the _____ to the top of the hill.

6. Something that has the shape of a tube is _____

7. Jill stopped watching the road _____ , and right then she had the accident.

8. Figure skating pairs must always be _____ carefully making their movements at the same time.

Understand What You Read

Write the answer to each question.

9. List two things Mark did to prepare to go to Straker's house.

_____

_____

10. Why does Mark move so carefully while he's watching Sue?

_____

_____

11. Why does Mark think Sue is there to kill the vampire?

_____

_____

Apply Your Skills

Circle the number of the best answer for each question.

12. Imagine that the author wanted to change the story and tell it from Sue's point of view. Which of the following sentences represents her point of view?
    (1) Mark had seen that guy Straker in town. . . .
    (2) She turned around and looked at him. . . .
    (3) It was a girl. He felt a sense of relief mingled with disappointment.
    (4) As she drew closer, he felt an urge to laugh bitterly. . . .
    (5) He felt her body tense, knew she was going to scream. . . .

13. Which of the following groups of words from the story tell the most about the setting?
    (1) Anything would be better than going up to that house alone.
    (2) Now he ran lightly up the carpeted incline . . . .
    (3) . . . she went on up the hill toward the break in the trees.
    (4) . . . the motor of Straker's car roared into life.
    (5) . . . yellow ash would burn longer and cleaner in the living room fireplace.

14. How might Mark act if he were preparing for a special holiday party?

    He would
    (1) not bother to think ahead and do things at the last minute
    (2) plan every detail long before the party
    (3) prepare somewhat and deal with things as they happened
    (4) make all of the preparations by himself
    (5) consult his father before doing anything

Connect with the Story

Write your answer to each question.

15. If you were rewriting this story from Sue's point of view, what would you have her think about Mark?

    _____

    _____

16. In this passage, Mark has decided he wants to team up with Sue. Do you prefer to have a partner or team with you when you attack a problem? Or do you prefer to handle problems by yourself? Give reasons for your answer.

    _____

    _____

Popular Novel

Popular Novel

Popular Novel

Vocabulary

posed

pranced

inhaled

intervals

baste

hesitantly

Popular novels are works of fiction that often focus on families, love, marriage, or work—issues that are important to all of us. Almost always, the characters face some sort of problem or conflict. These novels may entertain, but the best of them also express important ideas and values.

Relate to the Topic

The passage you are about to read is about three women who have known each other for a long time. Their feelings for each other are deep and loving. One of the women, Ciel, returns after a long absence. The reunion is joyous and tearful.

Have you ever had a reunion with someone you loved? What happened? How did you feel?

_____

_____

_____

Reading Strategy

READING DIALOGUE   Dialogue is the conversation between characters. You can learn a lot about a character through the dialogue. Characters reveal what they think and how they feel about each other. Remember that dialogue is enclosed in quotation marks. When a new character speaks, the author starts a new paragraph.

Read the first five paragraphs of the passage on page 119 and "hear" the dialogue in your head.

1.   How many people are in the conversation?

_____

Hint: Picture the people as you read. How many people are speaking?

2.   Read Mattie's comments. What do they tell you about her attitude toward Etta?

_____

Hint: Read paragraphs three and five.

The Women of Brewster Place

by Gloria Naylor

"Miss Johnson, you wanna dance?" A handsome teenager **posed** himself in a seductive dare before Etta. She ran her hand down the side of her hair and took off her apron.

"Don't mind if I do." And she **pranced** around the table.

"Woman, come back here and act your age." Mattie speared a rib off the grill.

"I am acting it—thirty-five!"

"Umph, you got *regrets* older than that."

The boy spun Etta around under his arms. "Careful, now, honey. It's still in working order, but I gotta keep it running in a little lower gear." She winked at Mattie and danced toward the center of the street.

Mattie shook her head. "Lord keep her safe, since you can't keep her sane." She smiled and patted her foot under the table to the beat of the music while she looked down the street and **inhaled** the hope that was bouncing off swinging hips, sauce-covered fingers, and grinning mouths.

A thin brown-skinned woman, carrying a trench coat and overnight case, was making her way slowly up the block. She stopped at **intervals** to turn and answer the people who called to her—"Hey, Ciel! Good to see you, girl!"

Ciel—a knot formed at the base of Mattie's heart, and she caught her breath. "No."

Ciel came up to Mattie and stood in front of her timidly. "Hi, Mattie. It's been a long time."

"No." Mattie shook her head slowly.

"I know you're probably mad at me. I should have written or at least called before now."

"Child." Mattie placed a hand gently on Ciel's face.

"But I thought about you all the time, really, Mattie."

"Child." Both of Mattie's hands cupped Ciel's face.

"I had to get away; you know that. I needed to leave Brewster Place as far behind me as I could. I just kept going and going until the highway ran out. And when I looked up, I was in San Francisco and there was nothing but an ocean in front of me, and since I couldn't swim, I stayed."

"Child. Child." Mattie pulled Ciel toward her.

"It was awful not to write—I know that." Ciel was starting to cry. "But I kept saying one day when I've gotten rid of the scars, when I'm really well and over all that's happened so that she can be proud of me, then I'll write and let her know."

"Child. Child. Child." Mattie pressed Ciel into her full bosom and rocked her slowly.

"But that day never came, Mattie." Ciel's tears fell on Mattie's chest as she hugged the woman. "And I stopped believing that it ever would."

"Thank God you found that out." Mattie released Ciel and squeezed her shoulders. "Or I woulda had to wait till the Judgment Day for this here joy."

She gave Ciel a paper napkin to blow her nose. "San Francisco, you said? My, that's a long way. Bet you ain't had none of this out there." She cut Ciel a huge slice of angel food cake on her table.

"Oh, Mattie, this looks good." She took a bite. "Tastes just like the kind my grandmother used to make."

"It should—it's her recipe. The first night I came to Miss Eva's house she gave me a piece of that cake. I never knew till then why they called it angel food—took one bite and thought I had died and gone to heaven."

Ciel laughed. "Yeah, Grandma could cook. We really had some good times in that house. I remember how Basil and I used to fight. I would go to bed and pray, God please bless Grandma and Mattie, but only bless Basil if he stops breaking my crayons. Do you ever hear from him, Mattie?"

Mattie frowned and turned to **baste** her ribs. "Naw, Ciel. Guess he ain't been as lucky as you yet. Ain't run out of highway to stop and make him think."

Drawing Conclusions A **conclusion** is an opinion or judgment you make after studying all the facts you have. The conclusion is not usually stated directly in what you read.

To draw a conclusion, use two or more stated ideas to come up with an idea that is not directly stated in the reading. You can conclude some things based on the facts that you find in the reading.

Which two facts from the passage support the conclusion that Ciel and Mattie have known each other for a very long time?
a. Ciel talks about events from long ago.
b. Ciel says that she has been living in San Francisco.
c. Ciel tells Mattie that it has been a long time since they have seen each other.

To draw the conclusion that Ciel and Mattie have known each other for a very long time, you "read between the lines." This means you have to go beyond what the passage actually says to reach this conclusion.

Etta came back to the table out of breath. "Well, looka you!" She grabbed Ciel and kissed her. "Gal, you looking good. Where you been hiding yourself?"

"I live in San Francisco now, Miss Etta, and I'm working in an insurance company."

"Frisco, yeah, that's a nice city—been through there once. But don't tell me it's salt water putting a shine on that face." She patted Ciel on the cheeks. "Bet you got a new fella."

Ciel blushed. "Well, I have met someone and we're sort of thinking about marriage." She looked up at Mattie. "I'm ready to start another family now."

. . . Mattie beamed.

"But he's not black." She glanced **hesitantly** between Etta and Mattie.

"And I bet he's not eight feet tall, and he's not as pretty as Billy Dee Williams, and he's *not* president of Yugoslavia, either," Etta said. "You know, we get so caught up with what a man *isn't*. It's what he is that counts. Is he good to you, child?"

"And is he good for you?" Mattie added gently.

"Very much so." Ciel smiled.

"Then, I'm baking your wedding cake." Mattie grinned.

"And I'll come dance at your reception." Etta popped her fingers.

Mattie turned to Etta. "Woman, ain't you done enough dancing today for a lifetime?"

"Aw, hush your mouth. Ciel, will you tell this woman that this here is a party and you supposed to be having a good time."

"And will you tell that woman," Mattie said, "that hip-shaking is for young folks, and old bags like us is supposed to be behind these tables selling food."

"You two will never change." Ciel laughed.

Visualizing Characters Sometimes characters in fiction are described in detail. Sometimes the author says only a little about how they look. Either way, characters become more alive if you can form some mental pictures of them.

To visualize a character, use all the details you can find about how the character looks. What the person does and says also helps create a mental picture. In the passage above, look at what Etta says and does. Also, look at what Mattie says to Etta or about her.

Based on details in the passage, which of the following is the best description of Etta Johnson?

    a.   middle-aged but energetic
    b.   awkward and shy

Thinking About the Story

Practice Vocabulary

The words below are in bold type in the passage. Study the way each word is used. Then match each word with its meaning. Write the letter.

_____ 1. posed

_____ 2. pranced

_____ 3. inhaled

_____ 4. intervals

_____ 5. baste

_____ 6. hesitantly

a. breathed in

b. spaces in time between events

c. brush liquid on roasting meat

d. in an unsure way

e. stood in a way intended to impress

f. walked in a proud, happy way

Understand What You Read

Write the answer to each question.

7. Where has Ciel been?

_____

_____

8. Who is Miss Eva, and what fact do you know about her?

_____

_____

9. Why do you think Ciel is hesitant after she tells Etta and Mattie that her boyfriend is not black?

_____

_____

10. How do Etta and Mattie feel about Ciel's new boyfriend?

_____

_____

11. How do you think Etta and Mattie feel about each other?

_____

_____

_____

Apply Your Skills

Circle the number of the best answer for each question.

12. What can you conclude about the setting of this passage? Where are these people?
    (1) at a family reunion
    (2) at Etta's birthday party
    (3) at an outdoor neighborhood party
    (4) at a San Francisco restaurant
    (5) at a wedding reception

13. What can you conclude about why Ciel left Brewster Place?
    (1) She had some kind of personal trouble.
    (2) She left to go to college.
    (3) She wanted to see the ocean.
    (4) Her grandma died.
    (5) Her friend Mattie sent her away.

14. Etta and Mattie are different in personality. Which sentence best describes their differences?
    (1) Etta thinks only of herself, while Mattie thinks mainly of others.
    (2) Etta gets angry easily, while Mattie is very calm.
    (3) Etta feels restless in Brewster Place, while Mattie is completely satisfied there.
    (4) Etta is an at-home type, while Mattie likes to go out and party.
    (5) Etta likes to go out and party, while Mattie is an at-home type.

Connect with the Story

Write your answer to each question.

15. Do you think of yourself as more like Etta or more like Mattie? Give reasons for your answer.

    _____

    _____

    _____

16. Could you be satisfied living in the same neighborhood all your life? Or are you more like Ciel, who needed to get away? Give reasons for your answer.

    _____

    _____

    _____

Folk Novel

Vocabulary

churned

listlessly

subsided

furrow

abode

relented

People have been telling certain tales over and over for centuries. These stories are called **folktales.** Folk novels retell these old stories, which are set in far-distant times and places.

Folktales often teach a lesson or explain how something began. Folktales also include ideas that are important to a group of people or a culture. By using a folktale as part of a longer story, a writer can show how events today are connected to the past.

Relate to the Topic

An important theme in the story you are about to read is the struggle for survival. The reader learns about this struggle in two ways. First, the fish struggle with the river as it floods and then dries up. Second, the early people struggled for survival when their crops died.

Is there a story in your family history, or in a family you know, about a struggle for survival? Most families have such a story. What is the story in your family or in a family you know?

_____

_____

_____

Reading Strategy

USING CONTEXT CLUES   Sometimes a story contains a word that the reader doesn't understand. One way to figure out the meaning of the word is to see how it is used in the sentence. Look at the words or phrases before or after the unknown word. They have clues about the meaning. The word "subside" is in the first sentence of the last paragraph on page 125. Read the sentence. Then answer the questions.

1. What does the word "subside" mean?

_____

Hint: Look at the surrounding words.

2. Which surrounding words give clues to the meaning of "subside"?

_____

Hint: Which words explain what happens to the water?

Bless Me, Ultima by Rudolfo A. Anaya

"You fish a lot?" I asked.

"I have always been a fisherman," he answered, "as long as I can remember—"

"You fish," he said.

"Yes. I learned to fish with my brothers when I was very little. Then they went to war and I couldn't fish anymore. Then Ultima came—" I paused.

"I know," he said.

"So last summer I fished. Sometimes with Jasón."

"You have a lot to learn—"

"Yes," I answered.

The afternoon sun was warm on the sand. The muddy waters after-the-flood **churned listlessly** south, and out of the deep hole by the rock in front of us the catfish came. They were biting good for the first fishing of summer. We caught plenty of channel catfish and a few small yellow-bellies.

"Have you ever fished for the carp of the river?"

The river was full of big, brown carp. It was called the River of the Carp. Everybody knew it was bad luck to fish for the big carp that the summer floods washed downstream. After every flood, when the swirling angry waters of the river **subsided,** the big fish could be seen fighting their way back upstream. It had always been so.

The waters would subside very fast and in places the water would be so low that, as the carp swam back upstream, the backs of the fish would raise a **furrow** in the water. Sometimes the townspeople came to stand on the bridge and watch the struggle as the carp splashed their way back to the pools from which the flood had uprooted them. Some of the town kids, not knowing it was bad luck to catch the carp, would scoop them out of the low waters and toss the fish upon the sand bars.

Identifying Figurative Language (Personification) Authors sometimes use language in a special way called personification. In personification, something that is not human is given human qualities. For example, an author might say that the wind whistled sadly through the trees. People can feel the emotion of sadness, but wind cannot. The author has used the word "sadly" to create a mood and make the reader think of a low, soft sound.

In the passage above, the author uses the word "angry" to describe the water. This is an example of personification that helps to create a mood. What does that word suggest to you?

  a. The level of the water was very low.
  b. The water was very rough and, perhaps, dangerous.

There the poor carp would flop until they dried out and died, then later the crows would swoop down and eat them.

Some people in town would even buy the carp for a nickel and eat the fish! That was very bad. Why, I did not know.

It was a beautiful sight to behold, the struggle of the carp to regain his **abode** before the river dried to a trickle and trapped him in strange pools of water. What was beautiful about it was that you knew that against all the odds some of the carp made it back and raised their families, because every year the drama was repeated.

"No," I answered, "I do not fish for carp. It is bad luck."

"Do you know why?" he asked and raised an eyebrow.

"No," I said and held my breath. I felt I sat on the banks of an undiscovered river whose churning, muddied waters carried many secrets.

"I will tell you a story," Samuel said after a long silence, "a story that was told to my father by Jasón's Indian—"

I listened breathlessly. The lapping of the water was like the tide of time sounding on my soul.

"A long time ago, when the earth was young and only wandering tribes touched the virgin grasslands and drank from the pure streams, a strange people came to this land. They were sent to this valley by their gods. They had wandered lost for many years but never had they given up faith in their gods, and so they were finally rewarded. This fertile valley was to be their home. There were plenty of animals to eat, strange trees that bore sweet fruit, sweet water to drink and for their fields of maíz [corn]—"

"Were they Indians?" I asked when he paused.

"They were *the people,*" he answered simply and went on. "There was only one thing that was withheld from them, and that was the fish called the carp. This fish made his home in the waters of the river, and he was sacred to the gods. For a long time the people were happy. Then came the forty years of the sun-without-rain, and crops withered and died, the game was killed, and the people went hungry. To stay alive they finally caught the carp of the river and ate them."

Identifying Point of View A story is often told through the eyes of only one character, the narrator. In that case, we are hearing the story from the narrator's point of view. In this story, we have a first-person narrator, identified by the word "I" in the first sentence. This point of view makes the action in a story seem very real.

Who is the narrator in this passage?
a. Samuel
b. We don't know his name.

I shivered. I had never heard a story like this one. It was getting late and I thought of my mother.

"The gods were very angry. They were going to kill all of the people for their sin. But one kind god who truly loved the people argued against it, and the other gods were so moved by his love that they **relented** from killing the people. Instead, they turned the people into carp and made them live forever in the waters of the river—"

The setting sun glistened on the brown waters of the river and turned them to bronze.

"It is a sin to catch them," Samuel said, "it is a worse offense to eat them. They are a part of *the people*." He pointed towards the middle of the river where two huge back fins rose out of the water and splashed upstream.

"And if you eat one," I whispered, "you might be punished like they were punished."

"I don't know," Samuel said. He rose and took my fishing line.

"Is that all the story?" I asked.

He divided the catfish we had caught and gave me my share on a small string. "No, there is more," he said. He glanced around as if to make sure we were alone. "Do you know about the golden carp?" he asked in a whisper.

"No," I shook my head.

"When the gods had turned the people into carp, the one kind god who loved the people grew very sad. The river was full of dangers to the new fish. So he went to the other gods and told them that he chose to be turned into a carp and swim in the river where he could take care of his people. The gods agreed. But because he was a god they made him very big and colored him the color of gold. And they made him the lord of all the waters of the valley."

Understanding Sequence One way an author can organize a story is by using sequence, or presenting events as they occur in time. To follow the sequence in a story, look for the order that things happen in time.

Sometimes that author uses words that help you know what the order of events is. Look for clue words such as "first," "second," "later," "then," "while," "before," "after," "during," and "since."

In Samuel's story, what happened after the people ate the carp?
a.   The gods became angry.
b.   The forty years of sun-without-rain began.

FOLK NOVEL

Check your answers on page 242.

Thinking About the Story

Practice Vocabulary

The words below are in bold type in the passage. Study the way each word is used. Then complete each sentence by writing the correct word.

churned	listlessly	subsided
furrow	abode	relented

1. The path left in the ground by a plow is called a _____

2. The boiling water _____ in the pot on the stove.

3. Samuel had no energy, so he lay _____ on his bed.

4. The woman knew she could change the run-down apartment into a cozy _____.

5. We waited until the flood _____ before we cleaned up the mess.

6. The parents sometimes _____ on their strict rules when their children gave good reasons for breaking those rules.

Understand What You Read

Write the answer to each question.

7. Why doesn't the narrator fish for carp?

_____

_____

8. In Samuel's story, why did the people eat the carp?

_____

_____

_____

9. In Samuel's story, why did the gods decide to save the people even though the people had eaten the carp?

_____

_____

_____

Apply Your Skills

Circle the number of the best answer for each question.

10. Which of the following phrases includes a personification?
    (1) the tide of time sounding on my soul
    (2) the struggle of the carp
    (3) muddied water carried many secrets
    (4) they turned the people into carp
    (5) forty years of the sun-without-rain

11. If the author had written the passage from Samuel's point of view, what might we not know?
    (1) that the boy thought of his mother while Samuel was talking
    (2) why the people ate the carp
    (3) why the gods agreed not to kill the people
    (4) that the kind god chose to be turned into a carp
    (5) that it was considered a sin to catch carp and a bigger sin to eat them

12. In the sequence of Samuel's story, when did the god become a golden carp?
    (1) while the people were eating the carp from the river
    (2) after the people had been turned into carp
    (3) after Samuel divided the catfish up with the boy
    (4) while the people were being turned into carp
    (5) before the gods got angry

Connect with the Story

Write your answer to each question.

13. In this passage, Samuel explains certain beliefs about the history and ways of his people. How have you learned the history and beliefs of your family or people? Explain your answer.

    _____

    _____

14. At the beginning of the story, the boy knows it's wrong to catch carp, but no one has ever told him why it is wrong. Do you think it's important to know *why* something is wrong? Or is it enough simply to know that it *is* wrong? Explain your answer.

    _____

    _____

    _____

Classic Short Story

Classic Short Story
Classic Short Story

Vocabulary

acute

dissimulation

sufficient

sagacity

stifled

suppositions

enveloped

unperceived

crevice

stealthily

A short story is a piece of fiction that is shorter than a novel but has a full plot. A short story usually has only a few main characters and takes place over a shorter time period than a novel. Writers have been publishing short stories in books, newspapers, and magazines for more than a century. A very famous writer of scary short stories was Edgar Allan Poe (1809–1849). His spine-chilling stories have been made into movies and TV shows.

Relate to the Topic

Most of the passage you are about to read takes place inside a dark bedroom where an old man sleeps. The narrator of the story describes his method for sneaking into that room at night, trying not to awaken the old man. The narrator imagines what the man in the bedroom is feeling after a sound awakens him one night.

Have you ever been awakened in the night by a sound, then lay there listening for every scratch or creak? Describe the experience. How did it feel?

_____

_____

_____

Reading Strategy

USING TITLES   Titles let readers know what stories are about. Sometimes a title is very clear and direct. Other times a title only gives hints or clues about the subject and mood of a story. Either way, the title is the first clue to what a story is going to be like. Read the title of the passage on page 131. Then answer the questions.

1. What does the title suggest about the mood of the story?

_____

Hint: Is this going to be a light-hearted story?

2. What does "tell-tale" mean?

_____

Hint: What does it mean to tell a tale on someone?

The Tell-Tale Heart by Edgar Allan Poe

True!—nervous—very, very dreadfully nervous I had been and am; but why *will* you say that I am mad? The disease had sharpened my senses—not destroyed—not dulled them. Above all was the sense of hearing **acute.** I heard all things in the heaven and in the earth. . . . How, then, am I mad? Hearken! and observe how healthily—how calmly I can tell you the whole story.

It is impossible to say how first the idea entered my brain; but once conceived, it haunted me day and night. Object there was none. Passion there was none. I loved the old man. He had never wronged me. He had never given me insult. For his gold I had no desire. I think it was his eye! Yes, it was this! One of his eyes resembled that of a vulture—a pale blue eye, with a film over it. Whenever it fell upon me, my blood ran cold; and so by degrees—very gradually—I made up my mind to take the life of the old man, and thus rid myself of the eye forever.

Using Definitions as Context Clues The context of a word or phrase is the language around it that gives clues to its meaning. Sometimes an author defines an unfamiliar word or phrase for the reader by using context clues. For example, in the passage above, the phrase "sharpened my senses" is used. By saying the opposite, "not destroyed—not dulled them," the author makes the meaning of the phrase clear. Definition clues are usually found after a word and are set off by commas or dashes.

In the passage above, the author uses the phrase "by degrees." Look for it. Based on the context clue, what is the meaning of this phrase?

a. doing something very gradually
b. making up one's mind

Now this is the point. You fancy me mad. Madmen know nothing. But you should have seen *me*. You should have seen how wisely I proceeded—with what caution—with what foresight—with what **dissimulation** I went to work! I was never kinder to the old man than during the whole week before I killed him. And every night, about midnight, I turned the latch of his door and opened it—oh, so gently! And then, when I had made an opening **sufficient** for my head, I put in a dark lantern, all closed, closed, so that no light shone out, and then I thrust in my head. Oh, you would have laughed to see how cunningly I thrust it in! I moved it slowly—very, very slowly, so that I might not disturb the old man's sleep. It took me an hour to place my whole head within the opening so far that I could see him as he lay upon his bed. Ha!—would a madman have been so wise as this? And then, when my head was well in the room, I undid the lantern cautiously—oh, so cautiously—cautiously (for the hinges creaked)—I undid it just so much that a single thin ray fell upon the vulture eye.

And this I did for seven long nights—every night just at midnight—but I found the eye always closed; and so it was impossible to do the work; for it was not the old man who vexed me, but his Evil Eye. And every morning, when the day broke, I went boldly into the chamber, and spoke courageously to him, calling him by name in a hearty tone, and inquiring how he had passed the night. So you see he would have been a very profound old man, indeed, to suspect that every night, just at twelve, I looked in upon him while he slept.

Upon the eighth night I was more than usually cautious in opening the door. A watch's minute hand moves more quickly than did mine. Never before that night had I *felt* the extent of my own powers—of my **sagacity.** I could scarcely contain my feelings of triumph. To think that there I was, opening the door, little by little, and he not even to dream of my secret deeds or thoughts. I fairly chuckled at the idea; and perhaps he heard me; for he moved on the bed suddenly, as if startled. Now you may think that I drew back—but no. His room was as black as pitch with the thick darkness (for the shutters were close fastened, through fear of robbers), and so I knew he could not see the opening of the door, and I kept pushing it on steadily, steadily.

I had my head in, and was about to open the lantern, when my thumb slipped upon the tin fastening, and the old man sprang up in the bed, crying out—"Who's there?"

I kept quite still and said nothing. For a whole hour I did not move a muscle, and in the meantime I did not hear him lie down. He was still sitting up in the bed listening;—just as I have done, night after night, hearkening to the death watches in the wall.

Understanding Mood The mood of a story is like the mood of a person. It can be tense and gloomy, light and joyous, or dark and frightening. An author has many ways of creating mood: telling what the characters are like, describing the setting, and indicating how quickly or slowly events occur.

In this story, the author creates the mood by introducing a peculiar and nervous character and making him sneak around in someone's dark bedroom. The language "hinges creaked," "vulture eye," and "stalked with his black shadow" also contributes to the mood.

What is the mood of this passage?
a. light and comical
b. dark and spooky

Presently I heard a slight groan, and I knew it was the groan of mortal terror. It was not a groan of pain or of grief—oh, no!—it was the low **stifled** sound that arises from the bottom of the soul when overcharged with awe. I knew the sound well. Many a night, just at midnight, when all the world slept, it has welled up from my own bosom, deepening, with its dreadful echo, the terrors that distracted me. I say I knew it well. I knew what the old man felt, and pitied him, although I chuckled at heart. I knew that he had been lying awake ever since the first slight noise, when he had turned in the bed. His fears had been ever since growing upon him. He had been trying to fancy them causeless, but could not. He had been saying to himself—"It is nothing but the wind in the chimney—it is only a mouse crossing the floor," or "it is merely a cricket which has made a single chirp." Yes, he had been trying to comfort himself with these **suppositions;** but he has found all in vain. *All in vain;* because Death, in approaching him, had stalked with his black shadow before him, and **enveloped** the victim. And it was the mournful influence of the **unperceived** shadow that caused him to feel—although he neither saw nor heard—to *feel* the presence of my head within the room.

When I had waited a long time, very patiently, without hearing him lie down, I resolved to open a little—a very, very little **crevice** in the lantern. So I opened it—you cannot imagine how, **stealthily,** stealthily—until, at length, a single dim ray, like the thread of the spider, shot from out the crevice and full upon the vulture eye.

It was open—wide, wide open—and I grew furious as I gazed upon it. I saw it with perfect distinctness—all a dull blue, with a hideous veil over it that chilled the very marrow in my bones; but I could see nothing else of the old man's face or person: for I had directed the ray as if by instinct, precisely upon the . . . spot.

And now have I not told you that what you mistake for madness is but over-acuteness of the senses?—now, I say, there came to my ears a low, dull, quick sound, such as a watch makes when enveloped in cotton. I knew *that* sound well too. It was the beating of the old man's heart. It increased my fury, as the beating of a drum stimulates the soldier into courage.

Predicting Outcomes Sometimes an author ends a story without telling what finally happened. The reader must figure out the ending. When you do that, you are predicting the outcome. You use the information presented in the story to predict what will happen.

The outcome you predict must fit the story. It must make sense with what you know about the characters and what has already happened in the story.

In the part of "The Tell-Tale Heart" you have read, you have seen how upset the narrator gets because of the old man's "vulture" eye. Now he has finally seen the eye in the middle of the night. What do you think he will do next?

   a.   He will probably go ahead with his plan to kill the old man.

   b.   He will probably get control of his feelings, sneak out of the room, and close the door.

Thinking About the Story

Practice Vocabulary

The words below are in bold type in the passage. Study the way each word is used. Then match each word with its meaning. Write the letter.

_____ 1. acute

_____ 2. stealthily

_____ 3. sufficient

_____ 4. enveloped

_____ 5. sagacity

_____ 6. stifled

_____ 7. suppositions

_____ 8. unperceived

_____ 9. crevice

_____ 10. dissimulation

a. not seen

b. surrounded

c. enough

d. wisdom

e. small crack

f. the process of disguising one's intentions

g. sharp

h. ideas assumed to be correct

i. held in

j. quietly and secretly

Understand What You Read

Write the answer to each question.

11. What about the old man bothered the narrator the most?

_____

_____

12. Why did the narrator enter the man's room for seven nights without carrying out his plan to kill him?

_____

_____

_____

13. According to the narrator, why couldn't the old man comfort himself and go back to sleep on the eighth night?

_____

_____

_____

Apply Your Skills

Circle the number of the best answer for each question.

14. Find the word "conceived" in the first line of the second paragraph of the passage. Using context clues, decide which of the following best defines the word.
    (1) put in words
    (2) entered the narrator's brain
    (3) haunted the narrator
    (4) insulted the narrator
    (5) wronged the old man

15. Which of the following phrases best establishes the mood of the story?
    (1) . . . when the day broke, I went boldly into the chamber.
    (2) I knew what the old man felt, and pitied him. . . .
    (3) . . . I found the eye always closed; and so it was impossible to do the work.
    (4) He had never given me insult.
    (5) For a whole hour, I did not move a muscle. . . .

16. Based on what you know of the narrator, what do you predict will happen after he kills the old man?
    (1) The sound of the old man's heartbeat will haunt the narrator.
    (2) The narrator will become more peaceful and relaxed.
    (3) The narrator will decide that he is mad after all.
    (4) The narrator will regret what he has done because the old man had always been kind to him.
    (5) The old man's eye will follow the narrator everywhere.

Connect with the Story

Write your answer to each question.

17. The narrator keeps saying that he is not crazy. Do you believe him? Why or why not?

    _____

    _____

18. Do you enjoy Poe's style of writing in this story? Explain your answer. Considering that most of Poe's writing has a similar dark mood, would you want to read more of his work? Why or why not?

    _____

    _____

Popular Short Story

Popular Short Story
Popular Short Story

Vocabulary

blend

circumstances

advantage

opportunities

pursuing

fabulous

Short stories and other types of popular fiction sometimes deal with problems between parents and children. A special kind of problem can come up if the parents moved to the United States from a different country. The immigrant parents may want to keep the traditions from their old country, but the American-born children may not. Recently, many young writers have explored these conflicts in fiction.

Relate to the Topic

The passage you are about to read is about a mother who is thinking about her adult daughter. The mother sees how different she is from her daughter who was raised as an American and has lost the Chinese ways of seeing and being. The mother has many feelings about these differences. She is sad, and proud, and confused.

How are you similar to your parents or children (if you have them) or different from them?

_____

_____

How do these similarities and differences make you feel?

_____

Reading Strategy

RELATING TO THE EXPERIENCE   Writers want their readers to relate to their stories, even if the stories are about unfamiliar things. This selection is about a Chinese mother and daughter. Even if you are not Chinese, you can understand their relationship. Read the first four paragraphs on page 137. Then answer the questions.

1. Describe the daughter's reaction to her mother.

_____

Hint: Is the daughter respectful of her mother?

2. Have you ever experienced a similar situation? Describe it.

_____

_____

Double Face   by Amy Tan

My daughter wanted to go to China for her second honeymoon, but now she is afraid.

"What if I **blend** in so well they think I'm one of them?" Waverly asked me. "What if they don't let me come back to the United States?"

"When you go to China," I told her, "you don't even need to open your mouth. They already know you are an outsider."

"What are you talking about?" she asked. My daughter likes to speak back. She likes to question what I say.

"Aii-ya," I said. "Even if you put on their clothes, even if you take off your makeup and hide your fancy jewelry, they know. They know just watching the way you walk, the way you carry your face. They know you do not belong."

My daughter did not look pleased when I told her this, that she didn't look Chinese. She had a sour American look on her face. Oh, maybe ten years ago, she would have clapped her hands—hurray!—as if this were good news. But now she wants to be Chinese, it is so fashionable. And I know it is too late. All those years I tried to teach her! She followed my Chinese ways only until she learned how to walk out the door by herself and go to school. So now the only Chinese words she can say are *sh-sh, houche, chr fan, and gwan deng shweijyau.* How can she talk to people in China with these words? . . . , choo-choo train, eat, close light, sleep. How can she think she can blend in? Only her skin and her hair are Chinese. Inside—she is all American-made.

It's my fault she is this way. I wanted my children to have the best combination: American **circumstances** and Chinese character. How could I know these two things do not mix?

I taught her how American circumstances work. If you are born poor here, it's no lasting shame. You are first in line for a scholarship. If the roof crashes on your head, no need to cry over this bad luck. You can sue anybody, make the landlord fix it. You do not have to sit like a Buddha under a tree letting pigeons drop their dirty business on your head. You can buy an umbrella. Or go inside a Catholic church. In America, nobody says you have to keep the circumstances somebody else gives you.

Comparing and Contrasting   Comparing shows how things are alike. Contrasting shows how things are different. In the passage, the mother says that Waverly has Chinese hair and skin. But her mother says that Waverly is different from the people in China in every other way.

What is one important way that Waverly is different from Chinese people?
   a.   She shows her feelings with a sour look.
   b.   She's afraid she'll have to stay in China.

She learned these things, but I couldn't teach her about Chinese character. How to obey parents and listen to your mother's mind. How not to show your own thoughts, to put your feelings behind your face so you can take **advantage** of hidden **opportunities.** Why easy things are not worth **pursuing.** How to know your own worth and polish it, never flashing it around like a cheap ring. Why Chinese thinking is best.

No, this kind of thinking didn't stick to her. She was too busy chewing gum, blowing bubbles bigger than her cheeks. Only that kind of thinking stuck.

"Finish your coffee," I told her yesterday. "Don't throw your blessings away."

"Don't be so old-fashioned, Ma," she told me, finishing her coffee down the sink. "I'm my own person."

And I think, How can she be her own person? When did I give her up?

Making Inferences When you make an inference, you figure out something that is suggested or implied by an author but not directly stated. You combine the facts you have with your own knowledge and experiences.

In this passage, the mother says, "Finish your coffee. Don't throw your blessings away." From this you can infer that the Chinese believe in not wasting what one has been given.

When the mother gives examples of "American circumstances," what can you infer as her meaning?

a. She believes that Americans have fewer opportunities than the Chinese do.

b. She believes Americans have more choices in life than Chinese people do.

My daughter is getting married a second time. So she asked me to go to her beauty parlor, her famous Mr. Rory. I know her meaning. She is ashamed of my looks. What will her husband's parents and his important lawyer friends think of this backward old Chinese woman?

"Auntie An-mei can cut me," I say.

"Rory is famous," says my daughter, as if she had no ears. "He does **fabulous** work."

So I sit in Mr. Rory's chair. He pumps me up and down until I am the right height. Then my daughter criticizes me as if I were not there. "See how it's flat on one side," she accuses my head. "She needs a cut and a perm. And this purple tint in her hair, she's been doing it at home. She's never had anything professionally done."

She is looking at Mr. Rory in the mirror. He is looking at me in the mirror. I have seen this professional look before. Americans don't really look at one another when talking. They talk to their reflections. They look at others or themselves only when they think nobody is watching. So they never see how they really look. They see themselves smiling without their mouth open, or turned to the side where they cannot see their faults.

"How does she want it?" asked Mr. Rory. He thinks I do not understand English. He is floating his fingers through my hair. He is showing how his magic can make my hair thicker and longer.

"Ma, how do you want it?" Why does my daughter think she is translating English for me? Before I can even speak, she explains my thoughts: "She wants a soft wave. We probably shouldn't cut it too short. Otherwise it'll be too tight for the wedding. She doesn't want it to look kinky or weird."

And now she says to me in a loud voice, as if I had lost my hearing, "Isn't that right, Ma? Not too tight?"

I smile. I use my American face. That's the face Americans think is Chinese, the one they cannot understand. But inside I am becoming ashamed. I am ashamed she is ashamed. Because she is my daughter and I am proud of her, and I am her mother but she is not proud of me.

Mr. Rory pats my hair more. He looks at me. He looks at my daughter. Then he says something to my daughter that really displeases her: "It's uncanny how much you two look alike!"

I smile, this time with my Chinese face. But my daughter's eyes and her smile become very narrow, the way a cat pulls itself small just before it bites. Now Mr. Rory goes away so we can think about this. I hear him snap his fingers. "Wash! Mrs. Jong is next!"

So my daughter and I are alone in this crowded beauty parlor. She is frowning at herself in the mirror. She sees me looking at her.

"The same cheeks," she says. She points to mine and then pokes her cheeks. She sucks them outside in to look like a starved person. She puts her face next to mine, side by side, and we look at each other in the mirror.

"You can see your character in your face," I say to my daughter without thinking. "You can see your future."

"What do you mean?" she says.

And now I have to fight back my feelings. These two faces, I think, so much the same! The same happiness, the same sadness, the same good fortune, the same faults.

I am seeing myself and my mother, back in China, when I was a young girl.

Identifying Conflict in Fiction Fiction is often based on a conflict between characters. The conflict can come from cultural differences, different opinions, or different ways of life. This passage is based on the conflict between Waverly and her mother.

What is an important conflict in this passage?

a. The mother does not like Mr. Rory, but the daughter does.

b. The mother is proud of the daughter, but the daughter is ashamed of the mother.

Thinking About the Story

Practice Vocabulary

The words below are in bold type in the passage. Study the way each word is used. Then complete each sentence by writing the correct word.

blend	circumstances	advantage
opportunities	pursuing	fabulous

1. I have not given up my goals. I am still _____ them.

2. The more education you have, the more _____ you are likely to have.

3. If things are mixed together enough, they will

   _____

4. She thought it would be _____ if she won the state lottery.

5. The scholarships for Chinese-Americans gave Waverly a financial

   _____

6. The difficult _____ Mrs. Jong grew up in did not stop her from trying to improve herself.

Understand What You Read

Write the answer to each question.

7. According to the mother, what does not mix?

   _____

   _____

8. Why do you think Waverly tells Mr. Rory what her mother wants?

   _____

   _____

9. What does Mr. Rory say just before he sends Mrs. Jong for her shampoo? Why do you think this bothers Waverly?

   _____

   _____

   _____

Apply Your Skills

Circle the number of the best answer for each question.

10. The mother compares and contrasts Chinese and American ways. According to her, which of the following is the most important difference?
    (1) The Chinese are more careful and quiet and observant than Americans.
    (2) The Chinese are poorer than Americans.
    (3) Chinese hair is different from American hair.
    (4) Americans wear more fancy jewelry than the Chinese.
    (5) Americans don't appreciate Chinese culture, while the Chinese love everything that is American.

11. From the mother's thoughts, what can you infer about the way the Chinese talk to each other?
    (1) They always look away from each other.
    (2) They look directly at each other.
    (3) They do not smile when talking.
    (4) They do not talk in public.
    (5) They tell each other their inner feelings.

12. The mother and daughter are in conflict about many things. For example, the mother thinks some of her daughter's ideas are silly. Which of the following shows how the mother feels about her daughter's ideas?
    (1) . . . now she is afraid.
    (2) "Don't be so old-fashioned . . ."
    (3) . . . her famous Mr. Rory.
    (4) . . . she is not proud of me.
    (5) "You can see your character in your face . . ."

Connect with the Story

Write your answer to each question.

13. In this passage, which of Mrs. Jong's "faces" do you like better? The Chinese one or the American one? Explain your answer.

    _____

    _____

14. Do you agree with the mother in this passage when she says that "Americans don't really look at each other when talking"? Explain your answer.

    _____

    _____

Adventure Story

Adventure Story
Adventure Story

Vocabulary

submerged

ceased

impede

miscalculated

veered

propelled

We love adventure stories because they keep us on the edge of our seats. In adventure stories, characters often battle with forces of nature. They climb mountains, fight hurricanes, and travel to distant countries—while you sit safely at home. You want to keep reading to find out if the characters can beat the odds and win.

Relate to the Topic

The passage you are about to read is about a man who is thrown overboard into whirling rapids while boating down a dangerous river. His friends and his dog attempt to save him.

Have you ever been in a dangerous situation? What was it?

_____

Did anyone help? What happened?

_____

_____

Reading Strategy

PICTURING CHARACTERS   Characters are the people or other creatures in a story. A writer has many ways of helping a reader form a picture of a character. Writers describe what the characters look like and how they sound. They also use action words to help the reader "see" what the characters are doing.

Read the first paragraph on page 143 and pay attention to the words that describe what a character looks like or is doing. Then answer the questions.

1. What words does the author use to describe Buck?

_____

Hint: Look at the last sentence in the first paragraph.

2. Who is Buck? How do you know?

_____

Hint: Look at the last sentence in the first paragraph.

The Call of the Wild by Jack London

Later on, in the fall of the year, he saved John Thornton's life in quite another fashion. The three partners were lining a long and narrow poling-boat down a bad stretch of rapids on the Forty-Mile Creek. Hans and Pete moved along the bank, snubbing [stopping the motion of an object with a rope, which is tied around a fixed object such as a tree or pole] with a thin Manila rope from tree to tree, while Thornton remained in the boat, helping its descent by means of a pole, and shouting directions to the shore. Buck, on the bank, worried and anxious, kept abreast of the boat, his eyes never off his master.

At a particularly bad spot, where a ledge of barely **submerged** rocks jutted out into the river, Hans cast off the rope, and, while Thornton poled the boat out into the stream, ran down the bank with the end in his hand to snub the boat when it had cleared the ledge. This it did, and was flying down-stream in a current as swift as a mill-race, when Hans checked it with the rope and checked too suddenly. The boat flirted over and snubbed in to the bank bottom up, while Thornton, flung sheer out of it, was carried down-stream toward the worst part of the rapids, a stretch of wild water in which no swimmer could live.

Buck had sprung in on the instant; and at the end of three hundred yards, amid a mad swirl of water, he overhauled Thornton. When he felt him grasp his tail, Buck headed for the bank, swimming with all his splendid strength. But the progress shoreward was slow, the progress down-stream amazingly rapid. From below came the fatal roaring where the wild current went wilder and was rent in shreds and spray by the rocks which thrust through like the teeth of an enormous comb.

Identifying Mood Mood is the overall feeling, or emotional atmosphere, of a story. As you read, look carefully for words the author has chosen to describe characters, actions, and places. These words create the mood of the story.

In the paragraph you have just read, the author creates the mood by describing Thornton's struggle in the dangerous river, and Buck's efforts to save him. The author uses words such as "fatal roaring" and "wild current." How would you describe the mood of this passage?

    a.   suspenseful

    b.   lighthearted

    c.   sad

The suck of the water as it took the beginning of the last steep pitch was frightful, and Thornton knew that the shore was impossible. He scraped furiously over a rock, bruised across a second, and struck a third with crushing force. He clutched its

ADVENTURE STORY

slippery top with both hands, releasing Buck, and above the roar of the churning water shouted: "Go, Buck! Go!"

Buck could not hold his own, and swept on downstream, struggling desperately, but unable to win back. When he heard Thornton's command repeated, he partly reared out of the water, throwing his head high, as though for a last look, then turned obediently toward the bank. He swam powerfully and was dragged ashore by Pete and Hans at the very point where swimming **ceased** to be possible and destruction began.

Synthesizing Ideas There are many things to keep track of in a story. For example, there are several characters, the situations they encounter, and the places where the action happens. Putting together information from different parts of the story can help you better understand the relationships between characters and the events in the plot. That's what synthesizing is: connecting information from different parts of the story.

For example, earlier in this story Buck jumped off a cliff just because Thornton told him to. Putting this fact together with the events from this passage tells you that Buck would do anything for Thornton.

You can also synthesize information from outside the story, such as information about the author, with facts from the story. Putting together these pieces of information can help you better understand the story, the author, or both.

The author of this story, Jack London, once said that "to live placidly (calmly) and complacently (contentedly) is not to live at all." If you take that information and put it together with information from this passage, which of the following conclusions makes the most sense?

a. Jack London lived through his writing.
b. Jack London led a happy life.
c. Jack London felt he hadn't really lived.

They knew that the time a man could cling to a slippery rock in the face of that driving current was a matter of minutes, and they ran as fast as they could up the bank to a point far above where Thornton was hanging on. They attached the line with which they had been snubbing the boat to Buck's neck and shoulders, being careful that it should neither strangle him nor **impede** his swimming, and launched him into the stream. He struck out boldly, but not straight enough into the stream. He discovered the mistake too late, when Thornton was abreast of him and a bare half-dozen strokes away while he was being carried helplessly past.

Hans promptly snubbed with the rope, as though Buck were a boat. The rope thus tightening on him in the sweep of the current, he was jerked under the surface, and under the surface he remained till his body struck against the bank and he was hauled out. He was half drowned, and Hans and Pete threw themselves upon him, pounding the breath into him and the water out of him. He staggered to his feet and fell down. The faint sound of Thornton's voice came to them, and though they could not make out the words of it, they knew that he was in his extremity. His master's voice acted on Buck like an electric shock. He sprang to his feet and ran up the bank ahead of the men to the point of his previous departure.

Again the rope was attached and he was launched, and again he struck out, but this time straight into the stream. He had **miscalculated** once, but he would not be guilty of it a second time. Hans paid out the rope, permitting no slack, while Pete kept it clear of coils. Buck held on till he was on a line straight above Thornton; then he turned, and with the speed of an express train headed down upon him. Thornton saw him coming, and, as Buck struck him like a battering ram, with the whole force of the current behind him, he reached up and closed with both arms around the shaggy neck. Hans snubbed the rope around the tree, and Buck and Thornton were jerked under the water. Strangling, suffocating, sometimes one uppermost and sometimes the other, dragging over the jagged bottom, smashing against rocks and snags, they **veered** in to the bank.

Applying Ideas You already have many skills that you apply in different day-to-day situations. For example, when you were younger you learned how to add and subtract. Now, you apply that skill in everyday situations, such as adding up the cost of items at the grocery store. You can do the same with an idea from a story. For example, knowing that a character is careful with money might help you predict what kind of car he or she would buy—probably an economy car rather than an expensive sports car. Being able to use information or ideas in new situations is an important skill to have, not just for reading, but for many things in life.

Based on what you have read about Thornton and Buck, which of the following is most likely to happen in this story?
a. Thornton punishes Buck for disobeying him.
b. Thornton is grateful and hopes that Buck isn't hurt.

Thornton came to, belly downward and being violently **propelled** back and forth across a drift log by Hans and Pete. His first glance was for Buck, over whose limp and apparently lifeless body Nig was setting up a howl, while Skeet was licking the wet face and closed eyes. Thornton was himself bruised and battered, and he went carefully over Buck's body, when he had been brought around, finding three broken ribs.

"That settles it," he announced. "We camp right here." And camp they did, till Buck's ribs knitted and he was able to travel.

Thinking About the Story

Practice Vocabulary

The words below are in bold type in the passage. Study the way each word is used. Then write each word next to its meaning.

submerged	**ceased**	**impede**
miscalculated	**veered**	**propelled**

1. came to an end _____

2. put under water _____

3. driven forward by a force _____

4. interfere with _____

5. changed direction or course _____

6. incorrectly solved a problem _____

Understand What You Read

Write the answer to each question.

7. What caused the boat to turn over?

_____

_____

_____

_____

8. Why did Buck swim back to the bank before saving Thornton?

_____

_____

_____

_____

9. Why did the men decide to camp right where they were?

_____

_____

_____

_____

Apply Your Skills

Circle the number of the best answer for each question.

10. Which of the following words best describes Thornton?
    (1) lazy
    (2) anxious
    (3) unforgiving
    (4) indifferent
    (5) tough

11. What is similar about Hans, Pete, and Buck?
    (1) They don't give up trying.
    (2) They like to make things easy.
    (3) They are each very self-involved.
    (4) They never delegate tasks to others.
    (5) They enjoy working alone.

12. Which of the following would Thornton probably enjoy?
    (1) working in an office
    (2) watching a hockey game on television
    (3) attending a formal dinner
    (4) camping alone on top of a mountain
    (5) skydiving with his trusted friends

Connect with the Story

Write your answer to each question.

13. If you were in Thornton's situation, would you react as he did? How would you react? Give reasons for your answer.

    _____

    _____

    _____

14. In the passage, Hans and Pete try to save Thornton by fixing the rope around Buck's neck and shoulders and sending him into the water. However, it causes Buck to almost drown. Have you ever been in a situation where what you did caused a problem you didn't expect? Explain.

    _____

    _____

    _____

Reading at Work

Retail Sales: Bookstore Clerk

Do you like working with people? If you do, you may choose to work in retail sales. This area involves a wide range of jobs in stores where people buy products for their home, work, or personal use. If you also like to read, then the retail sales job of bookstore clerk may be right for you.

Bookstore clerks should have good personal skills because they have a lot of interaction with customers. They can recommend books by a particular author, time period, or subject area. They must also have good math skills for working with inventory, prices, and discounts. Many bookstore clerks use computers and data entry skills to check whether a book is in stock or to order books from publishers or suppliers.

Look at the box showing some careers in retail sales.

Do any of the careers interest you? If so, which ones?

How could you find out more about those careers? On a separate piece of paper, write some questions that you would like to have answered. You can find out more information about those careers in the *Occupational Outlook Handbook* at your local library and online.

Some Careers in Retail Sales

Cashier
collects payment from customers and makes change; uses cash register and credit card scanners

Inventory Clerk
logs and prices; monitors and organizes stock

Service Sales Representative
sells and logs repair and warranty services; receives and returns items serviced

Sales Representative
presents products or services to customers

Use the material on the previous page and the bestseller list below to answer the questions that follow.

Bookstore clerks answer questions from customers. They often use tools like reference books, computer databases, and bestseller lists.

FICTION Bestsellers Week of April 27

Rank	Title	Author	Weeks on the Bestseller List
1	**Just Around the Corner**—Super sleuth Shelly Shift chases jewel thief around the globe.	Marcy Boone	3
2	**Fear of the Known**—Supernatural thriller set in 19th century Missouri.	Brian Jenkins	7
3	**Windy Days, Sleepless Nights**—Independent young woman climbs Mt. Everest and finds love.	Ellen Stein	2
4	**One More Byte**—Private Investigator Ray Fern hunts computer hacker.	Ray Lopez	10
5	**The Sky's the Limit**—Group of friends finds challenges in the Rocky Mountains.	Brett Young	5
6	**Let Me Hear It Again**—Bitter, ailing deaf woman finds hope and romance in the hospital.	Tanisha Jordan	22
7	**Aidan's Image**—Young family moves into haunted house.	Randy Moore	17
8	**Now You See It, Now You Don't**—Shelly Shift uncovers identity of murderous magician.	Marcy Boone	14

1. Put a check mark by each reason bookstore clerks use bestseller lists.

   _____ to suggest new books for their customers to read

   _____ to fill up the shelves in the bookstore

   _____ to keep the most popular books in stock

   _____ to make the bookstore look attractive

2. Which book has been on the bestseller list the longest?

   _____

3. What kinds of books do you enjoy reading? Name your favorite kind of book and explain why you like it.

   _____

   _____

   _____

   _____

Unit 2 Review
Fiction

Read the following passage from the novel *Mutation* by Robin Cook.

"But he's not crying?" questioned Victor. Doubt clouded his euphoria.

The resident lightly slapped the soles of Victor Jr.'s feet, then rubbed his back. Still the infant stayed quiet. "But he's breathing fine."

The resident picked up the bulb syringe and tried to suction Victor Jr.'s nose once again. To the doctor's astonishment, the newborn's hand came up and yanked the bulb away from the fingers of the resident and dropped it over the side of the infant care unit.

"Well that settles that," said the resident with a chuckle. "He just doesn't want to cry."

"Can I?" asked Victor, motioning toward the baby.

"As long as he doesn't get cold."

Gingerly, Victor reached into the unit and scooped up Victor Jr. He held the infant in front of him with both hands around his torso. He was a beautiful baby with strikingly blond hair. His chubby, rosy cheeks gave his face a picturesquely cherubic quality, but by far the most distinctive aspect of his appearance was his bright blue eyes. As Victor gazed into their depths he realized with a shock that the baby was looking back at him.

"Beautiful, isn't he?" said Marsha over Victor's shoulder.

"Gorgeous," Victor agreed. "But where did the blond hair come from? Ours is brown."

"I was blond until I was five," Marsha said, reaching up to touch the baby's pink skin.

Victor glanced at his wife as she lovingly gazed at the child. She had dark brown hair peppered with just a few strands of gray. Her eyes were a sultry gray-blue; her features quite sculptured: they contrasted with the rounded, full features of the infant.

"Look at his eyes," Marsha said.

Victor turned his attention back to the baby. "They are incredible, aren't they? A minute ago I'd have sworn they were looking right back at me."

"They are like jewels," Marsha said.

Victor turned the baby to face Marsha. As he did so he noticed the baby's eyes remained locked on his! Their turquoise depths were as cold and bright as ice. Unbidden, Victor felt a thrill of fear.

Questions 1 through 6 refer to the passage on page 150.

Find the numbered words in the passage. Study the way each word is used. Then match each word with its meaning. Write the letter.

_____ 1. euphoria

_____ 2. gingerly

_____ 3. cherubic

a. carefully

b. angel-like

c. extreme happiness

Circle the number of the best answer for each question.

4. What can you conclude about how Marsha feels about her child?

She feels
(1) proud
(2) puzzled
(3) worried
(4) uninterested
(5) surprised

5. Newborn babies cannot focus their eyes. What can you infer from Victor's noticing "the baby's eyes remained locked on his"?
(1) The baby is not a newborn infant.
(2) Victor has poor eyesight.
(3) The baby is not normal.
(4) The baby is not Victor's son.
(5) Victor knows a lot about babies.

6. Which of the following best describes what Victor thinks about the baby's eyes?

He thinks the baby's eyes are
(1) ugly
(2) beautiful
(3) warm
(4) loving
(5) frightening

Read the following passage from the novel *The Grapes of Wrath* **by John Steinbeck.**

And the migrants streamed in on the highways and their hunger was in their eyes, and their need was in their eyes. They had no argument, no system, nothing but their numbers and their needs. When there was work for a man, ten men fought for it— fought with a low wage. If that fella'll work for thirty cents, I'll work for twenty-five.

If he'll take twenty-five, I'll do it for twenty.

No, me, I'm hungry. I'll work for fifteen. I'll work for food. The kids. You ought to see them. Little boils, like, comin' out, an' they can't run aroun'. Give 'em some windfall fruit, an' they bloated up. Me. I'll work for a little piece of meat.

And this was good, for wages went down and prices stayed up. The great owners were glad and they sent out more handbills to bring more people in. And wages went down and prices stayed up. And pretty soon now we'll have serfs again.

And now the great owners and the companies invented a new method. A great owner bought a cannery. And when the peaches and the pears were ripe he cut the price of fruit below the cost of raising it. And as cannery owner he paid himself a low price for the fruit and kept the price of canned goods up and took his profit. And the little farmers who owned no canneries lost their farms, and they were taken by the great owners, the banks, and the companies who also owned the canneries. As time went on, there were fewer farms. The little farmers moved into town for a while and exhausted their credit, exhausted their friends, their relatives. And then they too went on the highways. And the roads were crowded with men ravenous for work, murderous for work.

And the companies, the banks worked at their own doom and they did not know it. The fields were fruitful, and starving men moved on the roads. The granaries were full and the children of the poor grew up rachitic [with spine problems], and the pustules of pellagra [sores caused by a skin disease] swelled on their sides. The great companies did not know that the line between hunger and anger is a thin line. And money that might have gone to wages went for gas, for guns, for agents and spies, for blacklists, for drilling. On the highways the people moved like ants and searched for work, for food. And the anger began to ferment.

Questions 7 through 12 refer to the passage on page 152.

Write the word that best completes each sentence.

hunger   work   cannery   anger

7. The migrants were competing for _____ so that they could feed their children.

8. The companies and banks did not understand that they would cause their own doom. They did not understand the thin line between _____ and _____

9. One way a great owner increased profits was to buy a _____

Circle the number of the best answer for each question.

10. Which of the following phrases is the best meaning of the word "ferment" as it is used in this passage?
    (1) to grow slowly
    (2) to make beer
    (3) to grow older
    (4) to make people sick
    (5) to die down quickly

11. Which of the following words best describes the mood in this passage?
    (1) calm
    (2) delighted
    (3) forgiving
    (4) uneasy
    (5) quiet

12. What do the words "ravenous" and "murderous" suggest about how the people felt about getting work?
    (1) They felt uninterested.
    (2) They felt that they deserved work.
    (3) They felt confident.
    (4) They felt desperate.
    (5) They felt that they could always find work.

■ **Read the following passage from the novel *Ramona* by Helen Hunt Jackson.**

Capitan was leaping up, putting his paws on Alessandro's breast, licking his face, yelping, doing all a dog could do, to show welcome and affection.

Alessandro laughed aloud. Ramona had not more than two or three times heard him do this. It frightened her. "Why do you laugh, Alessandro?" she said.

"To think what I have to show you, my Señorita," he said. "Look here;" and turning towards the willows, he gave two or three low whistles, at the first note of which Baba came trotting out of the copse [small group of trees] to the end of his lariat, and began to snort and whinny with delight as soon as he perceived Ramona.

Ramona burst into tears. The surprise was too great.

"Are you not glad, Señorita?" cried Alessandro, aghast. "Is it not your own horse? If you do not wish to take him, I will lead him back. My pony can carry you, if we journey very slowly. But I thought it would be joy to you to have Baba."

"Oh, it is! it is!" sobbed Ramona, with her head on Baba's neck. "It is a miracle,— a miracle. How did he come here? And the saddle too!" she cried, for the first time observing that. "Alessandro," in an awe-struck whisper, "did the saints send him? Did you find him here?" It would have seemed to Ramona's faith no strange thing, had this been so.

"I think the saints helped me to bring him," answered Alessandro, seriously, "or else I had not done it so easily. I did but call, near the corral-fence, and he came to my hand, and leaped over the rails at my word, as quickly as Capitan might have done. He is yours, Señorita. It is no harm to take him?"

"Oh, no!" answered Ramona. "He is more mine than anything else I had; for it was Felipe gave him to me when he could but just stand on his legs; he was only two days old; and I have fed him out of my hand every day till now; and now he is five. Dear Baba, we will never be parted, never!" and she took his head in both her hands, and laid her cheek against it lovingly.

Find the words in the passage. Study the way each word is used. Then complete each sentence by writing the correct word.

yelping   lariat   trotting   perceived

13. Sarah saw things differently; she _____ that people were angry with her.

14. He tied the end of the _____ to the post.

15. I couldn't hear you over the loud _____ of the animals.

16. The horse was _____ so quickly that Joe couldn't stop it.

Circle the number of the best answer for each question.

17. What or who is Baba?
    (1) a pony
    (2) a dog
    (3) a horse
    (4) an employee
    (5) Felipe's son

18. Why is Ramona so happy to see Baba?
    (1) because it was a surprise for Alessandro
    (2) because the saints brought him
    (3) because he had her saddle
    (4) because Felipe had lost him
    (5) because she had been separated from him

19. What can you infer about Ramona and Alessandro?
    (1) Ramona always loved Alessandro.
    (2) Alessandro isn't very generous towards Ramona.
    (3) Ramona dislikes Alessandro's gift.
    (4) Alessandro wants to please Ramona.
    (5) Ramona is frightened by Alessandro.

Reading Extension

In this unit you have read samples of many types of fiction. Which piece did you like the best? Would you like to read the book that it came from or something else by that author? Turn to the Annotated Bibliography on pages 257–258 of this book. Write down the name of the book and the author. Make a plan to go to a library or bookstore soon to get that book or another one by that author.

Mini-Test • Unit 2

 This is a 15-minute practice test. After 15 minutes, mark the last number you finished. Then complete the test and check your answers. If most of your answers were correct but you did not finish, try to work faster next time.

Directions: Choose the one best answer to each question.

Questions 1 through 3 refer to the following passage.

WHY IS THIS DIARY INTERESTING?

He had found the diary during one of those cold, rainy spells that sometimes occur in summer. Bored, he'd wandered into the old carriage house, which served
(5) as a garage.

He climbed the rickety steps to the stuffy, dusty loft, and for lack of something better to do, began rummaging through the boxes he found there.

(10) The first one was filled with utterly useless odds and ends: rusty old lamps; faded, outdated clothing; pots and pans and a scrub board; chipped vanity sets, the glass on the mirrors cracked or
(15) blurred. They all were the sorts of items one shoves out of sight with the intention of fixing or giving away, and then forgets altogether.

Another box held thick albums, the
(20) pages crumbling, filled with pictures of stiffly posed, stern-faced people refusing to share their emotions with the camera.

A third contained books, dusty, swollen from humidity, the type faded. He'd
(25) always been a reader, but even though only fourteen at the time, he could glance through these titles and dismiss them. No hidden masterpieces in the lot.

A dozen more boxes proved to be filled
(30) with equally worthless junk.

In the process of throwing everything back into the boxes, he came across a rotted leather binder that had been hidden in what looked like another photo
(35) album. He opened it and found it stuffed with pages, every one of them covered with writing.

The first entry was dated, September 7, 1891. It began with the words
(40) "Madeline is dead by my hand."

Mary Higgins Clark, *On the Street Where You Live*

1. What is the mood at the beginning of the passage?

   (1) gloomy
   (2) optimistic
   (3) fearful
   (4) curious
   (5) overwhelmed

2. What is the condition of the attic?

   (1) hot and humid
   (2) rusty and outdated
   (3) messy and cluttered
   (4) chipped and cracked
   (5) neat and organized

3. Based on the ending, what is the main character likely to do next with the diary?
   He will
   (1) put it back where he found it
   (2) call someone for help
   (3) tear it up
   (4) think about throwing it away
   (5) read it with interest

WHAT DOES NAT SEE?

He looked out to sea and watched the crested breakers, combing green. They rose stiffly, curled, and broke again, and because it was ebb tide the roar was
(5) distant, more remote, lacking the sound and thunder of the flood.

Then he saw them. The gulls. Out there, riding the seas.

What he had thought at first to be the
(10) white caps of the waves were gulls. Hundreds, thousands, tens of thousands . . .They rose and fell in the trough of the seas, heads to the wind, like a mighty fleet at anchor, waiting on the tide. To
(15) eastward, and to the west, the gulls were there. They stretched as far as his eye could reach, in close formation, line upon line. Had the sea been still they would have covered the bay like a white cloud,
(20) head to head, body packed to body. Only the east wind whipping the sea to breakers hid them from the shore.

Nat turned, and leaving the beach climbed the steep path home. Someone
(25) should know of this. Someone should be told. Something was happening, because of the east wind and the weather, that he did not understand. He wondered if he should go to the call box by the bus stop
(30) and ring up the police. Yet what could they do? What could anyone do? Tens and thousands of gulls riding the sea there, in the bay, because of storm, because of hunger. The police would think him mad,
(35) or drunk, or take the statement from him with great calm. "Thank you. Yes, the matter has already been reported. The hard weather is driving the birds inland in great numbers."

Daphne Du Maurier, "The Birds"

4. Why was Nat alarmed?

Because
(1)   the sea was at ebb tide
(2)   there was going to be a flood
(3)   the east wind whipped the sea
(4)   the sea was completely full of gulls
(5)   the sea was still

5. How does Nat think the police will react to him if he contacts them about what he has seen?

He thinks the police will
(1)   arrest him
(2)   not take him seriously
(3)   take him home to his wife
(4)   refuse to take his statement
(5)   tell him to stay away from the sea

6. Later in the story, Nat boards up the windows of his bedroom and fills up the chimney bases in his house.

Based on the information in the passage, why do you think Nat did these things?
(1)   The weather was beginning to turn cold.
(2)   His house was in need of insulation.
(3)   He was afraid of an attack by the gulls.
(4)   The police did not take him seriously.
(5)   His wife had asked him to repair the house.

3 UNIT

Drama

A **drama,** or play, is a story written to be acted out. Plays are meant to be performed in front of an audience of people, even though sometimes we can just read them. A play can be funny, serious, or both, but a good play will hold our attention, perhaps make us laugh or cry, and make us think.

The word "drama" is sometimes used to refer to all plays. Other times it refers only to serious plays, not musicals or comedies.

Have you ever seen a play on a stage? _____

Did you enjoy the play? How did it affect you?

_____

Thinking About Drama

You may not realize how much plays are part of your daily life. Think about the times you have seen or heard plays.

Check the box for each activity you did.

- ☐ Did you attend a school play?
- ☐ Did you act in a play?
- ☐ Did you try to write or make up a play?
- ☐ Did you listen to a play on the radio?
- ☐ Did you see a friend act in a play?
- ☐ Did you watch a television drama or comedy?
- ☐ Did you attend a community theatre production?
- ☐ Did you go to a Broadway show?

Write some other experiences you have had with drama.

_____

_____

_____

Previewing the Unit

In this unit, you will learn:

- how dramas about popular topics help us see ourselves more clearly
- how social drama helps us become aware of important social issues
- how comedy can reflect our lives with a touch of humor
- how plays can entertain us
- how plays can make us think
- how plays can make us laugh

Lesson 21	Popular Drama
Lesson 22	Social Drama
Lesson 23	Comedy

Popular Drama

Vocabulary

improvising

spontaneous

superstition

ravenously

glimmer

Most **plays** are written about topics that people can relate to their own lives, such as family, work, and relationships. These plays are called **popular drama.** In popular drama, the characters face some type of conflict. The characters change during the course of the play and give the audience something to think about.

Relate to the Topic

In the play you are about to read, the characters are planning a birthday surprise. Meg and Babe are lighting the candles on a cake to surprise their sister, Lenny.

Have you ever been to a surprise party? Who was the party for? How did the person feel about the surprise?

_____

_____

_____

Reading Strategy

READING DIALOGUE   Dialogue is the conversation among characters in a play. The dialogue tells a lot about the characters — their interests, their motives, their feelings.

When you read a play, notice that a character's name is given first, followed by what the character says. No quotation marks are used. Whenever a new character speaks, a new paragraph is started. This makes it easy to follow who is speaking.

Read the title and first six lines of dialogue on page 161. Then answer the questions.

1. What are the names of the characters?

_____

Hint: Look on the left side of the page.

2. What are the characters doing?

_____

Hint: What are the characters talking about?

Crimes of the Heart by Beth Henley

MEG: But, Babe, we've just got to learn how to get through these real bad days here. I mean, it's getting to be a thing in our family. *(Slight pause as she looks at Babe)* Come on, now. Look, we've got Lenny's cake right here. I mean, don't you wanna be around to give her her cake, watch her blow out the candles?

BABE: *(Realizing how much she wants to be here)* Yeah, I do, I do. 'Cause she always loves to make her birthday wishes on those candles.

MEG: Well, then we'll give her her cake and maybe you won't be so miserable.

BABE: Okay.

MEG: Good. Go on and take it out of the box.

BABE: Okay. *(She takes the cake out of the box. It is a magical moment.)* Gosh, it's a pretty cake.

MEG: *(Handing her some matches)* Here now. You can go on and light up the candles.

BABE: All right. *(She starts to light the candles.)* I love to light up candles. And there are so many here. Thirty pink ones in all, plus one green one to grow on.

MEG: *(Watching her light the candles)* They're pretty.

BABE: They are. *(She stops lighting the candles.)* And I'm not like Mama. I'm not so all alone.

MEG: You're not.

BABE: *(As she goes back to lighting candles)* Well, you'd better keep an eye out for Lenny. She's supposed to be surprised.

MEG: All right. Do you know where she's gone?

BABE: Well, she's not here inside—so she must have gone on outside.

MEG: Oh, well, then I'd better run and find her.

BABE: Okay; 'cause these candles are gonna melt down. *(Meg starts out the door.)*

MEG: Wait—there she is coming. Lenny! Oh, Lenny! Come on! Hurry up!

Making Inferences When you make an **inference,** you figure out something that the author suggests but does not state directly. To make an inference, use the facts that are given and what you already know to decide what the suggestion is.

The author does not tell us that Meg, Babe, and Lenny are sisters. Instead she gives clues to help us make this inference. Meg says "it's getting to be a thing in our family." Babe mentions how much Lenny always loves to make birthday wishes. Both of these ideas plus the familiar way the characters talk to each other lead the reader to believe that the characters are sisters.

At the beginning of the play, it seems as though Babe had been planning to leave before the birthday surprise. Which idea supports this inference?

a. Meg asks Babe whether she wants to be around to give Lenny the cake.
b. Meg tells Babe to light the candles.

BABE:	*(Overlapping and* **improvising** *as she finishes lighting the candles)* Oh, no! No! Well, yes—Yes! No, wait! Wait! Okay! Hurry up! *(Lenny enters. Meg covers Lenny's eyes with her hands.)*
LENNY:	*(Terrified)* What? What is it? What?
MEG/BABE:	Surprise! Happy birthday! Happy birthday to Lenny!
LENNY:	Oh, no! Oh, me! What a surprise! I could just cry! Oh, look: *Happy Birthday, Lenny—A Day Late!* How cute! My! Will you look at all those candles—it's absolutely frightening.
BABE:	*(A* **spontaneous** *thought)* Oh, no, Lenny, it's good! 'Cause—'cause the more candles you have on your cake, the stronger your wish is.
LENNY:	Really?
BABE:	Sure!
LENNY:	Mercy! *(Meg and Babe start to sing.)*
LENNY:	*(Interrupting the song)* Oh, but wait! I—can't think of my wish! My body's gone all nervous inside.
MEG:	. . . Lenny—Come on!
BABE:	The wax is all melting!
LENNY:	My mind is just a blank, a total blank!
MEG:	Will you please just—
BABE:	*(Overlapping)* Lenny, hurry! Come on!
LENNY:	Okay! Okay! Just go!
	(Meg and Babe burst into the "Happy Birthday" song. As it ends, Lenny blows out all the candles on the cake. Meg and Babe applaud loudly.)
MEG:	Oh, you made it!
BABE:	Hurray!
LENNY:	Oh, me! Oh, me! I hope that wish comes true! I hope it does!
BABE:	Why? What did you wish for?
LENNY:	*(As she removes the candles from the cake)* Why, I can't tell you that.
BABE:	Oh, sure you can—
LENNY:	Oh, no! Then it won't come true.

Identifying Conflict in Drama Plays are often based on a **conflict** or problem between characters. Sometimes the conflict comes from the situation that is occurring. This type of conflict may last for only a short time before it is quickly resolved. A brief conflict can create a feeling of suspense or excitement.

In the passage above, a minor conflict happens when Lenny is supposed to blow out the candles on the cake. The reader is briefly left in suspense. Which of the following describes the conflict in the passage?

a. Lenny is upset because her sisters are celebrating her birthday a day late.

b. Meg and Babe become impatient with Lenny when she can't decide what to wish for.

BABE: Why, that's just **superstition!** Of course it will, if you made it deep enough.

MEG: Really? I didn't know that.

LENNY: Well, Babe's the regular expert on birthday wishes.

BABE: It's just I get these feelings. Now, come on and tell us. What was it you wished for?

MEG: Yes, tell us. What was it?

LENNY: Well, I guess it wasn't really a specific wish. This—this vision just sort of came into my mind.

BABE: A vision? What was it of?

LENNY: I don't know exactly. It was something about the three of us smiling and laughing together.

BABE: Well, when was it? Was it far away or near?

LENNY: I'm not sure; but it wasn't forever; it wasn't for every minute. Just this one moment and we were all laughing.

BABE: Then, what were we laughing about?

LENNY: I don't know. Just nothing, I guess.

MEG: Well, that's a nice wish to make.
        (Lenny and Meg look at each other a moment.)

MEG: Here, now, I'll get a knife so we can go ahead and cut the cake in celebration of Lenny being born!

BABE: Oh, yes! And give each one of us a rose. A whole rose apiece!

LENNY: *(Cutting the cake nervously)* Well, I'll try—I'll try!

MEG: *(Licking the icing off a candle)* Mmmm—this icing is delicious! Here, try some.

BABE: Mmmm! It's wonderful! Here, Lenny!

LENNY: *(Laughing joyously as she licks icing from her fingers and cuts huge pieces of cake that her sisters bite into **ravenously**)* Oh, how I do love having birthday cake for breakfast! How I do!
        *(The sisters freeze for a moment laughing and eating cake. The lights change and frame them in a magical, golden, sparkling **glimmer;** saxophone music is heard. The lights dim to blackout, and the saxophone continues to play.)*

Determining Plot The **plot** of a story or drama is the series of events that create the action. The events of a plot can be described in the order in which they happen. A scene in a play has a plot. The first event of the plot for this scene is Meg and Babe planning a birthday surprise for Lenny. Which two items are also events in the plot of this scene?

a. Lenny is surprised by the birthday cake.

b. Babe is an expert on birthday wishes.

c. Lenny is persuaded to tell her wish.

Thinking About the Play

Practice Vocabulary

The words below are in bold type in the passage. Study the way each word is used. Then complete each sentence by writing the correct word.

improvising **spontaneous** **superstition**

ravenously **glimmer**

1. The young man ate ———————; it was as if he hadn't eaten for days.

2. We saw a soft ——————— of light shining down on the water.

3. I made up the story as I went along because I enjoy

   ———————.

4. Knocking on wood for good luck is a ———————.

5. The audience was so surprised that they broke into

   ——————— applause.

Understand What You Read

Write the answer to each question.

6. What wish does Lenny make as she blows out her birthday candles?

   _____

   _____

7. What does Babe mean when she says "keep an eye out for Lenny"? Why do you think she says this?

   _____

   _____

8. What is the superstition that is mentioned in the passage?

   _____

   _____

9. What do you think helped make the birthday celebration such a surprise?

   _____

   _____

Apply Your Skills

Circle the number of the best answer for each question.

10. You can infer from the scene that Babe seems to make up "facts" as she goes along. Which detail supports this inference?
    (1) She thinks the cake is pretty.
    (2) She loves to light up candles.
    (3) She says that she's not like her mother.
    (4) She says that Lenny's wish will come true if she makes it deep enough.
    (5) She wants everyone to get a piece of cake with a rose on it.

11. Which line best shows there is a conflict among the sisters?
    (1) ". . . we've just got to learn how to get through these real bad days here."
    (2) "Well, she's not inside—so she must have gone on outside."
    (3) "My mind is just a blank, a total blank!"
    (4) "Why, I can't tell you that."
    (5) "Why that's just superstition!"

12. Based on the information in the passage, what do you think might have happened earlier in the plot?
    (1) The family were getting along well.
    (2) Meg was causing problems in the family.
    (3) Lenny said she hated birthday celebrations.
    (4) Babe was taking saxophone lessons.
    (5) All the sisters were having problems.

Connect with the Play

Write your answers in the space provided.

13. Do you think Lenny's wish has been granted? Why or why not?

    _____

    _____

14. You have probably made a wish at some time. What was it? Did it come true? Did you do anything that helped it come true?

    _____

    _____

15. Have you ever felt nervous and unable to think the way Lenny did when she had to make a birthday wish? When was it? What happened?

    _____

    _____

Social Drama

Vocabulary

consulting

expectantly

labored

deplore

quizzical

affirmation

Some plays, known as social dramas, deal with major social issues. For example, a social drama might deal with the issue of prejudice against a minority group or individual. These plays describe conflicts that are not always solved in the play. A social drama may take a humorous or serious approach to an issue, or a combination of both.

Relate to the Topic

The title of the play you are about to read, *A Raisin in the Sun*, comes from a poem by the African-American poet Langston Hughes. The play deals with a possible neighborhood conflict.

Has there ever been any kind of conflict between neighbors where you live? What was done about it? What do you think should have been done?

_____

_____

_____

_____

Reading Strategy

UNDERSTANDING STAGE DIRECTIONS   Stage directions tell actors where to move on the stage or how to say their lines. For example, the stage directions may tell an actor to walk very slowly, or to speak in a very fast, excited voice. Stage directions are in parentheses and italics so they are easy to find.

Read the first seven lines of the play on page 167. Then answer the questions.

1. Write the first stage direction for "Man."

_____

Hint: Find the italic words in parentheses.

2. What do you think is written on the piece of paper?

_____

Hint: Look at what the Man says after he glances at the slip of paper.

A Raisin in the Sun by Lorraine Hansberry

BENEATHA:	Sticks and stones may break my bones but . . . words will never hurt me! *(Beneatha goes to the door and opens it as Walter and Ruth go on with the clowning. Beneatha is somewhat surprised to see a quiet-looking middle-aged white man in a business suit holding his hat and a briefcase in his hand and **consulting** a small piece of paper.)*
MAN:	Uh—how do you do, miss. I am looking for a Mrs.—*(He looks at the slip of paper.)* Mrs. Lena Younger?
BENEATHA:	*(Smoothing her hair with slight embarrassment)* Oh—yes, that's my mother. Excuse me. *(She closes the door and turns to quiet the other two)* Ruth! Brother! Somebody's here. *(Then she opens the door. The man casts a curious quick glance at all of them.)* Uh—come in please.
MAN:	*(Coming in)* Thank you.
BENEATHA:	My mother isn't here just now. Is it business?
MAN:	Yes . . . well, of a sort.
WALTER:	*(Freely, the Man of the House)* Have a seat. I'm Mrs. Younger's son. I look after most of her business matters. *(Ruth and Beneatha exchange amused glances.)*
MAN:	*(Regarding Walter, and sitting)* Well—My name is Karl Lindner . . .
WALTER:	*(Stretching out his hand)* Walter Younger. This is my wife—*(Ruth nods politely.)*—and my sister.
LINDNER:	How do you do.
WALTER:	*(Amiably, as he sits himself easily on a chair, leaning with interest forward on his knees and looking **expectantly** into the newcomer's face)* What can we do for you, Mr. Lindner!
LINDNER:	*(Some minor shuffling of the hat and briefcase on his knees)* Well—I am a representative of the Clybourne Park Improvement Association—
WALTER:	*(Pointing)* Why don't you sit your things on the floor?

Drawing Conclusions About Characters Unlike stories, plays don't usually include descriptions of the **characters.** Stage directions and characters' words and actions give clues about what the characters are like.

The stage directions describe Walter's attitude. They also describe the way he greets the guest and how the women react. Walter states that he looks after his mother's business matters. From these clues, the reader gets the sense that Walter sees himself as the head of the household, the one in control. Which stage direction gives the reader a clue about what Ruth and Beneatha think of Walter's attitude?

    a.   *(Ruth and Beneatha exchange amused glances.)*

    b.   Beneatha *(Smoothing her hair with slight embarrassment)*

LINDNER:	Oh—yes. Thank you. *(He slides the briefcase and hat under the chair.)* And as I was saying—I am from the Clybourne Park Improvement Association and we have had it brought to our attention at the last meeting that you people—or at least your mother—has bought a piece of residential property at—*(He digs for the slip of paper again.)*—four o six Clybourne Street . . .
WALTER:	That's right. Care for something to drink? Ruth, get Mr. Lindner a beer.
LINDNER:	*(Upset for some reason)* Oh—no, really. I mean thank you very much, but no thank you.
RUTH:	*(Innocently)* Some coffee?
LINDNER:	Thank you, nothing at all.
	(Beneatha is watching the man carefully.)
LINDNER:	Well, I don't know how much you folks know about our organization. *(He is a gentle man; thoughtful and somewhat **labored** in his manner.)* It is one of these community organizations set up to look after—oh, you know, things like block upkeep and special projects and we also have what we call our New Neighbors Orientation Committee . . .
BENEATHA:	*(Drily)* Yes—and what do they do?
LINDNER:	*(Turning a little to her and then returning the main force to Walter)* Well— it's what you might call a sort of welcoming committee, I guess. I mean they, we, I'm the chairman of the committee—go around and see the new people who move into the neighborhood and sort of give them the lowdown on the way we do things out in Clybourne Park.
BENEATHA:	*(With appreciation of the two meanings, which escape Ruth and Walter)* Un-huh.
LINDNER:	And we also have the category of what the association calls—*(He looks elsewhere.)*—uh—special community problems . . .

Recognizing Theme A **theme** is an idea that runs through the entire passage. It is a general truth about life, or human nature, suggested in a story. In the passage Lindner wants to discuss something with the Youngers. His words and actions indicate that he seems very uncomfortable.

1. Which two items support the idea that Lindner is uncomfortable talking to the Youngers?
   a. He shuffles his hat and briefcase.
   b. He uses words like "oh," "uh," and "well" often.
   c. The Youngers offer him coffee.

2. From what you have read so far, you know that Lindner is white and you can infer that the Youngers are African-Americans. What do you think the author is trying to suggest about human nature by the way he writes about Lindner's behavior?
   a. People often feel uncomfortable when meeting new neighbors.
   b. People can become uncomfortable with people they see as different.

BENEATHA:	Yes—and what are some of those?
WALTER:	Girl, let the man talk.
LINDNER:	*(With understated relief)* Thank you. I would sort of like to explain this thing in my own way. I mean I want to explain to you in a certain way.
WALTER:	Go ahead.
LINDNER:	Yes. Well. I'm going to try to get right to the point. I'm sure we'll all appreciate that in the long run.
BENEATHA:	Yes.
WALTER:	Be still now!
LINDNER:	Well—
RUTH:	*(Still innocently)* Would you like another chair—you don't look comfortable.
LINDNER:	*(More frustrated than annoyed)* No, thank you very much. Please. Well—to get right to the point I—*(A great breath, and he is off at last)* I am sure you people must be aware of some of the incidents which have happened in various parts of the city when colored people have moved into certain areas—*(Beneatha exhales heavily and starts tossing a piece of fruit up and down in the air.)* Well—because we have what I think is going to be a unique type of organization in American community life—not only do we **deplore** that kind of thing—but we are trying to do something about it. *(Beneatha stops tossing and turns with a new and **quizzical** interest to the man.)* We feel—*(gaining confidence in his mission because of the interest in the faces of the people he is talking to)*—we feel that most of the trouble in this world, when you come right down to it—*(He hits his knee for emphasis.)*—most of the trouble exists because people just don't sit down and talk to each other.
RUTH:	*(Nodding as she might in church, pleased with the remark)* You can say that again, mister.
LINDNER:	*(More encouraged by such **affirmation**)* That we don't try hard enough in this world to understand the other fellow's problem. The other guy's point of view.

Summarizing It is sometimes helpful to **summarize** speeches by finding the main idea and the most important supporting details. This will help you understand what the speaker is really trying to say.

In Lindner's speech, he mentions incidents that have happened when African-American families have moved into white neighborhoods, that his association is trying to do something about it, and that people should sit down and talk to each other. What main idea is supported by these details?

a. Lindner wants new people to join committees to help keep the neighborhood clean.

b. He thinks that an African-American family moving into Clybourne Park is a "special community problem."

c. Lindner wants the Youngers to help plan a neighborhood party.

Thinking About the Play

Practice Vocabulary

The words below are in bold type in the passage. Study the way each word is used. Then complete each sentence by writing the correct word.

consulting	expectantly	labored
deplore	quizzical	affirmation

1. If you give an _____, it shows that you agree.

2. A person with a _____ look is likely to be curious about something.

3. He's _____ a mechanic before buying a used car.

4. If you _____ an action, you strongly dislike it.

5. A patient who has _____ breathing has difficulty inhaling and exhaling.

6. The student was _____ awaiting the results of the test.

Understand What You Read

Write the answer to each question.

7. Which character seems to be suspicious of Lindner? Give one clue that supports your answer.

   _____

   _____

8. At first how do the Youngers treat their visitor?

   _____

   _____

9. What do you think Lindner is referring to when he mentions "special community problems"?

   _____

   _____

10. Why do you think Lindner is uncomfortable?

   _____

   _____

Apply Your Skills

Circle the number of the best answer for each question.

11. Based on Lindner's approach to the Younger family, what do you think he will probably do to solve the problem?
    (1) threaten them
    (2) ask them to join the association
    (3) suggest in a nice way that they sell the house
    (4) learn to accept the family
    (5) have them arrested for disturbing the peace

12. Lindner suggests that racial problems exist because people are quick to judge, without thinking about the other person's point of view. Which statement supports this theme?
    (1) Lindner's organization includes a welcoming committee.
    (2) Lindner went to talk to the family about the property Mrs. Younger bought.
    (3) There have been race riots in Clybourne Park.
    (4) Lindner suggests that people should sit down and talk.
    (5) The Youngers have protested against African-American people.

13. In the passage, Lindner says the purpose of the Clybourne Park Improvement Association is to ensure that the neighborhood is properly maintained and that new people understand and follow the "rules." Which detail supports this main idea?
    (1) The organization looks after upkeep and special projects.
    (2) Mrs. Younger has bought property in the neighborhood.
    (3) Walter explains that he handles Mrs. Younger's business affairs.
    (4) The association prefers not to address any issues about racial conflict.
    (5) Mr. Lindner turns down Walter and Ruth's offer of a drink.

Connect with the Play

Write your answer to each question.

14. If you were a member of the Younger family, how would you respond to Lindner's speech? Explain.

    _____

    _____

15. Have you or someone you know had an experience with some kind of prejudice? Was the prejudice suggested or was it stated directly? Was the problem resolved? Explain.

    _____

    _____

Comedy

LESSON 23

Vocabulary

prominent

cliché

spectacular

frantic

traditional

indicted

Many plays are written to make the audience laugh. A play that is meant to be funny is called a **comedy.** Sometimes the characters in a comedy have serious problems or conflicts, but the way they behave or handle the situation makes the play funny. A comedy can have misunderstandings between characters, physical mishaps, or silly dialogue. In most comedies, the characters overcome their problems and there is a happy ending.

Relate to the Topic

In the play you are about to read, the characters are meeting for the first time and don't appear to have much in common. Think about a time when you met someone for the first time. What happened?

_____

_____

Reading Strategy

VISUALIZING CHARACTERS When you read a play, use the words, actions, and stage directions to picture the characters in your mind. To bring characters to life, pay attention to what they say, their interactions with each other, and how they react in different situations. Look for clues in the dialogue and stage directions.

Read the first four lines of dialogue on page 173. Then answer the questions.

1. Based on the first three lines, which of the following is the most likely description of Gorgeous?
   a. awkward and shy
   b. confident and bold
   Hint: Think about what her name suggests.

2. Which of the following details is the most helpful in giving readers a clue to Gorgeous's character?
   a. "Well it's obvious, isn't it?"
   b. "I also just met your sister Pfeni."
   Hint: Read Gorgeous' first lines in the passage.

The Sisters Rosensweig
by Wendy Wasserstein

MERV:	And you must be Gorgeous. We were just talking about you.
GORGEOUS:	And how I got my name! Well, it's obvious, isn't it! Thanks for leaving the door open. I feel like Elijah.
MERV:	I also just met your sister Pfeni.
GORGEOUS:	Aren't my sisters fabulous? They're really such funsy people!
MERV:	I wouldn't say your sister Sara is "funsy."
GORGEOUS:	Maybe you should marry her.
MERV:	I've only spent five minutes with her.
GORGEOUS:	So what? Some people know at first sight. People call me from the Massachusetts Turnpike because they've just met someone at a rest stop and have fallen in love.
MERV:	And you speak to these people?
GORGEOUS:	Have you ever been to Boston?
MERV:	My son lives there.
GORGEOUS:	Well, if you ever listen to the radio when you visit your son, you'd know that everyone calls Dr. Gorgeous. *Begins to sing her theme song.*

Call Dr. Gorgeous, ring, ring, ring,
Call Dr. Gorgeous, ring, ring, ring.

Mimes picking up a phone.

"Hello, I'm Dr. Gorgeous, how can I help you?" Isn't that great! Isn't that funsy! I just have the best time. I'm sorry, I didn't catch your name.

Understanding the Author's Purpose The author, or playwright, has a reason for making the characters say and do certain things. The playwright might want to entertain the reader with silly dialogue, help the reader understand what type of personality a character has, or show the reader why a character feels or acts the way he or she does.

When Gorgeous starts singing her theme song, it serves two purposes. One of these is to add to the humorous feeling in the play. The other is to show that Gorgeous is a self-centered person.

Circle each bit of dialogue that shows Gorgeous is self-centered.
a. "I feel like Elijah." (Elijah is a prophet.)
b. "Maybe you should marry her."
c. "...everyone calls Dr. Gorgeous"
d. "Isn't that great!"
e. "I'm sorry, I didn't catch your name."

MERV:	Mervyn Kant.
GORGEOUS	*helps herself to nuts from a dish*: Merlin, let me tell you something. I was a Newton housewife with four wonderful kids. My husband, Henry, is a very **prominent** attorney. We have a very comfortable lifestyle. In other words, everything was going just great, but I needed just a little sparkle to make it all perfect.
MERV:	So you're the sister who did everything right. You married the attorney, you had the children, you moved to the suburbs.
GORGEOUS:	Now, don't make me into a **cliché.** I am much more than that. Merlin, I am one of the first real jugglers. I love nuts and they're just terrible for you. Ucch! I'm so fat! I ate like a pig! Honey, do me a favor, give me one more and then put these on the other table. Sara shouldn't keep things like this around the house. The Dr. Gorgeous Show is hoping to make the leap from radio to cable. You know that absolutely everything shows on television.
MERV:	I'm sure you'll have no problem.
GORGEOUS:	Sara, who is such a brilliant woman, says I could have a **spectacular** career in communications. Talking has always come easily to me.
MERV:	Yes, you're very natural.
GORGEOUS:	In fact, my first show really happened by accident. So many women in the Newton Temple Beth El sisterhood wanted to know how I managed in our **frantic** modern times to maintain a warm **traditional** home, that they begged me to give a speech to their local chapter. Well, as it happens, P. S., who should be in the audience but Rabbi Carl Pearlstein, the host of "Newton at Sunrise." Pearlstein was so impressed with my presentation that he invited me on his show.

Applying Ideas Applying an idea means taking an idea in a play and using, or applying, that idea to another situation. For example, if you know that a character is very particular about what she wears, you can predict what the character might wear in the next scene of the play when she goes to a formal dinner party. First, think about what you know about a character, and then apply what you know to a different situation.

1. Based on what you know about Gorgeous, what would she most likely do if she were at a restaurant and found a fly in her soup?
   a. walk out of the restaurant without saying a word
   b. discuss the issue at length with the waiter
   c. quickly and quietly get rid of the fly

2. What do you think Gorgeous would do if someone told her that her show was terrible and that her advice was not helpful?
   a. talk to other people to find out if they liked her show or not
   b. think deeply about how she could improve her show
   c. dismiss the statement and claim the person was just jealous

MERV:	I've heard of Pearlstein. Didn't he write *I Learned Everything but Handwriting in First Grade*?
GORGEOUS:	Try *Learning to Love Again, Learning to Live Again*. Only twenty-six months on every bestseller list.
MERV:	Of course. He was recently **indicted.**
GORGEOUS:	Rabbi Pearlstein is a great man. His accountant was evil.
MERV:	I think we use the same one. I'm sorry, please tell me what happened next.
GORGEOUS:	I became a regular on Pearlstein's show. Then he was indicted, and the rest is history. Now you just mention Dr. Gorgeous anywhere in suburban Boston, Framingham, Natick, or Lynn, and they all know who I am. Merlin, I am what they call a real middle-aged success story. And I am having a ball. It's really funsy.
MERV:	Your husband must be very proud.
GORGEOUS:	He is thrilled. And so supportive.
MERV:	I have only one more question. When did you become a doctor?
GORGEOUS:	You've heard of Dr. Pepper?
MERV:	Yes.
GORGEOUS:	So I'm Dr. Gorgeous. *Laughs and takes his arm.*

Synthesizing Ideas When you synthesize ideas, you put different ideas together to come up with a new idea that gives you a broader and deeper understanding of what you are reading. For example, imagine that you are reading a play that begins with a lot of action and movement. The main character speaks in a fast and energetic manner, and events in the play seem to happen quickly. You might put these different aspects of the play together to conclude that the play is going to have an exciting ending.

You can also gain extra insight into the characters by putting together information you learn about them. For example, Gorgeous thinks that Rabbi Pearlstein is a great man even though he was indicted for a crime. She also thinks her sister Sara is fun although Mervyn disagrees with her. Putting this information together, you might conclude that Gorgeous does not necessarily know the truth about things.

If we then add the idea that Gorgeous tends to be self-centered, we can conclude that she doesn't see herself as she really is. Gorgeous might be incorrect when she says that her husband is thrilled and supportive or that many women in the Temple Beth El sisterhood wanted her advice on how to maintain a warm, traditional home.

After synthesizing these ideas, which of the following statements about Gorgeous is most likely to be true?

a. Gorgeous is actually a doctor.
b. Gorgeous does not really have a show.
c. Gorgeous's show is not very well-known.

Thinking About the Play

Practice Vocabulary

The words below are in bold type in the passages. Study the way each word is used. Then complete each sentence by writing the correct word.

prominent	**cliché**	**spectacular**
frantic	**traditional**	**indicted**

1. Someone charged with a crime must then be_____.

2. Fireworks are often a_____ sight.

3. A_____ member of the community is well respected.

4. The child's parents were_____ when they thought he was missing.

5. An overused phrase is a_____.

6. Turkey with stuffing is a _____ Thanksgiving meal for many people.

Understand What You Read

Write the answer to each question.

7. What kind of work does Gorgeous do?

_____

8. What does Gorgeous mean when she says she doesn't want to be made into a cliché?

_____

_____

9. What does Gorgeous mean when she says that she needed a little sparkle in her life?

_____

10. What does the author mean by the statement "You've heard of Dr. Pepper?"

_____

Apply Your Skills

Circle the number of the best answer for each question.

11. Why does the author have Gorgeous call Mervyn "Merlin"?
    To show that Gorgeous
    (1) knows Mervyn so well that she calls him by a nickname
    (2) sometimes has trouble hearing
    (3) is a mean and spiteful woman
    (4) does not pay much attention to other people
    (5) is too playful and silly with her friends

12. Based on the information in the passage, how would Mervyn respond if someone insulted him?
    (1) He would ignore the insult.
    (2) He would become angry.
    (3) He would become depressed.
    (4) He would challenge the person who insulted him.
    (5) He would wonder what he had done wrong.

13. In the passage, Gorgeous makes many statements about how wonderful her life has been, and Mervyn makes statements such as "Yes, you're very natural" and "When did you become a doctor?" Based on this information, what can you conclude?
    (1) Mervyn has a lot of sympathy for Gorgeous.
    (2) Mervyn doesn't realize that Gorgeous is exaggerating.
    (3) Mervyn is tired and wants to go home.
    (4) Mervyn always thinks the best of people.
    (5) Mervyn tends to be sarcastic.

Connect with the Play

Write your answer to each question.

14. Have you ever listened to a radio talk show where people call in for advice? What was your opinion of the show? Why?

    _____

    _____

    _____

15. If you ran into Gorgeous at a party, what would you think of her?

    _____

    _____

    _____

Reading

Theater: Stage Manager

Some Careers in Theater

Have you ever wondered who is in charge of making everything run smoothly in a play? There is much more to a play than the actors getting on stage in costumes and saying their lines. Someone needs to schedule rehearsals, talk with the production staff, and organize the many aspects of the play. That person is the stage manager.

A stage manager needs to have good organizational skills and be good at working with people. He or she must be able to communicate what the director wants to the production staff, and vice versa. A stage manager has to coordinate the work of many people: the costume designer, the lighting technician, the director, the actors, and the set designer.

Look at the box showing some careers in theater.

- Do any of the careers interest you? If so, which ones?

- How could you find out more about those careers? On a separate piece of paper, write some questions that you would like to have answered. You can find out more about those careers in the *Occupational Outlook Handbook* at your local library and online.

Properties Coordinator supervises the building of the set and props; tracks the position of props during rehearsals and shows

Sound Designer amplifies the performers' voices and musical instruments; provides sound effects; supervises the sound technician

House Manager supervises the areas of the theatre that the audience uses; prepares the seating area and lobby; supervises ticket-taking, seating, intermission, and ushers

Read the following article about a stage manager. Then answer the questions.

What Does a Stage Manager Do All Day?

Many people have asked me what I do as a stage manager. Because they do not see me or my work on stage—I am not an actor or a costume designer—people aren't clear about how I spend my time at work. Just think of it this way—someone has to organize everyone involved in the production of a play. That person is me.

I am responsible for running the entire performance. I give cues to the actors and make sure they are moving around the stage the way the director wants them to. I find all the props and furniture, and I manage the cost of these items. I run the backstage and onstage areas during performances and supervise the tearing down of the set when the show has ended. I also coordinate everything between the director and the other staff, such as the lighting director and costume designer.

I have always been very good at organization. When I started my job as an assistant stage manager at the Pittsburgh Playhouse, I learned how to be a great organizer of both people and things. I love my current job, but in my next job I hope to be stage manager for a big Broadway musical like *Phantom of the Opera*.

1. What is the main idea of this article?
   (1) Being a stage manager is a difficult but fulfilling career.
   (2) There are many kinds of jobs in theater, such as being a lighting designer.
   (3) The job of a stage manager requires the ability to organize a variety of tasks.
   (4) Running a stationery store is probably easier than being a stage manager.
   (5) *Phantom of the Opera* is a major Broadway musical.

2. What was the author's purpose in writing this article?
   (1) to show his friends what a good stage manager he is
   (2) to explain what a stage manager does
   (3) to persuade the reader to become a stage manager
   (4) to entertain the reader with stories about being a stage manager
   (5) to try to get a job as a stage manager for *Phantom of the Opera*

3. Write down three tasks of a stage manager that you would enjoy. What skills are needed for each of those tasks?

_____

_____

Unit 3 Review
Drama

Read the following passage from the play *The Tomorrow Radio* by Robyn Reeves.

NARRATOR:	Marcos and Adela Perez, a husband-and-wife team of scientists, are working on a project in their lab at home. For several years they have been trying to discover evidence of life on other planets by picking up radio signals from deep outer space. Their work has been expensive, however, and their money is about to run out. . . .
ADELA:	Marcos, wait a minute. . . . I'm not sure. It sounds like—words.
NARRATOR:	The sounds become clearer, and Marcos and Adela are able to make out a voice. . . .
RADIO VOICE:	. . . And now, a weather forecast for tomorrow.
ADELA:	What next? I never thought we'd be crossing sound waves with an ordinary radio broadcast. . . .
RADIO VOICE:	Today's rain will turn into light showers tonight. Tonight will be slightly cooler. Sunday will be mostly cloudy. The high will be in the low fifties. . . .
ADELA:	That's odd. It's not raining here. The announcer said "tomorrow's weather" and then talked about the weather for Sunday. But tomorrow is Saturday.
RADIO VOICE:	Here are today's football scores. Dartmouth beat Yale in New Haven, 20 to 17. And here's a big upset. Indiana stunned Ohio State, 35 to 7! In the South . . . *(Static)*
ADELA:	This is incredible! How could he have these football scores now? None of these games will be played until tomorrow. . . . This is no ordinary broadcast. . . .
MARCOS:	*(Looking over her shoulder)* What are you doing?
ADELA:	I'm writing down the football scores. If this thing is as good as it seems to be, we may never have to worry about money again!
RADIO VOICE:	And that's the last of the football scores. This completes our broadcast day. Join me tomorrow, Sunday, at 10:00 A.M. for a sports and weather update. Until then . . . *(Music plays, then static)*
MARCOS:	I still can't believe it. A radio that tells the future! . . . Think of all the good that people could do if they knew what was going to happen a day early. . . . And think of all the bad that could be done too. If this radio ever got into the wrong hands. . . .
NARRATOR:	The radio suddenly crackles to life once more.
RADIO VOICE:	I've just been handed a special news bulletin. The River Bridge in Sommerville has just collapsed. So far, one person is known dead. Stay tuned for more details. *(Static again then silence)*

UNIT 3 DRAMA

Questions 1 through 7 refer to the passage on page 180.

Write the answer to each questions.

1. How are Adela and Marcos trying to discover evidence of life on other planets?

   _____

2. The action of the play takes place on what day of the week?

   _____

3. Why does Adela say, "If this thing is as good as it seems to be, we may never have to worry about money again"?

   _____

4. What is the relationship between Adela and Marcos?

   _____

Circle the number of the best answer for each question.

5. Why were Adela and Marcos surprised by the broadcast?
   They
   (1) didn't expect the radio to ever receive anything
   (2) were trying to contact scientists in other countries
   (3) were expecting to receive radio signals from outer space
   (4) expected to receive ordinary radio broadcasts
   (5) had turned the radio off

6. After hearing the news bulletin about the collapse of the bridge, what could they use the radio to do?
   (1) make money
   (2) fool people
   (3) prove there's life on other planets
   (4) do something good
   (5) hear an ordinary broadcast

7. After hearing the last broadcast, what do you predict Adela and Marcos will do next?
   They will
   (1) say nothing and continue their research
   (2) try to sell the radio to make money for their lab
   (3) wait to see if the bridge collapses before they tell anyone
   (4) go to the authorities and try to convince them that the bridge will collapse
   (5) try to find out where the broadcast is coming from

Read the following passage from the play *An Ideal Husband* by Oscar Wilde.

JAMES:	Lord Caversham has been waiting for some time in the library for Sir Robert. I told him your lordship was here.
LORD GORING:	Thank you. Would you kindly tell him I've gone?
JAMES:	*(bowing)* I shall do so, my lord. *(Exit servant.)*
LORD GORING:	Really, I don't want to meet my father three days running. It is a great deal too much excitement for any son. I hope to goodness he won't come up. Fathers should be neither seen nor heard. That is the only proper basis for family life. Mothers are different. Mothers are darlings. *(Throws himself down into a chair, picks up a paper and begins to read it.)* *(Enter LORD CAVERSHAM.)*
LORD CAVERSHAM:	Well, sir, what are you doing here? Wasting your time as usual, I suppose?
LORD GORING	*(throws down paper and rises)*: My dear father, when one pays a visit it is for the purpose of wasting other people's time, not one's own.
LORD CAVERSHAM:	Have you been thinking over what I spoke to you about last night?
LORD GORING:	I have been thinking about nothing else.
LORD CAVERSHAM:	Engaged to be married yet?
LORD GORING:	*(genially)*: Not yet; but I hope to be before lunch-time.
LORD CAVERSHAM	*(caustically)*: You can have till dinner-time if it would be of any convenience to you.
LORD GORING:	Thanks awfully, but I think I'd sooner be engaged before lunch.
LORD CAVERSHAM:	Humph! Never know when you are serious or not.
LORD GORING:	Neither do I, father.
LORD CAVERSHAM:	Why don't you propose to that pretty Miss Chiltern?
LORD GORING:	I am of a very nervous disposition, especially in the morning.
LORD CAVERSHAM:	I don't suppose there is the smallest chance of her accepting you.
LORD GORING:	I don't know how the betting stands today.
LORD CAVERSHAM:	If she did accept you she would be the prettiest fool in England.
LORD GORING:	That is just what I should like to marry. A thoroughly sensible wife would reduce me to a condition of absolute idiocy in less than six months.
LORD CAVERSHAM:	You don't deserve her, sir.
LORD GORING:	My dear father, if we men married the women we deserved, we should have a very bad time of it.

Questions 8 through 13 refer to the passage on page 182.

Write the answer to each question.

8. What does Lord Caversham think of Miss Chiltern?

   _____

9. What does Lord Goring mean when he says, "I don't know how the betting stands today"?

   _____

10. How would you describe Lord Caversham?

   _____

Circle the number of the best answer for each question.

11. What is meant by "If we men married the women we deserved, we should have a very bad time of it"?
    (1) Women don't deserve good men.
    (2) Women are all no good.
    (3) Men are too good for women.
    (4) Men don't deserve good women.
    (5) Men should not get married.

12. Which of the following best shows that Lord Goring does not take many things seriously?
    (1) "Would you kindly tell him I've gone?"
    (2) "Fathers should be neither seen nor heard."
    (3) "Mothers are darlings."
    (4) "I have been thinking about nothing else."
    (5) "Thanks awfully, but I think I'd sooner be engaged before lunch."

13. Which of the following best describes the tone in the entire passage?
    (1) calm
    (2) forgiving
    (3) irritated
    (4) desperate
    (5) comic

Reading Extension

Think about a movie, play, or television show that you have seen recently. Write a brief summary of it, including a description of the main characters, the main idea, and supporting details.

Mini-Test • Unit 3

This is a 15-minute practice test. After 15 minutes, mark the last number you finished. Then complete the test and check your answers. If most of your answers were correct but you did not finish, try to work faster next time.

Directions: Choose the <u>one best answer</u> to each question.

<u>Questions 1 through 8</u> refer to the following passage.

WHY IS BOOLIE UPSET WITH HIS MOTHER?

BOOLIE: Mama, the car didn't just back over the driveway and land on the Pollard's garage all by itself. You had it in the wrong
(5) gear.

DAISY: I did not!

BOOLIE: You put it in reverse instead of drive. The police report shows that.

(10) DAISY: You should have let me keep my La Salle.

BOOLIE: Your La Salle was eight years old.

DAISY: I don't care. It never would have
(15) behaved this way. And you know it.

BOOLIE: Mama, cars don't behave. They are behaved upon. The fact is you, all by yourself, demolished
(20) that Packard.

DAISY: Think what you want. I know the truth.

BOOLIE: The truth is you shouldn't be allowed to drive a car anymore.

(25) DAISY: No.

BOOLIE: Mama, we are just going to have to hire somebody to drive you.

DAISY: No *we* are not. This is my
(30) business.

BOOLIE: Your insurance policy is written so that they are going to have to give you a brand-new car.

DAISY: Not another Packard, I hope.

(35) BOOLIE: Lord Almighty! Don't you see what I'm saying?

DAISY: Quit talking so ugly to your mother.

BOOLIE: Mama, you are seventy-two
(40) years old and you just cost the insurance company twenty-seven hundred dollars. You are a terrible risk. Nobody is going to issue you a policy after this.

(45) DAISY: You're just saying that to be hateful.

BOOLIE: Okay. Yes. Yes I am. I'm making it all up. Every insurance company in America is lined up
(50) in the driveway waving their fountain pens and falling all over themselves to get you to sign on. Everybody wants Daisy Wertham, the one
(55) woman in the history of driving to demolish a three-week-old Packard, a two-car garage and a freestanding tool shed in one fell swoop!

(60) DAISY: You talk so foolish sometimes, Boolie.

Alfred Uhry, *Driving Miss Daisy*

184

1. Why can't Daisy drive anymore?

   (1) She is too old to drive her car safely.
   (2) She wrecked Boolie's car and he is
       very angry.
   (3) Boolie can't afford to buy another car.
   (4) Her neighbors are angry with her for
       destroying their garage.
   (5) She can't drive Packards and needs to
       own a LaSalle.

2. Which statement best explains why Daisy
   and Boolie are having an argument?

   (1) Daisy and Boolie dislike each other.
   (2) Daisy and Boolie are not nice people.
   (3) Daisy and Boolie are both stubborn.
   (4) Daisy and Boolie like different cars.
   (5) Daisy and Boolie talk too much.

3. Which of the following best characterizes
   Boolie?

   He is
   (1) intimidated by Daisy
   (2) embarrassed by Daisy
   (3) worried about Daisy
   (4) frustrated with Daisy
   (5) cold-hearted towards Daisy

4. Based on the information in the passage,
   which of the following is most likely to
   happen when Daisy gets a driver?

   (1) She will secretly be relieved not to
       drive anymore.
   (2) She will insist on choosing the driver.
   (3) She will dislike him at the beginning.
   (4) She will enjoy having someone to talk
       to.
   (5) She will become depressed that she
       has lost her independence.

5. Why does Daisy say "You're just saying that
   to be hateful"? (lines 45–46)

   (1) Daisy's son doesn't treat her well.
   (2) Daisy and her son like to joke around.
   (3) Daisy hates her son.
   (4) Daisy doesn't believe her son.
   (5) Daisy may be losing her mind.

6. Which of the following best describes
   Boolie's tone at the end of this passage?
   (lines 47–59)

   (1) sarcastic
   (2) compassionate
   (3) humorous
   (4) serious
   (5) violent

7. Which of the following best describes the
   tone of the entire passage?

   (1) playful
   (2) thoughtful
   (3) argumentative
   (4) puzzled
   (5) suspenseful

8. Later in the play, after Daisy has had a
   driver for many years, he visits her in a
   nursing home. Daisy asks Boolie to leave
   them alone, and they share a piece of pie.
   What change does this show in Daisy?

   She has changed from
   (1) hateful to devoted
   (2) energetic to shy
   (3) angry to humiliated
   (4) sarcastic to loving
   (5) resistant to accepting

Poetry

Poetry is a special type of writing that uses vivid language to appeal to our senses and imagination. Poets—like the famous American poet Maya Angelou in this picture—use words to create images we can see, hear, feel and taste. Poems are usually arranged in a special way on the page. Some poems rhyme, while others do not. Poems express different moods, tell stories, share feelings, and make readers think.

What is your favorite poem? Why do you like it? _____

_____

_____

Thinking About Poetry

You have probably read more poetry than you realize. Think about the times you have come across poetry in your life.

Check the box for each activity you did.

- ☐ Did you recite nursery rhymes as a child?
- ☐ Did you read children's books with lots of rhymes?
- ☐ Did you ever try to write a poem to express your feelings?
- ☐ Did you read poetry in school?
- ☐ Did you take a book of poems out of the library?
- ☐ Did you read a poem in a newspaper or magazine?
- ☐ Did you browse the poetry section in a bookstore?
- ☐ Did you read a poem that a friend had written?
- ☐ Did you listen to a song with poetic lyrics?

Write some other experiences you have had with poetry.

_____

_____

_____

Previewing the Unit

In this unit, you will learn:

- how popular poetry helps us look at our lives

- how classic poetry reflects the experiences of people years ago yet still relates to modern life

Lesson 24	Popular Poetry
Lesson 25	Classic Poetry
Lesson 26	Classic Poetry

Popular Poetry

Poetry uses language in a special way. **Poets** want readers to use their senses to experience a scene. Poets do not just give facts or information. Instead, they choose words carefully to convey feelings or experiences. They often use vivid words that bring a picture, or an image, to the reader's mind.

Popular poetry includes works that have been recently written. The poems are about events in modern-day life. They may be about the ordinary things people do in their day-to-day lives or about ideas that people can imagine.

Vocabulary

countenance

awkward

mantel

extend

precious

embrace

Relate to the Topic

The character in the first poem you will read is thirty-eight years old and somewhat disappointed with her life. She had expected to be more than she is.

How do you feel about your own life? Are you doing what you expected to be doing?

_____

_____

Reading Strategy

UNDERSTANDING POEMS   To understand a poem, pay careful attention to its form, rhyme, rhythm and speaker. A poem isn't organized like prose. Instead, it is organized into lines and stanzas. A stanza is a group of lines. In some poems, the lines of poetry end in words that rhyme. The speaker is the person talking in the poem. The speaker is not necessarily the poet, but is often a character the poet creates.

Read the first seven lines of the poem on page 189. Then answer the questions.

1. Is this poem divided into stanzas?_____
   Hint: Remember that stanzas are groups of lines in a poem, similar to paragraphs.

2. Does the poem have a rhyming pattern?_____
   Hint: Look for rhyming words at the ends of the lines.

188

UNIT 4 POETRY

the thirty eighth year

by Lucille Clifton

the thirty eighth year
of my life,
plain as bread
round as a cake
an ordinary woman.

an ordinary woman.

i had expected to be
smaller than this,
more beautiful
wiser in afrikan ways,
more confident,
i had expected
more than this.

i will be forty soon.
my mother once was forty.

my mother died at forty four,
a woman of sad **countenance**
leaving behind a girl
awkward as a stork.
my mother was thick,
her hair was a jungle and
she was very wise
and beautiful
and sad.

Identifying Figurative Language Figurative language is a way of using words in different and unusual ways to create a vivid picture. One type of figurative language occurs when poets compare two things that are very different. In the passage above, the speaker compares her mother's hair to a jungle. The word "jungle" creates the image of wild and untamed things. Through this figurative language, the reader can picture the mother's hair being wild, or hard to control.

In this first part of the poem, the speaker describes herself as "plain as bread." What point is she making about herself?

a.   She thinks that she is a good cook.

b.   She thinks that she is not very pretty or special in any way.

Check your answers on page 250.

i have dreamed dreams
for you mama
more than once.
i have wrapped me
in your skin
and made you live again
more than once.
i have taken the bones you hardened
and built daughters
and they blossom and promise fruit
like afrikan trees.
i am a woman now.
an ordinary woman.

in the thirty eighth
year of my life,
surrounded by life,
a perfect picture of
blackness blessed.
i had not expected this
loneliness.

if it is western,
if it is the final
europe in my mind,
if in the middle of my life
i am turning the final turn
into the shining dark
let me come to it whole
and holy
not afraid
not lonely

out of my mother's life
into my own
into my own.

i had expected more than this.
i had not expected to be
an ordinary woman.

Summarizing You can summarize a poem by finding the main idea and supporting details. Which statement best summarizes the feelings of the speaker in this poem?

a. She feels disappointed that she is getting older and is no longer young and beautiful.

b. She feels disappointed that she is not as wise and beautiful as her mother was.

A Picture on the Mantel

by James Lafayette Walker

All he knew about his mom
Was the picture of her face
That always seemed to have been on
The **mantel** by a vase.
He didn't have the love that every
Child of five should know
That only mothers can **extend**
Mixed with a warming glow.
One day while shopping with his dad
He stopped and gave a stare
"Look, Dad, look, can't you see
That's mother over there?"
"That isn't mother," said the dad
"Your mother's now with God."
"Are you sure, Dad, are you sure?"
Dad gave a knowing nod.
The dad said "Please excuse my son"
As tears welled in his eyes
"He's too young to understand
when someone **precious** dies."
The child said to the lady,
"But you have my mother's face."
He longed for her to hold him
In a mother's fond **embrace.**
"Are you a mother?" He then asked
"Why yes," she sadly smiled
"Will you hold me close?" he begged
The mother held the child.

Identifying Details Details that support the main idea can help you understand what the characters are thinking and feeling. The little boy in this poem is unsure about what happened to his mother. The father understands how confused his son feels. He explains this to the woman in the store. The father shows his understanding in two ways. The details that show this are the knowing nod and the tears in his eyes. Which two details show that the boy in the poem is confused?

a. He asks his father if he is sure his mother is with God.

b. He wonders if a stranger might be his mother.

c. He has a picture of his mother on the mantel.

Check your answers on page 250.

Thinking About the Poems

Practice Vocabulary

The words below are in bold type in the poems. Study the way each word is used. Then write each word next to its meaning.

countenance   awkward   mantel

extend   precious   embrace

1. a hug _____

2. the shelf above a fireplace _____

3. very valuable _____

4. offer _____

5. clumsy _____

6. face _____

Understand What You Read

Write the answer to each question.

7. What four things had the speaker in "the thirty eighth year" expected to be at the age of 38?

   _____

   _____

8. In what way are the speaker in "the thirty eighth year" and the boy in "A Picture on the Mantel" alike?

   _____

   _____

9. What is the boy in "A Picture on the Mantel" looking for? Does he find it?

   _____

   _____

10. The woman in "A Picture on the Mantel" was not the boy's mother. Why do you think she gave him a hug?

   _____

   _____

Apply Your Skills

Circle the number of the best answer for each question.

11. The speaker in "the thirty eighth year" says "i have wrapped me in your skin." What does she mean by this?
    (1) Her mother bothered her.
    (2) She wore her mother's clothes.
    (3) She has tried to be like her mother.
    (4) She looks exactly like her mother.
    (5) She misses her mother very much.

12. Which of the following details would you include in a summary of "A Picture on the Mantel?"
    (1) The mother's picture was placed next to the vase.
    (2) While shopping with his dad, the boy stopped and stared.
    (3) The child doesn't understand what happened to his mother.
    (4) The dad gave a knowing nod.
    (5) The child asked, "Are you my mother?"

13. The speaker in "the thirty eighth year" wants to live the rest of her life on her own terms. Which line from the poem supports this idea?
    (1) i am . . . an ordinary woman.
    (2) i have dreamed dreams for you mama more than once.
    (3) i had expected to be smaller than this . . .
    (4) i will be forty soon.
    (5) . . . out of my mother's life into my own . . .

Connect with the Poems

Write your answer to each question.

14. If you were the boy's father in "A Picture on the Mantel," what would you tell your son? How would you help him understand the situation?

    _____

    _____

    _____

15. Both poems are about people who have lost someone close to them. Have you ever lost someone you felt very close to? What do you miss most about that person?

    _____

    _____

    _____

Classic Poetry

Vocabulary

diverged

claim

trodden

arrayed

fluttered

minuet

Classic poems have stood the test of time. Although they were written years ago, they are still read and enjoyed by people today. These poems appeal to people of all ages. They speak about experiences and emotions that are common to everyone.

Relate to the Topic

We are faced with important choices and decisions every day. The first poem you will read, "The Road Not Taken," is about choosing what direction to take in life.

What is an important decision that you have made? What helped you to decide?

_____

_____

_____

Reading Strategy

READING A POEM ALOUD   When you read a poem aloud, listen for the sound, rhyme, and rhythm of the words. They create an almost musical effect. These sounds help to express the poem's feeling. Some poems repeat sounds. For example, a repeated "s" sound in a poem about a snake can make the poem come alive with the sound of hissing. The rhythm of the poem is a regular beat that you can hear in a poem. Read aloud the first five lines of the poem on page 195 and listen for the sound and rhythm of the words. Then answer the questions.

1. Write down two words that rhyme in the poem.

    _____

    Hint: Read the words at the end of each line in the first five lines of the poem.

2. What kind of music is this poem similar to?
    a.   hip-hop
    b.   a waltz
    Hint: Does the poem sound active and upbeat or slower and more thoughtful?

194   UNIT 4 POETRY

The Road Not Taken by Robert Frost

Two roads **diverged** in a yellow wood,
And sorry I could not travel both
And be one traveler, long I stood
And looked down one as far as I could
To where it bent in the undergrowth;

Then took the other, as just as fair,
And having perhaps the better **claim,**
Because it was grassy and wanted wear;
Though as for that the passing there
Had worn them really about the same,

And both that morning equally lay
In leaves no step had **trodden** black.
Oh, I kept the first for another day!
Yet knowing how way leads on to way,
I doubted if I should ever come back.

I shall be telling this with a sigh
Somewhere ages and ages hence:
Two roads diverged in a wood, and I—
I took the one less traveled by,
And that has made all the difference.

Using Context Clues Sometimes you will see an unfamiliar word or phrase when you read a passage. To figure out the meaning of an unfamiliar word, study the words and phrases around it. These surrounding words are the context. The context contains clues that can help you figure out the meaning of the word.

The word "undergrowth" appears in the fifth line of the poem. The clues "yellow wood," "grassy," and "in leaves" suggest that this scene takes place in a forest. Now look at the two words that make up the compound word "undergrowth." These clues help you to guess that "undergrowth" means "the plants that grow close to the ground in a forest."

Find the phrase "wanted wear" in the second stanza. Can you figure out from the context what this phrase means? "Wanted wear" means "had not been used much." Which two context clues from the rest of the poem could help a reader figure out the meaning of "wanted wear"?

  a.   no step had trodden
  b.   Two roads diverged in a wood
  c.   the one less traveled by

  Check your answers on page 251.

Richard Cory by Edwin Arlington Robinson

Whenever Richard Cory went down town,
We people on the pavement looked at him:
He was a gentleman from sole to crown,
Clean favored, and imperially slim.

And he was always quietly **arrayed,**
And he was always human when he talked;
But still he **fluttered** pulses when he said,
"Good-morning," and he glittered when he walked.

And he was rich—yes, richer than a king—
And admirably schooled in every grace:
In fine, we thought that he was everything
To make us wish that we were in his place.

So on we worked, and waited for the light,
And went without the meat, and cursed the bread;
And Richard Cory, one calm summer night,
Went home and put a bullet through his head.

Recognizing Theme The **theme** of a piece of writing is an idea that states a general truth about life or an insight into human nature. The theme is usually not stated directly. Readers have to analyze all the events and look for supporting details in order to decide for themselves what the theme is. Some stories or poems have more than one theme.

Reread the lines "We people on the pavement . . ." and " . . . wish that we were in his place." This shows that the ordinary people on the street admired Richard Cory and wished that they were in his place. These lines support one theme of the poem—that people often want to be something they are not.

1. Which line also supports the theme that people often want to be something they are not?
   a. And he was always human when he talked;
   b. In fine, we thought that he was everything. . .
   c. Went home and put a bullet through his head.

2. Another theme in this poem could be that wealth or money doesn't necessarily make a person happy. What detail supports this theme?
   a. Richard Cory was richer than a king and schooled in every grace.
   b. Even though Richard Cory seemed to have everything, he killed himself.
   c. Richard Cory glittered when he walked.

The Minuet by Mary Mapes Dodge

Grandma told me all about it,
Told me so I couldn't doubt it,
How she danced, my grandma danced; long ago—
How she held her pretty head,
How her dainty skirt she spread,
How she slowly leaned and rose—long ago.

Grandma's hair was bright and sunny,
Dimpled cheeks, too, oh, how funny!
Really quite a pretty girl—long ago.
Bless her! why, she wears a cap,
Grandma does, and takes a nap
Every single day: and yet
Grandma danced the **minuet**—long ago.

"Modern ways are quite alarming,"
Grandma says, "but boys were charming"
(Girls and boys she means, of course) "long ago."
Brave but modest, grandly shy;
She would like to have us try
Just to feel like those who met
In the graceful minuet—long ago.

Restating the Main Idea Remember that the main idea is an important idea in a paragraph, passage, or stanza. This important idea is supported by details. All forms of literature, including poems, have one or several main ideas. Sometimes the author tells us directly what the main idea is. Other times we have to think about the events and details in a section of writing in order to figure out the main idea.

After you have figured out the main idea in a section of writing, you can **restate** it. To restate a main idea, you figure out how to put the main idea into different words. The main idea of the first six lines of the poem is that Grandma described how she danced. This main idea can be restated. One way to restate it would be to say that Grandma paid a lot of attention to how she danced.

Reread the last seven lines of the poem. One way to state the main idea of this section is that Grandma would like her grandchildren to experience the things she experienced as a young girl. How could you restate this main idea?

a. Grandma is living in the past. She needs to realize that times have changed and today things are different.

b. Grandma thinks that the old ways were good, and she wishes that today's young people could feel the way she did.

Thinking About the Poems

Practice Vocabulary

The words below are in bold type in the poems. Study the way each word is used. Then complete each sentence by writing the correct word.

diverged	**claim**	**trodden**
arrayed	**fluttered**	**minuet**

1. More than a century ago, a popular dance was the
   _____.

2. Over the summer, hikers have _____ this path through the woods.

3. The road _____ at the fork, and we didn't know which way to go.

4. When people have dressed up for a special occasion, they have _____ themselves in nice clothing.

5. The butterfly _____ its wings and flew away.

6. If you say you have a right to something, you are making a
   _____.

Understand What You Read

Write the answer to each question.

What did the speaker in "The Road Not Taken" do before he chose which road to take?

_____

_____

8. In "The Minuet," why did the speaker say that the way Grandma looked long ago was "funny"?

_____

_____

9. Why is it a surprise to find out that Richard Cory killed himself?

_____

_____

Apply Your Skills

Circle the number of the best answer for each question.

10. Use context clues to figure out the meaning of the phrase "just as fair" from "The Road Not Taken." It means
    (1) just as long
    (2) just as attractive
    (3) just as important
    (4) just as traveled
    (5) just as dark

11. To the townspeople, Richard Cory appeared to have everything, including wealth and happiness. At the end we find out this is not true. Which of the following sayings best states this theme in "Richard Cory"?
    (1) A bird in the hand is worth two in the bush.
    (2) An apple a day keeps the doctor away.
    (3) You can't judge a book by its cover.
    (4) You can't change a sow's ear into a silk purse.
    (5) Money is the root of all evil.

12. The main idea of "The Road Not Taken" could be stated as follows: the speaker took the road less traveled, and it turned out to be the better choice. How could this main idea be restated?
    (1) If you do what everyone else does, you can get in trouble.
    (2) It is not always a good idea to break away from the pack and do your own thing.
    (3) When you travel, it's a good idea to take the route that most people follow.
    (4) People don't always make the best decisions in life.
    (5) Sometimes you can get more out of life if you do something different and don't just follow the crowd.

Connect with the Poems

Write your answer to each question.

13. If you were the speaker in "The Road Not Taken," how would you feel about the choice you made? Give reasons for your answer.

    _____

    _____

14. Richard Cory killed himself even though he seemed to have everything. What reasons might explain why Richard Cory killed himself?

    _____

    _____

Classic Poetry

Poems become classics because they focus on topics that are important to many people, such as love, work, nature, and conflict. However, poems with similar topics may be very different from each other. Each poet has a special point of view and writes in a particular way.

Vocabulary

passionate

outright

breadth

strive

slackened

jutted

Relate to the Topic

The poems you are about to read are love poems. However, they each have something very different to say about the subject. In the first poem the speaker gives advice about love.

Have you ever been in love? What advice would you give?

_____

_____

_____

Reading Strategy

FOLLOWING PUNCTUATION IN POEMS   Punctuation in poetry is not always like punctuation in other types of writing. For example, in some poems each line begins with a capital letter even if it is not a proper noun or a new sentence. However, poets often do use punctuation for the same purposes as prose writers. For example, a period means the end of a sentence or a complete thought.

When you read a poem, notice whether a line ends with punctuation or flows right into the next line. Read the first four lines of the poem on page 201. Then answer the questions.

1. What type of punctuation is used within the lines of this poem?

_____

   Hint: Skim the first five lines of the poem.

2. Read the poem, paying attention to the punctuation. Which word describes the poem?
   a.   flowing
   b.   abrupt
   Hint: Does the punctuation tell you to stop at the ends of the lines?

Never Give All the Heart by W.B. Yeats

Never give all the heart, for love
Will hardly seem worth thinking of
To **passionate** women if it seem
Certain, and they never dream
That it fades out from kiss to kiss;
For everything that's lovely is
But a brief, dreamy, kind delight.
O never give the heart **outright,**
For they, for all smooth lips can say,
Have given their hearts up to the play.
And who could play it well enough
If deaf and dumb and blind with love?
He that made this knows all the cost,
For he gave all his heart and lost.

Understanding Word Choice The first time you read a poem, pay attention to the literal meaning of the poem. Is the poem about a horse race? Or is the poem describing the day a famous person died? Then read it again and think about the images it brings to mind.

To create images, poets choose their words very carefully. For example, a poet may use the word "daffodil" instead of "flower" to describe what he or she sees. This word choice creates a more exact picture, or image, in the mind of the reader.

Poets also choose words that suggest something in particular about the feeling or idea in the poem. For example, daffodils are more likely to make the reader think of bright, happy things than if the poet had chosen a different type of flower, such as a thorny, dark red roses.

As you read a poem, remember that the poet has chosen each word carefully. The poet's word choice will influence your understanding of the meaning of the poem, as well as your reaction to the images and feelings that the poem suggests.

1. What is the effect of the poet using the word "passionate" to describe the women?
   a. "Passionate" conveys the intensity of their feelings.
   b. "Passionate" shows they are too emotional.

2. What idea does the phrase "deaf and dumb and blind with love" communicate?
   a. The poet thinks that people in love are silly and he has no respect for them.
   b. Being in love is a handicap that makes a person unable to play the game of love.

Check your answers on page 252.

Sonnet 43 by Elizabeth Barrett Browning

How do I love thee? Let me count the ways.
I love thee to the depth and **breadth** and height
My soul can reach, when feeling out of sight
For the ends of Being and ideal Grace.
I love thee to the level of everyday's
Most quiet need, by sun and candle-light.
I love thee freely, as men **strive** for Right;
I love thee purely, as they turn from Praise.
I love thee with the passion put to use
In my old griefs, and with my childhood's faith.
I love thee with a love I seemed to lose
With my lost saints,—I love thee with the breath,
Smiles, tears, of all my life!—and, if God choose,
I shall but love thee better after death.

Recognizing Repetition Many poems contain words or sounds that are repeated. Repetition can be used to create a musical effect, to engage our emotions, and to emphasize important ideas. Pay particular attention to words or phrases that are repeated in a poem. They are probably very important to the poem's meaning.

Words that rhyme (sounds that are repeated at the ends of words—"lime" and "mime," for example) are often placed at the end of the lines in a particular pattern. For instance, every other line may end with words that rhyme. In this poem, not all of the rhymes are exact—for example, the words "ways" and "Grace," and "use" and "lose," are used in a pattern but do not rhyme exactly. Their sounds are very similar, but they are not actually the same.

The rhyme, repetition, and word choice of a poem can make it seem fast or slow, and give it a regular or irregular beat. This is called the rhythm of the poem.

1. List two pairs of words in the poem that rhyme exactly.

_____

2. Which of the following best describes the rhythm of this poem?
    a. pounding and energetic
    b. even and thoughtful
    c. irregular and mixed up

3. What is the effect of repeating the words "I love thee"?
    a. It emphasizes how deeply the speaker loves this person.
    b. It emphasizes the fact that the speaker is insisting too strongly.

The Taxi by Amy Lowell

When I go away from you
The world beats dead
Like a **slackened** drum.
I call out for you against the **jutted** stars
And shout into the ridges of the wind.
Streets coming fast,
One after the other,
Wedge you away from me,
And the lamps of the city prick my eyes
So that I can no longer see your face.
Why should I leave you,
To wound myself upon the sharp edges of the night?

Recognizing Theme The theme of a poem is the most important idea the poet is trying to express in the poem. It is the underlying meaning of the poem. To find the theme, ask yourself "What is the most important idea in this poem?"

The theme is different from the topic of the poem. The topic of a poem might be love or war, for example, but the theme would be a more specific idea, such as "It is human nature to love." The theme of a poem is usually not stated directly. You might have to figure out the theme by putting together all the different ideas in the poem to see what they have in common.

You can find clues to the theme in the poet's choice of words, the rhythm, the length of the lines, in fact, in everything about the poem. Look at the poem's title, the poet's observations, and the objects in the poem. When you decide what you think the theme is, make sure that it is true for the whole poem and not just part of it.

1. What is the topic of this poem?
   a. taking a taxi ride through the city at night
   b. taking a taxi ride away from a loved one

2. What is the theme of the poem?
   a. It is painful to be separated from a loved one.
   b. Nights can be lonely and uncomfortable, especially in a taxi.
   c. It's hard to maintain relationships in a city.

Thinking About the Poems

Practice Vocabulary

The words below are in bold type in the poems. Study the way each word is used. Then complete each sentence by writing the correct word.

passionate	outright	breadth
strive	slackened	jutted

1. After paying off his loan, Ben will own the car
   _____.

2. The instructor demonstrated the _____ of his knowledge about history.

3. The mountains _____ into the sky.

4. The rope _____ as they slowly released it.

5. Someone who feels very strongly about something is
   _____.

6. If someone works hard to achieve something, they _____ to achieve that goal.

Understand What You Read

Write the answer to each question.

7. Why does the speaker in "Never Give All the Heart" advise the reader not to give all one's heart? _____

   _____

8. In "Sonnet 43," what is meant by "I love thee by . . . sun and

   candle-light"? _____

   _____

9. In "The Taxi," what does the speaker mean by the phrase "Wedge you away from me"? _____

   _____

10. How are the speakers in "Never Give All the Heart" and "Sonnet 43"

    different? _____

    _____

Apply Your Skills

Circle the number of the best answer for each question.

11. In "The Taxi," which image best gives the impression of pain?
    (1) the world beating
    (2) the streets coming fast
    (3) no longer seeing the person's face
    (4) asking why she should leave
    (5) the sharp edges of the night

12. Which of the following is a characteristic of "Never Give All the Heart"?
    (1) rhyming lines
    (2) complex word choice
    (3) repeating sounds at the beginning of the lines
    (4) stanzas of even length
    (5) heavy punctuation

13. Which of the following best states the theme of "Sonnet 43"?
    (1) I love you with the faith of a child.
    (2) I love you like a lost part of myself.
    (3) I love you during quiet times.
    (4) I love you totally and completely.
    (5) I love you even though you've gone away.

Connect with the Poems

Write your answer to each question.

14. The speaker in "Never Give All the Heart" is most likely a man speaking about being in love with a woman. Do you think his advice—holding back in order to be able to play the game of love—holds true for anyone who is in love? Explain.

    _____

    _____

    _____

15. Have you or someone you know ever experienced a difficult ending to a relationship? Were there any mixed feelings about leaving? What happened?

    _____

    _____

    _____

Reading at Work

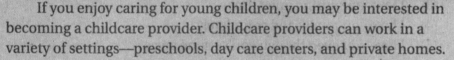

Service: Childcare Provider

If you enjoy caring for young children, you may be interested in becoming a childcare provider. Childcare providers can work in a variety of settings—preschools, day care centers, and private homes.

Most providers care for infants, toddlers, preschoolers, or elementary grade students after school. Providers who work with very young children devote much of their time to caring for the children's basic health, social, emotional, and play needs. Providers working with preschoolers and kindergartners may find themselves spending more time on the social and educational development of the children.

Childcare providers should have patience, a basic knowledge of child development, good listening and reasoning skills, and a strong interest in nurturing and teaching children.

Look at the box showing some careers in service.

- Do any of the careers interest you? If so, which ones?

- How could you find out more about those careers? On a separate piece of paper, write some questions that you would like to have answered. You can find out more information about those careers in the *Occupational Outlook Handbook* at your local library and online.

Library Assistant helps librarians and patrons by locating and delivering requested materials

Lunchroom Attendant/ Recess Aide monitors students in lunchrooms or cafeterias and in play areas

Preschool Aide helps children and teachers with the day's functions, lessons, and activities

Teacher Aide provides clerical and instructional support for classroom teachers and students

Read the passage. Then answer the questions.

Happy Lands Day Care Center
Guidelines for Selecting Poems and Stories for Children

At Happy Lands Day Care Center, we believe in building a love of reading and literature in the children in our care. We believe that children of all ages benefit from being read to. We encourage our providers to share a wide variety of stories, songs, and poems with the children.

Please be responsible about the types of stories, poems, and songs you choose to share with the children. Keep in mind the following suggestions when selecting your material:

- Select materials with vocabulary that is appropriate for the ages of the children in your class.
- Evaluate the content of the material. Make sure the material will not frighten or confuse the children. Material with adult themes of violence, abuse, and disaster is not appropriate for children.
- Vary the types of material you share with the children. Expose them to different rhythms in songs and poetry and to different kinds of stories.
- Use good judgment. If you have a question about the material, don't use it or ask the Center Director if it is appropriate.

1. The guidelines above encourage providers to
   (1) let the children choose which materials should be read aloud
   (2) share stories, poems, or songs with adult themes with the children
   (3) let the Center Director select all material for the children
   (4) expose the children to a wide variety of stories, poems, and songs
   (5) select materials that appeal to a wide range of ages

2. Why does the day care center believe providers should read to children?
   (1) It helps keep them quiet and well-behaved.
   (2) Otherwise, children become violent and abusive.
   (3) The center wants children to develop a love of reading and literature.
   (4) Children don't hear stories, poems, and songs anywhere else.
   (5) Providers need activities to fill up the children's time at the center.

3. According to the descriptions, which selection would not be appropriate for children at the Happy Lands Day Care Center?
   (1) "Merrily We Roll Along," a happy song with a catchy melody
   (2) "Greedy Dog," a delightful poem about a dog who will eat anything
   (3) "The Old Field," a sad poem about a field abandoned by children and animals
   (4) "The Turkey," a funny poem about a turkey's bad luck on Christmas
   (5) "The Wild Hog," a poem about a mean hog who kills many men

4. What is your favorite children's story or song? Write the name of the story or song. Then explain why you like it.

_____

_____

Read the poem "Pillow" by John Updike.

Plump mate to my head, you alone absorb,
through your cotton skin, the thoughts behind my bone
skin of skull. When I weep, you grow damp.
When I turn, you comply. In the dark,
you are my only friend, the only kiss
my cheek receives. You are my bowl of dreams.
Your underside is cool, like a second chance,
like a little leap into the air when I turn
you over. Though you would smother me,
properly applied, you are, like the world
with its rotating mass, all I have. You accept
the strange night with me, and are depressed
when the morning discloses your wrinkles.

Questions 1 through 6 refer to the poem on page 208.

Write the answer to each question.

1. How does the speaker feel about his pillow?

   _____

   _____

2. What is the one negative thing the pillow can do?

   _____

   _____

Circle the number of the best answer for each question.

3. Which of the following statements applies to the poem?
   (1) It uses rhyming words.
   (2) It uses punctuation in a regular way.
   (3) It is divided into stanzas.
   (4) It is about a serious topic.
   (5) It does not use repetition.

4. Which of the following is the speaker referring to when he says "like a little leap into the air when I turn you over"?
   (1) his body as he turns over
   (2) the fresh coolness of his pillow
   (3) the cool night air
   (4) the dream that he's having
   (5) his comfortable bed

5. What is the most likely reason the poet uses the word "depressed" to describe the pillow?
   (1) to show the speaker is extremely unhappy
   (2) to show that the pillow is overused and a new one is needed
   (3) to show the pillow is indented and to suggest unhappiness
   (4) to show that the speaker believes his pillow has human feelings
   (5) to show how the strange night has affected the pillow

6. Which of the following best states the theme of the poem?
   (1) The speaker has had this pillow for many years and is very attached to it.
   (2) The speaker is comforted by and feels less alone because of his pillow.
   (3) The speaker feels smothered by his life and by the pillow.
   (4) The speaker loves cuddling up with his pillow at night.
   (5) The speaker feels sorry for himself and the pillow.

Read the poem "Getting Out" by Cleopatra Mathis.

That year we hardly slept, waking like inmates
who beat the walls. Every night
another refusal, the silent work
of tightening the heart.
Exhausted, we gave up; escaped
to the apartment pool, swimming those laps
until the first light relieved us.

Days were different: FM and full-blast
blues, hours of guitar "you gonna miss me
when I'm gone." Think how you tried
to pack up and go, for weeks stumbling
over piles of clothing, the unstrung tennis rackets.
Finally locked into blame, we paced
that short hall, heaving words like furniture.

I have the last unshredded pictures
of our matching eyes and hair. We've kept
to separate sides of the map,
still I'm startled by men who look like you.
And in the yearly letter, you're sure to say
you're happy now. Yet I think of the lawyer's bewilderment
when we cried, the last day. Taking hands
we walked apart, until our arms stretched
between us. We held on tight, and let go.

Questions 7 through 12 refer to the poem on page 210.

Write the answer to each question.

7. The poem describes how the couple acted during one particular year. What happened after that year?

   _____

8. What is the first thing the speaker talks about?

   _____

9. What can you conclude that the speaker has done with most of the couple's photographs?

   _____

Circle the number of the best answer for each question.

10. What does the phrase "heaving words like furniture" suggest the couple was doing?
    (1) arguing bitterly
    (2) throwing chairs at each other
    (3) rearranging the furniture
    (4) moving out of the apartment at the same time
    (5) throwing books at each other

11. What is the best meaning of the phrase "kept to separate sides of the map"?
    (1) They kept a map in the middle of the apartment.
    (2) They needed a map to find their way around.
    (3) They live in different parts of the country.
    (4) They had an apartment that was laid out like a city street.
    (5) They always argued about where to live.

12. The speaker seems sad but sure that the divorce was right. Which of the following phrases from the poem best expresses this feeling?
    (1) tightening the heart
    (2) relieved us
    (3) you gonna miss me
    (4) paced that short hall
    (5) held on tight, and let go

Reading Extension

In this unit you have read samples of several types of poems. Which poem did you like the best? Would you like to read more poems by this poet? Turn to the Annotated Bibliography on pages 257–258 of this book. Write down the name of the book and the author. Plan to get that book or another one by that poet.

Mini-Test • Unit 4

GED PRACTICE

This is a 15-minute practice test. After 15 minutes, mark the last number you finished. Then complete the test and check your answers. If most of your answers were correct but you did not finish, try to work faster next time.

Directions: Choose the one best answer to each question.

Questions 1 through 3 refer to the following poem.

WHAT DOES A CHILD'S YARD LOOK LIKE?

Homes where children live exude a
    pleasant rumpledness,
like a bed made by a child, or a yard
    littered with balloons.
(5) To be a child again one would need to
    shed details
till the heart found itself dressed in the
    coat with a hood.
Now the heart has taken on gloves and
(10)   mufflers,
the heart never goes outside to find
    something to "do."
And the house takes on a new face,
    dignified.
(15) No lost shoes blooming under bushes.
No chipped trucks in the drive.
Grown-ups like swings, leafy plants, slow-
    motion back and forth.
While the yard of a child is strewn with
(20)   the corpses
of bottle-rockets and whistles,
anything whizzing and spectacular,
    brilliantly short-lived.
Trees in children's yards speak in clearer
(25)   tongues.
Ants have more hope. Squirrels dance as
    well as hide.
The fence has a reason to be there, so
    children can go in and out.
(30) Even when the children are at school, the
    yards glow
with the leftovers of their affection,
the roots of the tiniest grasses curl toward
    one another
(35) Like secret smiles.

Naomi Shihab Nye, "Where Children Live"

1. Which statement best summarizes the first stanza?

(1) Children don't make their beds very neatly.
(2) Children leave things in the yard.
(3) Children's homes are quiet.
(4) Children have messy homes.
(5) Children's homes are enjoyably messy.

2. What is meant by "To be a child again one would need to shed details"? (lines 5–6)

(1) One should enjoy life's simple pleasures.
(2) One needs to keep a clean home.
(3) One should have a simple schedule.
(4) One needs to know unimportant facts.
(5) One should dress warmly.

3. Which sentence best states the poem's theme?

(1) Children create disorder.
(2) Adults prefer slow motion.
(3) Animals and ants enjoy children.
(4) Children bring warmth and joy.
(5) Adults should try to remember childhood.

Questions 4 through 8 refer to the following poem.

WHO IS WALKING TOO FAST?

"Don't go so fast," I called,
but my father always forgot.
Helpless, I reached to clutch
his coattails until his hand
(5)   surrounded mine and towed me on.
What knowledge of me did
his hand record?
What angers were given
to my childish keeping—to await
(10) this instant, years later,
when I'm reproached: "Go slow."
Memories swell. He stops to rest.
A small victory implodes. So brief
the time before my child
(15) will triumph over me
for hurts I caused, unknowing,
back on our deep-rutted road.

Celia Gilbert, "The Walk"

4. Based on the information in the poem, what type of boss would the speaker most likely be?

One who is
(1)   considerate
(2)   strict
(3)   unfair
(4)   relaxed
(5)   generous

5. What does the poet mean by "our deep-rutted road" (line 17)?

(1)   their memories that are fading
(2)   their house on a dirt road
(3)   their usual path
(4)   their long, complex past
(5)   their deep dislike of each other

6. Which of the following best describes the main idea of this poem?

(1)   The speaker dislikes her father.
(2)   The speaker is worried about her son.
(3)   Families are very complicated.
(4)   Childhood experiences affect us through life.
(5)   No one knows how they affect their children.

7. If the speaker were punished unfairly by her parents, what would she most likely do?

(1)   calmly explain to her parents why she thought the punishment was unfair
(2)   serve her punishment without question
(3)   whine until she got her way
(4)   make a promise to herself to never treat her children the same way
(5)   sneak out of her room at night

8. In another poem, the poet says her mother had "the will to shape a world of her devising." Based on this information and on the poem, how did the poet most likely view her parents?

As
(1)   helpless
(2)   powerful
(3)   uncaring
(4)   devoted
(5)   distracted

Language Arts, Reading

Name: _____ **Class:** _____ **Date:** _____

1 ① ② ③ ④ ⑤   11 ① ② ③ ④ ⑤

2 ① ② ③ ④ ⑤   12 ① ② ③ ④ ⑤

3 ① ② ③ ④ ⑤   13 ① ② ③ ④ ⑤

4 ① ② ③ ④ ⑤   14 ① ② ③ ④ ⑤

5 ① ② ③ ④ ⑤   15 ① ② ③ ④ ⑤

6 ① ② ③ ④ ⑤   16 ① ② ③ ④ ⑤

7 ① ② ③ ④ ⑤   17 ① ② ③ ④ ⑤

8 ① ② ③ ④ ⑤   18 ① ② ③ ④ ⑤

9 ① ② ③ ④ ⑤   19 ① ② ③ ④ ⑤

10 ① ② ③ ④ ⑤   20 ① ② ③ ④ ⑤

LANGUAGE ARTS, READING

Directions

This is a 33-minute practice test. After 33 minutes, mark the last number you finished. Then complete the test and check your answers. If most of your answers were correct but you did not finish, try to work faster next time.

The PreGED Reading Posttest consists of passages from nonfiction, fiction, drama, and poetry. Each passage is followed by multiple choice questions about the reading material.

Read each passage. Then answer the questions that follow. Refer back to the reading material as often as necessary when answering the questions.

Each passage is preceded by a "purpose question." The purpose question gives a reason for reading the material. Use these purpose questions to help focus your reading. You are not required to answer these purpose questions.

Record your answers on the answer sheet on page 214. You may make a photocopy of this page. To record your answer, fill in the numbered circle on the answer sheet that corresponds to the answer you select for each question in the posttest.

EXAMPLE

Mabel crawled up the stairs and with great effort pushed against the powerful wind to open the hatch onto the deck of the boat. What she saw concerned her greatly. The sky was pitch black with swirling clouds, and enormous waves at least twelve feet high were rising against the sides of the boat.

Which of the following best describes the tone?

(1) calm
(2) humorous
(3) suspenseful
(4) absurd
(5) sorrowful

(On Answer Sheet)

① ② ● ④ ⑤

The correct answer choice is 3.

If you do not use the answer sheet provided, mark your answers on each test page by circling the correct answer for each question.

Go on to the next page.

Directions: Choose the <u>one best answer</u> to each question

<u>Questions 1 through 5</u> refer to the following passage.

WHAT IS HELEN TRYING TO LEARN?

I remember the morning that I first asked the meaning of the word "love." This was before I knew many words. I had found a few early violets in the garden and brought them to my teacher. She tried to kiss me: but at that time I did not like to have any one kiss me except my mother. Miss Sullivan put her arm gently round me and spelled into

(5) my hand, "I love Helen."

"What is love?" I asked.

She drew me closer to her and said, "It is here," pointing to my heart, whose beats I was conscious of for the first time. Her words puzzled me very much because I did not then understand anything unless I touched it.

(10) I smelt the violets in her hand and asked, half in words, half in signs, a question which meant, "Is love the sweetness of flowers?"

"No," said my teacher.

Again I thought. The warm sun was shining on us.

"Is this not love?" I asked, pointing in the direction from which the heat came. "Is

(15) this not love?"

It seemed to me that there could be nothing more beautiful than the sun, whose warmth makes all things grow. But Miss Sullivan shook her head, and I was greatly puzzled and disappointed. I thought it strange that my teacher could not show me love.

(20) A day or two afterward I was stringing beads of different sizes in symmetrical groups—two large beads, three small ones, and so on. I had made many mistakes, and Miss Sullivan had pointed them out again and again with gentle patience. Finally I noticed a very obvious error in the sequence and for an instant I concentrated my attention on the lesson and tried to think how I should have arranged the beads. Miss

(25) Sullivan touched my forehead and spelled with decided emphasis, "Think."

In a flash I knew that the word was the name of the process that was going on in my head. This was my first conscious perception of an abstract idea.

For a long time I was still—I was not thinking of the beads in my lap, but trying to find a meaning for "love" in the light of this new idea. The sun had been under a cloud

(30) all day, and there had been brief showers; but suddenly the sun broke forth in all its southern splendor.

Again I asked my teacher, "Is this not love?"

"Love is something like the clouds that were in the sky before the sun came out," she replied.

Helen Keller, *The Story of My Life*

1. Which of the following statements best summarizes the main idea?

   (1) Helen learns some new words from her teacher, Miss Sullivan.
   (2) Helen becomes aware of her thoughts for the first time.
   (3) Helen learns the meaning of abstract ideas such as "love."
   (4) Helen finally learns to feel affection for Miss Sullivan.
   (5) Helen successfully learns how to string beads in a pattern.

2. Miss Sullivan spells words into Helen's hand in sign language, and Helen talks partly in sign. These details support which inference?

   (1) Miss Sullivan does not know how to talk.
   (2) Helen is not very smart.
   (3) Miss Sullivan cares for Helen.
   (4) Miss Sullivan cannot see.
   (5) Helen is hearing impaired.

3. If Helen were learning how to knit, how would she most likely go about it?

   (1) She would express frustration and anger at her mistakes.
   (2) She would thoughtfully keep trying until she succeeded.
   (3) She would learn quickly and then lose interest in the activity.
   (4) She would learn but not share her accomplishment.
   (5) She would refuse to ask for help and insist on doing it herself.

4. Which of the following best explains the author's choice of words in saying that Helen pointed "in the direction from which the heat came"?

   (1) It was more interesting than saying she pointed at the sun.
   (2) It showed that Helen was blind and did not see the sun.
   (3) It described the day as having lovely, warm summer weather.
   (4) It demonstrated how Helen liked to use her hands when she spoke.
   (5) It emphasized that feeling the hot sun was like feeling love.

5. When Miss Sullivan first met Helen, Helen wildly misbehaved, ate with her hands, threw tantrums, and was unable to communicate.

   Based on this and the information in the passage, what does this suggest about Miss Sullivan?

   (1) She was a highly skilled teacher.
   (2) She wanted to give up on Helen.
   (3) She was very strict with Helen.
   (4) She knew when to get extra help.
   (5) She was always cheerful with Helen.

Go on to the next page.

WILL TOM AND BECKY FIND THEIR WAY HOME?

It was but a little while before a certain indecision in his manner revealed another fearful fact to Becky—he could not find his way back!

"Oh, Tom, you didn't make any marks!"

"Becky, I was such a fool! Such a fool! I never thought we might want to come
(5) back! No—I can't find the way. It's all mixed up."

"Tom, Tom, we're lost! we're lost! We never can get out of this awful place! Oh, why *did* we ever leave the others!"

She sank to the ground and burst into such a frenzy of crying that Tom was appalled with the idea that she might die, or lose her reason. He sat down by her and
(10) put his arms around her; she buried her face in his bosom, she clung to him, she poured out her terrors, her unavailing regrets, and the far echoes turned them all to jeering laughter. Tom begged her to pluck up hope again, and she said she could not. He fell to blaming and abusing himself for getting her into this miserable situation; this had a better effect. She said she would try to hope again, she would get up and follow
(15) wherever he might lead if only he would not talk like that. For he was no more to blame than she, she said.

So they moved on again—aimlessly—simply at random—all they could do was to move, keep moving. For a little while, hope made a show of reviving—not with any reason to back it, but only because it is its nature to revive when the spring has not
(20) been taken out of it by age and familiarity with failure.

By and by Tom took Becky's candle and blew it out. This economy meant so much! Words were not needed. Becky understood, and her hope died again. She knew that Tom had a whole candle and three or four pieces in his pockets—yet he must economize.

(25) By and by, fatigue began to assert its claims; the children tried to pay no attention, for it was dreadful to think of sitting down when time was grown to be so precious; moving, in some direction, in any direction, was at least progress and might bear fruit; but to sit down was to invite death and shorten its pursuit.

Mark Twain, *The Adventures of Tom Sawyer*

6. Which of the following statements best restates the main idea of lines 18–20?

   (1) Hope usually stays only for a brief while.
   (2) Hope comes back more easily for the young.
   (3) Hope usually has no good reason to back it.
   (4) Hope is like walking with a spring in your step.
   (5) Hope is natural for people, both old and young.

7. What is meant by the phrase "to sit down was to invite death and shorten its pursuit"? (line 28)

   (1) They will be more likely to die if they don't keep moving.
   (2) They are being pursued by someone who wants to kill them.
   (3) They will die from exhaustion if they sit down.
   (4) They will admit to being so tired they want to die if they sit down.
   (5) They feel that death is a friend to them and not to be feared.

8. What would Tom probably do if Becky decisively laid out a plan?

   (1) groan and make fun of her idea
   (2) follow his own plan instead
   (3) thank her and follow her plan
   (4) pretend the plan was his idea
   (5) tell her that she is a fool

9. Based on the information in lines 22–24, which of the following statements would Tom most likely make if the paragraph were written from his point of view?

   (1) There is no hope! We will die here.
   (2) I know we are about to be rescued.
   (3) Perhaps the darkness will comfort Becky.
   (4) I will save this; we may be here a while.
   (5) I am so frightened of the dark!

10. Mark Twain wrote several novels, including one with a character named Huck Finn. Huck escapes from his father, meets a runaway slave, and journeys down the Mississippi River with him on a raft.

    Based on this information and the passage, what type of stories did Mark Twain write?

    (1) romance
    (2) adventure
    (3) mystery
    (4) biography
    (5) science fiction

Questions 11 through 15 refer to the following passage.

WHAT ARE THIS FATHER AND SON ARGUING ABOUT?

LYONS: Come on, Pop, Mr. Bono don't want to hear all that. Let me have the ten dollars. I told you Bonnie working.

(5) TROY: What that mean to me? "Bonnie working." I don't care if she working. Go ask her for the ten dollars if she working. Talking about "Bonnie working." Why ain't

(10) you working?

LYONS: Aw, Pop, you know I can't find no decent job. Where am I gonna get a job at? You know I can't get no job.

(15) TROY: I told you I know some people down there. I can get you on the rubbish if you want to work. I told you that the last time you came by here asking me for something.

(20) LYONS: Naw, Pop . . . thanks. That ain't for me. I don't wanna be carrying nobody's rubbish. I don't wanna be punching nobody's time clock.

TROY: What's the matter, you too good to

(25) carry people's rubbish? Where you think that ten dollars you talking about come from? I'm just supposed to haul people's rubbish and give my money to you cause

(30) you too lazy to work. You too lazy to work and wanna know why you ain't got what I got.

ROSE: What hospital Bonnie working at? Mercy?

(35) LYONS: She's down at Passavant working in the laundry.

TROY: I ain't got nothing as it is. I give

you that ten dollars and I got to eat beans the rest of the week.

(40) Naw . . . you ain't getting no ten dollars here.

LYONS: You ain't got to be eating no beans. I don't know why you wanna say that.

(45) TROY: I ain't got no extra money. Gabe done moved over to Miss Pearl's paying her the rent and things done got tight around here. I can't afford to be giving you every

(50) payday.

LYONS: I ain't asked you to give me nothing. I asked you to loan me ten dollars. I know you got ten dollars.

(55) TROY: Yeah, I got it. You know why I got it? Cause I don't throw my money away out there in the streets. You living the fast life . . . wanna be a musician . . . running around in

(60) them clubs and things . . . then, you learn to take care of yourself. You ain't gonna find me going and asking nobody for nothing. I done spent too many years without.

(65) LYONS: You and me is two different people, Pop.

TROY: I done learned my mistake and learned to do what's right by it. You still trying to get something

(70) for nothing. Life don't owe you nothing. You owe it to yourself. Ask Bono. He'll tell you I'm right.

LYONS: You got your way of dealing with the world . . . I got mine. The only

(75) thing that matters to me is the music.

August Wilson, *Fences*

11. Which of the following best restates the sentence "You and me is two different people, Pop"?

    (1) You and I understand each other, Pop.
    (2) I do not respect the way you live your life, Pop.
    (3) You are too old to enjoy yourself, Pop.
    (4) We will never get along very well, Pop.
    (5) What is right for you isn't right for me, Pop.

12. Based on the information in the passage, what do you think might have happened before?

    (1) Troy had been badly cheated by Lyons.
    (2) Lyons had helped Troy by giving him money.
    (3) Lyons had been laid off from a steady job.
    (4) Troy had told Lyons he should get a job.
    (5) Lyons had been spending money on music lessons.

13. What conclusion can you draw about Troy's character?

    (1) He is bitter about having to work so hard.
    (2) He is independent and proud of himself.
    (3) He is cruel and enjoys making Lyons feel bad.
    (4) He doesn't care whether or not Lyons changes his attitude.
    (5) He is worried that Lyons doesn't respect him.

14. In what way are the two men similar?

    (1) They both learn from their mistakes.
    (2) They both have strong opinions.
    (3) They both hate working for others.
    (4) They both are sneaky and manipulative.
    (5) They both like to criticize each other.

15. In another part of the play, Troy talks with his other son, Cory. Cory wants Troy's permission to play on the football team. Troy realizes that Cory will have to leave his job at the A&P to join the team.

    Based on this and the information in the excerpt, what response is Troy most likely to have?

    (1) Troy will insist that Cory not play football.
    (2) Troy will talk to the football coach about Cory.
    (3) Troy will have Cory's mother talk to him.
    (4) Troy will be happy that Cory is good at football.
    (5) Troy will worry that Cory might not succeed.

Questions 16 through 20 refer to the following poem.

DOES THE SNOWMAN REACT TO THE BOY?

Boy at the Window

Seeing the snowman standing all alone
In dusk and cold is more than he can bear.
The small boy weeps to hear the wind prepare.
A night of gnashings and enormous moan.
(5) His tearful sight can hardly reach to where
The pale-faced figure with bitumen eyes
Returns him such a god-forsaken stare
As outcast Adam gave to Paradise.

The man of snow is, nonetheless, content,
(10) Having no wish to go inside and die.
Still, he is moved to see the youngster cry.
Though frozen water is his element,
He melts enough to drop from one soft eye
A trickle of the purest rain, a tear
(15) For the child at the bright pane surrounded by
Such warmth, such light, such love, and so much fear.

Richard Wilbur, "Boy at the Window"

16. Which of the following is most clearly implied by the poem?

    (1) The boy is upset about something more than the snowman.
    (2) The boy is angry at his parents for yelling at him.
    (3) The snowman can comfort the boy better than anyone else can.
    (4) The snowman makes life much easier for the boy.
    (5) The boy should not have left the snowman outside alone.

17. What in particular has caused the boy to become so worried about the snowman?

    (1) The snowman is alive and has feelings.
    (2) The weather is becoming stormier.
    (3) The snowman has been crying.
    (4) The night is moving in quickly.
    (5) The wind is knocking over the snowman.

18. What else is probably true about the snowman?

    (1) The snowman was built by the boy.
    (2) The snowman has a carrot nose.
    (3) The snowman has been there a long time.
    (4) The snowman will melt during the night.
    (5) The snowman thinks the house is Paradise.

19. What would the boy be most likely to do if he found a stuffed animal thrown out in the trash?

    (1) The boy would leave it in the trash.
    (2) The boy would take it home and clean it.
    (3) The boy would invent a story about it.
    (4) The boy would give it to someone.
    (5) The boy would wonder why it was there.

20. Which of the following best describes the tone of this poem?

    (1) puzzled
    (2) envious
    (3) angry
    (4) sad
    (5) sarcastic

Posttest Evaluation Chart

The chart below will help you determine your strengths and weaknesses in reading and interpreting different forms of literature and other written material.

Directions

Check your answers on pages 254–256. On the chart below, circle the number of each question that you answered correctly on the Posttest. Count the number of questions you answered correctly in each row. Write the number in the Total Correct space in each row. (For example, in the Fiction row, write the number correct in the blank before *out of 5*.) Complete this process for the remaining rows. Then add the four totals to get your Total Correct for the whole Posttest.

Content Areas	Questions	Total Correct	Pages
Nonfiction (Pages 14–97)	1, 2, 3, 4, 5,	_____ out of 5	Pages 52–57
Fiction (Pages 98–157)	6, 7, 8, 9, 10	_____ out of 5	Pages 142–147
Drama (Pages 158–185)	11, 12, 13, 14, 15	_____ out of 5	Pages 160–165
Poetry (Pages 186–213)	16, 17, 18, 19, 20	_____ out of 5	Pages 188–193

TOTAL CORRECT FOR POSTTEST _____ out of 20

If you answered fewer than 15 questions correctly, determine which of the four content areas you need to study further. Go back and review the material in those areas. Page numbers to refer to for practice are given in the right-hand column above.

PRETEST

PAGE 5

1. Clemens threw a fastball that was slightly more manageable, so Sosa was able to hit it. In other words, the fastball was not quite as fast as the previous ones Clemens had thrown, and it was in a better location.

2. Details that support the conclusion: Sosa's hit silenced a very excited crowd of over 34,000 fans; Clemens never seemed to recover; Clemens walked a couple of batters and gave up a couple of hits; and Sosa's team won the game.

3. **(5) Sosa's first big league home run was a memorable event.** This main idea is supported by all of the details in the passage. The other options are factual but only refer to parts of the passage.

4. **(2) Roger Clemens would be a challenge for Sosa.** Sierra was warning Sosa that he'd be up against an excellent pitcher, Roger Clemens. Sierra tells Sosa that he should prepare for this and reminds him that he is a rookie.

5. **(2) energetic** The author, who is Sosa, uses words such as "exploded" and "pushed" to add to the energetic, excited feeling of the piece.

PAGE 7

6. There are several possibilities: the spacious dining hall, the red-lacquered lattice windows, the clean dining hall, and the full restaurant.

7. Several answers are possible. Old Man Li wanted to eat everything, but he didn't want to spend money. He felt torn between these two impulses. He let his daughter order to avoid the discomfort of making a decision.

8. **(5) He is very fond of his daughter.** There are many details that support this statement, including the description of May Li being strong, like her mother. In addition, he had a desire to have a good

meal with her and let her order something, perhaps expensive, from the menu.

9. **(2) very strong** This is clear from the simile in the passage, "She was as strong as a cow. . . ." The passage does not mention the other options.

10. **(5) He was quite tired from the walk.** There are several details that support this. Old Man Li comments on the long distance they have walked, he wipes the perspiration from his brow twice, and he eventually gives in and lets May Li carry his luggage for him.

PAGE 9

11. He will change, or they can live like brother and sister.

12. Nora will probably leave. The stage directions say that she has put on her cloak, hat, and shawl.

13. **(3) gap** The clue to the meaning is given by the words "opened between us" and "fill it up." The other options are not logical substitutes for "abyss."

14. **(2) He does not really understand what Nora wants.** Torvald keeps making the wrong suggestions in his effort to get Nora to stay. Option 1 is incorrect because this is what he offers to do, not what he has done. Options 3 and 5 are the opposite of what is suggested about his character. The passage does not mention option 4.

15. **(3) treated her like a pet or a toy** This option is correct because a skylark is a bird and a doll is a toy; this suggests how Torvald thought of Nora. Option 1 is incorrect because Torvald tells Nora that she thinks and talks like a child. The passage does not mention option 2. Option 4 is incorrect because it is a suggestion that Torvald makes but Nora rejects. Option 5 is incorrect because Nora does not like the way Torvald has treated her.

PAGE 11

16. Opening the wound/scar again is more painful each successive time.

17. Answers may include many of the images mentioned in the first stanza: see the sun on the upland slopes, feel the wind stir through the grass, or see the river flow.

18. It looks very smooth, still, and clear.

19. **(1) All creatures suffer when they are trapped.** The bird is a symbol for any being that is not free. The poet understands its pain because people feel the same way when they are trapped. Option 2 is incorrect because it is too specific to be a general truth about life. The passage does not support option 3. Option 4 is a general truth about life, but not the one suggested by this poem. Option 5 is incorrect because singing is an expression of pain in the poem, not a way to solve the problem.

20. **(3) yearning** This option is correct because the bird wants what it cannot have. Options 1, 2, and 5 are the opposites of the emotion in the poem. The poem does not mention option 4.

21. **(4) a blues song** This option is correct because the blues express painful emotions and a search for something. Options 1, 2, 3, and 5 are incorrect because they are generally not songs that express pain.

PAGE 12

22. **(1) specifically designed** A customized tennis program is one where the instruction is geared towards the needs of the individual instead of being more general to fit everyone.

23. **(3) It wants to build its business by teaching all levels of tennis.** The opening two sentences state that all levels of experience are welcome, and that the center wants to introduce as many people as possible to the sport of tennis. Teaching all levels will increase the number of people using the center's facilities and therefore increase its business.

24. **(1) friendly and encouraging** Several details from the passage demonstrate the friendly and encouraging attitude—for example, "It's great exercise!" and "Anyone can learn to play and enjoy tennis."

UNIT 1: NONFICTION

LESSON 1

PAGE 16

Many answers are possible. Brochures and advertisements can help people find out about new medicines and treatments. They can be helpful in learning more about preventing illnesses and in finding out what questions you can ask your doctor.

1. The author is concerned about how watching a lot of television affects a child's ability to learn. The words "Too Much" in the title are a clue.

2. Yes. The third heading states that television weakens a child's reading skills.

PAGE 17

a

PAGE 18

1. b   2. b

PAGE 19

1. a and b   2. a

PAGES 20–21

1. allergic
2. enhanced
3. symptoms
4. clarity
5. hypnotized
6. antibiotics
7. There are three reasons given in the brochure: television can shorten a child's attention span, weaken a child's language skills, and weaken a child's reading skills.
8. When sound effects and music are ignored, it becomes apparent that the

characters speak in short phrases and incomplete sentences.

9. Antibiotics fight to kill bacteria that can cause some sore throats and earaches.

10. Answers should include two of the claims made about the CD player: its sound is of high quality and can fill a concert hall; the sound has a clarity never before possible from a small CD player; and you'll never want to listen to music on any other CD player again.

11. **(2) Watching television may weaken a child's language skills.** The heading for paragraph 3 states the main idea of that paragraph. Only option 2 restates that idea. While options 1 and 3 may be true, these ideas are not the focus of the brochure. Options 4 and 5 are false according to the information in the brochure.

12. **(5) For antibiotics to work well, you need to take them on a schedule.** The second tip says to take the medicine at the same time every day. This is the only option mentioned in the list of tips. Options 1, 2, 3, and 4 are all false statements according to the facts in the brochure.

13. **(5) Be the first among your friends to own the CD player that** *Music World* **called the "Invention of the Year."** Option 4 is the only statement that includes a fact about the CD player, that it was called the "Invention of the Year" by *Music World.* The other options appeal to the readers' emotions or make unfounded claims.

14. Many answers are possible. Answers should include the name of the product, the information that inspired the purchase, and an opinion about whether the advertising claims were true.

15. Many answers are possible. Answers should express an opinion and include reasons for the opinion. Some might state that watching a lot of television is bad for adults because it takes time away from more worthwhile activities. The quick cuts and flashing lights may shorten an adult's

attention span in the same way that it can shorten a child's. Others might not think watching a lot of television is bad for adults.

LESSON 2

PAGE 22
Many answers are possible. Some might say that they signed a lease or a credit card statement but did not read all of the "fine print." People who have had trouble understanding a document may have asked questions of the person who gave them the document.

1. Section 1: General Information
2. Section 2: Work Experience

PAGE 23
1. a   2. b

PAGE 24
1. b
2. b Every patient should sign Lines 13 and 15. Only patients who want their benefits paid directly to the dentist sign Line 14.

PAGE 25
1. a   2. a

PAGES 26–27
1. constitute   2. references
3. specify   4. introductory
5. authorize   6. certify
7. This question must be answered by applicants who are under 18 years old.
8. The purpose of box 2 is to find out how the patient is related to the employee who has the dental insurance.
9. Box 13 requires a signature so that information about treatment and dental history can be released to the insurance company.
10. The interest rate will increase to 19.9% if the cardholder is late paying his or her bill twice during a six-month period.
11. **(4) how much money you made at your last job** Section 2 is where you would list your previous work experience. The salary

you received at your last job is part of the information you would include in this section.

12. (3) **The employee should sign and date line 14.** Line 4 of the instructions tells the employee to sign and date line 14 in order to have the payment sent directly to the dentist. Options 1, 2, and 5 cannot be correct because every employee filing a claim must fill out boxes 1 through 4, sign line 15, and attach the dental bill to the form. Only employees who have other dental insurance should check box 11, so option 4 is incorrect.

13. (5) **if you use your card to borrow cash** These words introduce the information about cash advances in section E. They make it clear that the credit card can also be used to get cash. Options 1 and 2 are found in the section on cash advances but refer to the fee, not the term "cash advance." Option 3 applies to the introductory rate in section A. Option 4 appears in section C, not section E.

14. Many answers are possible. Answers may include any of these ideas: always read the instructions on a form carefully; provide all the information the form requires; print neatly; and make sure all answers are true and complete.

15. Many answers are possible. Answers should express an opinion about how legal documents should be written and include reasons or personal experiences to support the opinion.

LESSON 3

PAGE 28

Some people have been in an emergency situation, while others have not. Those who have might describe where it happened, what happened, and how they responded. Those who haven't been in an emergency situation might imagine what type of emergency could happen, such as a fire or an injury.

People who have been in an emergency situation might describe what they actually did. Those who have not might mention using written instructions or common sense.

1. Answers will vary but might include information about sick days and vacation days, any dress code that the company might have, or procedures for making a complaint about a supervisor.

2. No. The title of the section indicates that it is about employee policies, not emergency procedures.

PAGE 29

1. a   2. b

PAGE 30

1. a   2. c

PAGE 31

1. b   2. b

PAGES 32–33

1. malfunction
2. probationary
3. affix
4. contaminated
5. eligible
6. reinstated
7. The supervisor will give the employee a written evaluation.
8. An employee can use sick leave for any illness, for pregnancy, for doctor or dentist visits, or for illness in the employee's immediate family.
9. The discs may become warped.
10. (4) **Family Leave** If your friend is going to need to take more than a few days off, she will need some type of leave. Family Leave allows an employee to take off up to four months. Options 1 and 2 are not about taking a leave of absence. Neither Maternity Leave (option 3) nor Vacation Leave (option 5) apply to this situation.
11. (3) **Line up the plus and minus signs on the batteries and battery compartment.** The second paragraph of the document

describes how to properly insert batteries into the remote control. One of the steps is matching the plus and minus signs on the batteries with those inside the battery compartment.

12. **(5) dispose of the paper towels in a red trash bag** Step 2 of the safety procedure on page 31 has two parts. The first gives the instruction to wipe up the fluids with paper towels. The second part tells the worker to dispose of the paper towels in a red trash bag—option 5. Option 2 is unnecessary in this situation. Options 1, 3, and 4 come later in the procedure.

13. Many answers are possible. Answers should include reasons to support the *yes* or *no* response. Some might say it is important to read the entire employee handbook as soon as possible after starting a new job because the handbook may contain information that your supervisor has forgotten to tell you. In addition, once an employee is given a handbook, it becomes his or her responsibility to know what is in it.

14. Many answers are possible. Answers should include a description of the features of the perfect instruction manual and an explanation of how these would make the manual easy to understand.

LESSON 4

PAGE 34

Some people have been called to serve on a jury and served, others have been called but have not served. Some have not been called for jury duty because they are not registered voters, or their name just hasn't come up for jury duty yet. Those who have been called to serve and those who have served might briefly explain their experiences.

1. Answers should include three of the boldfaced words or phrases on page 35.
2. The word "summoned" is important because it states the main idea of the document—that the person must appear for jury service, The word "exempt" is important because it indicates the only situations in which a person can be excused from jury duty.

PAGE 35
c

PAGE 36
1. b   2. b

PAGE 37
1. c   2. c

PAGES 38–39
1. exempt   2. incur
3. liability   4. retained
5. prospective   6. summoned
7. There are two acceptable reasons for being excused from jury duty: (1) having a child under ten years old who would have to be left unsupervised and (2) being the primary caregiver of an invalid.
8. The car dealer might change his mind about the value of a trade-in vehicle if the car has been damaged or altered in any way, other than normal wear and tear, before the trade-in deal is final.
9. The landlord could spend the security deposit if there is damage to the apartment or if the tenant doesn't live up to any part of the legal agreement.
10. **(2) a person unable to care for himself or herself** The context clues are often the words or phrases surrounding the unfamiliar word. In this case, the clue for the meaning of "invalid" appears directly after the word—"a person of any age who is an invalid and therefore unable to care for himself or herself."
11. **(4) If the buyer doesn't buy the new car or doesn't follow the agreement, the seller can keep the deposit and, if necessary, charge the buyer extra money.** This is the only option that summarizes correctly what the section says.

12. **(1) call the tenant for permission to enter** Based on the passage, the tenant needs to agree to allow the landlord to enter the apartment, but the tenant cannot be unreasonable about this. The landlord will want to check with the tenant in advance to be sure he has permission to enter.

13. Some people have bought or sold a used car. In some cases, there may not have been any written agreement (if the car was bought from a friend, for example). Those who have signed a written agreement can explain their experiences.

14. Most people will have experience with signing an apartment lease and can discuss their concern or displeasure with parts of the agreement. For example, they may have wanted to have pets, but the lease did not allow it. Or, the rent was higher than they'd hoped. Or, perhaps, the landlord included additional requirements on the lease that displeased them, such as no overnight guests, no subletting, or no parking in the driveway.

LESSON 5

PAGE 40

Many answers are possible. Most people can remember this experience and can tell how they felt. For example, people may discuss the first time they slept away from home as a child, moved to a new house or apartment, or traveled to a new country.

1. Answers will vary but might include the following: Why is this his first time on a subway? Is he from a small town that doesn't have subways? What city is he in? Why is he going to Harlem?

2. Answers will vary, but might include the following: Who is he? Where is he from? What year is this? How old is he?

PAGE 41

b

PAGE 42

a and c

PAGE 43

c

PAGES 44–45

1. marquee
2. dazzled
3. anchorage
4. fraternity
5. flurry
6. Hughes spent his time learning everything he could about Harlem. His activities included visiting the Harlem Branch Library and the Lincoln Theatre.
7. Hughes dreamed of being Harlem's poet.
8. His final grades included three Bs and a C.
9. He had few skills and he was an African-American.
10. They did not get along.
11. **(3) Hughes spent hardly any time on campus and all the time he could in Harlem or downtown.** If Hughes had liked the university, he would have spent more time there. Options 1 and 5 have nothing to do with Columbia University. Option 2 describes Hughes' feelings about Harlem, not about the university. Option 4 tells Hughes' grades, but it doesn't show how he feels about Columbia University.
12. **(3) It is a publication that includes poetry.** The facts that he met the editors at *The Crisis* while in New York City and that his poem appeared in that publication support the idea that *The Crisis* is some kind of publication that includes poetry. The passage does not support the remaining options.
13. **(5) try to make a living writing poetry** The passage describes how much Hughes liked to write poetry and how he dreamed of being Harlem's poet. Option 1 is wrong because Hughes' father never answered the letter. Option 2 is wrong because Hughes didn't like Columbia University. The material does not support options 3 and 4.

14. Hughes' father was probably angry because his son quit school. Not replying would be a way to express that anger.

15. Many answers are possible. Responses should reflect feelings, dreams, hopes, or disappointments about a particular place.

LESSON 6

PAGE 46

Many answers are possible and might include inventions such as the television, the automobile, the radio, the telephone, or the computer. Events might include the two world wars, other wars (Korea, Vietnam), the founding of the United States, or the signing of the Bill of Rights. A sample is given below.

I think that the telephone is one of the greatest inventions that has had a significant impact on society. If we didn't have the telephone (or any other communication technology invented since then—computers, for instance), then it would take a long time to communicate with a relative or friend who lived far away. It would make the world seem much larger, and the town in which we live would be even more important to our lives.

1. Luis W. Alvarez
2. Since the first three paragraphs describe two projects that Alvarez was involved in, it is reasonable to predict that he will participate in further scientific experiments.

PAGE 47
  b and c

PAGE 48
  b

PAGE 49
  b and c

PAGES 50–51
  1. radiation   2. fossil
  3. radar   4. nuclear
  5. geologist   6. inspire

7. Alvarez may be best known for his idea that about 65 million years ago a body from space hit Earth, causing a giant explosion. He suggested that dust from the explosion covered Earth, blocked the sun, and killed most plants and animals.

8. Many answers are possible. He built the hydrogen bubble chamber, developed a radar system, and worked on the atom bomb that ended World War II.

9. Alvarez helped to develop the bomb. He also witnessed the bombing and worked with the team that measured the energy released by the blast.

10. Alvarez received the Nobel Prize in 1968. In 1988, a newly discovered asteroid was named in his honor.

11. (3) **They proved that the large amount of iridium could not have come from erupting volcanoes.** Proving that the iridium came from space rather than from volcanoes would have required extensive scientific tests. Options 1 and 2 are hypotheses. Options 4 and 5 are true but don't include evidence of careful testing practices.

12. (2) **Future wars would be avoided.** Alvarez referred to this possible cause-and-effect relationship in a letter to his son. The passage does not support the other options.

13. (2) **A clay layer formed on Earth at the same time that the dinosaurs disappeared.** This option is correct because there is no evidence of fossils in the layer. Option 1 is a hypothesis, not a fact. Option 4 is true but does not support the conclusion. Option 3 does not discuss the differences between the layers and why they are important. Option 5 does not explain the animals' death.

14. Many answers are possible. Some people might be more afraid of war because of the terrible destructive capabilities of nuclear weapons. Others might feel safer because the destructive power of the

weapons would deter governments from starting wars.

15. Many answers are possible. Accomplishments or inventions might relate to medical care, food production, transportation, communication technology, science, interpersonal relationships, or other topics.

LESSON 7

PAGE 52

Answers will vary but might include trying to settle disputes or differences between family members, friends, or children. This experience might be described as challenging, difficult, or rewarding, depending on the particular experience.

Most people have been away from home at least for a vacation, or perhaps to find work in a new location or to care for a family member. Responses might include feelings of homesickness or other feelings.

1. evening   2. on a train

PAGE 53

b

PAGE 54

b

PAGE 55

c

PAGES 56–57

1. d   2. c   3. e   4. a
5. f   6. b   7. b   8. a
9. Black Elk left home to perform with Buffalo Bill's Wild West Show. He wanted to learn about the white man's ways so he could help his people live in peace with the new settlers.
10. Black Elk thought that New York City was too big and crowded. He didn't like the way the people treated one another.
11. The weather was rough and stormy.

12. **(4) the end of the Native American way of life** This option is supported by Black Elk saying that throwing away the animals was like throwing away part of the power of his people. The material does not support options 1, 2, 3, and 5.
13. **(5) He felt like he had lost his spirit.** For a holy man, being without a vision is like having no spiritual support. Option 1 uses the wrong meaning of the word vision. Options 2 and 3 are not supported by the passage. Option 4 is wrong because Black Elk faces death bravely.
14. **(3) Black Elk performed for six months with the Wild West Show in London.** The last statement of the story says that they stayed in London for 6 moons (6 months). Options 1, 2, 4, and 5 all happened before Black Elk got to London.
15. The Wasichus had a different way of life than the Sioux. Black Elk was unhappy living this way because it seemed like a strange, cruel, spiritless way to live.
16. Many answers are possible. Some people might have adapted to the situation in which they felt out of place. Other people might have tried to change the situation or escape from it.

LESSON 8

PAGE 58

Most people will agree that the dollar is worth less than it was during their childhood. A sample answer is below.

When I was in grade school, I could go to the corner store and buy a handful of candy for a dollar. Now, I'm lucky to be able to buy a cup of coffee for a dollar.

1. No. The author thinks most people need directions on giving directions.
2. Answers will vary. People who think others are bad at giving directions might say that it's difficult to remember the number of traffic lights before taking a turn, or that knowing how to get

somewhere is very different from being able to tell someone else how to get there.

3. Answers will vary. Some people find it easy to give directions; others find it difficult. People who think it is easy might say that they know their town very well, or that they can picture a map of their town in their head while giving directions. People who find it difficult might list some of the same reasons given for question one for why other people are bad at giving directions.

PAGE 59

b

PAGE 60

a and c

PAGE 61

humorous

1. obligations   2. abruptly
3. retain   4. realign
5. prior   6. hierarchy
7. People who are not familiar with the streets in many cities may have difficulty finding their way around.
8. The government in Washington no longer understands the value of a dollar.
9. Arkins is critical of the government. She uses a sarcastic tone in her writing.
10. **(5) If America wants to save gas, it ought to . . . give everyone directions on how to give directions.** This option is humorous because it offers a highly unlikely solution to a problem. Options 1–4 are examples of factual statements.
11. **(2) "Money Management—Government Style"** This is the best match for both the tone and the content of the article. It is broad enough to cover the main point of the article—about how government spending affects everyday people—and it fits the article's humorous, ironic tone.

12. **(2) Both essays could be considered complaints.** This option states a similarity between the two essays; therefore, it is a comparison. Option 1 describes a cause-effect relationship between making money and spending it. Options 3, 4, and 5 don't mention similarities among two or more items.
13. Many answers are possible. Topics might range from the personal to the political. Answers should include a suggestion for solving the problem.

LESSON 9

PAGE 64

Answers will vary. Some people believe peace is possible, others don't. There will be a variety of opinions on how peace might be achieved.

1. This article looks at the idea of peace during an unpeaceful time—an air raid.
2. The author's purpose is to persuade the reader that it's possible to fight for freedom without the use of weapons.

PAGE 65

a and c

PAGE 66

b and c

PAGE 67

b

PAGES 68–69

1. subdued   2. disarmament
3. sterile   4. imperative
5. compensate
6. She describes the feeling as "dull dread."
7. Without creative outlets, men will return to fighting as an instinctive response.
8. When the fear has gone, the mind instinctively tries to create. Fond memories return.
9. **(3) The young airman . . . is driven by voices in himself. . . .** This option is a judgment, or opinion, and cannot be

proved true. Options 1, 4, and 5 are wrong because they are facts about what is happening. Option 2 is wrong because it is a quotation from someone other than the author.

10. **(3) to compare women's responsibilities with men's** To explain how difficult it would be for men to give up fighting, the author compares something women might be asked to do to achieve peace—give up childbearing. Option 1 is wrong because the passage does not suggest that women are better than men. The essay does not support options 2, 4, and 5.

11. **(4) We must free him from the machine.** In this statement the author uses the strong word "must" to motivate the reader to act. Options 1 and 2 are not supported by the essay. Options 3 and 5 are quotations, not the author's ideas.

12. Many answers are possible. Most people would think about their personal safety and fear the possibility of being killed.

13. Many answers are possible. Issues might be related to politics, health, charitable contributions, or other topics. Answers should include the outcome of the persuasive effort.

LESSON 10

PAGE 70

Answers should include what the person spoke out about and what the result was.

1. Answers will vary but might include the following: Who was courageous? What was the courageous action or stand? Where did it happen? When did this happen? Why did this person do this courageous thing?

2. Answers will vary but might include the following: What year did this happen? What is the athlete's first name? What type of athlete was he? What did he want to make a gesture about?

PAGE 71

1. b   2. b

PAGE 72

a and c

PAGE 73

a

PAGES 74–75

1. deprived   2. irrevocable
3. reprimanded   4. vindication
5. calculated   6. gesture

7. The Olympic audience included people from many countries. Some would not understand a protest spoken in English.

8. Norman wore an Olympic Project for Human Rights button.

9. Smith wasn't expected to win the final race because Carlos had achieved the best time in the semifinals and because Smith had injured a leg muscle in the second semifinal.

10. They felt angry about racial injustice in the United States. As African-American men, they believed they weren't treated fairly by the International Olympic Committee.

11. **(2) He slowed down.** "I pulled back on the reins" is a figurative way of saying that Carlos intentionally slowed down. The material does not support options 1, 3, and 5. Option 4 is the opposite of the facts stated in the passage.

12. **(4) Carlos would have won the race and set a world record.** This is supported by the statement "America deprived our society of seeing what the world record would have been." The passages do not support options 1, 3, and 5. Option 2 is not true because Smith hurt himself before the final race began.

13. **(3) They were suspended from the rest of the Olympic Games.** This option is supported by the fact that Norman was severely reprimanded, so it is likely that Carlos and Smith were too. The article does not support options 1, 4, and 5. Option 2 is wrong because Brundage, the

president of the International Olympic Committee, was not a strong supporter of civil rights issues.

14. A gesture can be understood by everyone, no matter what language they speak. Also, gestures can sometimes be more powerful than words.

15. Many answers are possible. Responses may focus on racism, sexism, religious or cultural discrimination, or other issues involving injustice or unfair treatment. Answers should include a method of protest.

LESSON 11

PAGE 76

Answers will vary. It is a life of privilege, but that privilege has its drawbacks. The drawbacks include the intense scrutiny by the media, which was a big problem for Princess Diana.

1. Answers will vary depending on a person's likes and dislikes.
2. Answers will vary but might include the history, the celebrities, or a general human interest.

PAGE 77

b

PAGE 78

1. b   2. a

PAGE 79

1. a
2. a, b, c, and d
3. Answers will vary, but should include all of the information from the answers given for question two. Below is an example of a possible answer.

This 8-day, 11-hour miniseries on the Windsors balances the past, present, and future coverage of the royals. It includes interviews with celebrities, the Queen's Jubilee (which included a rock concert), and takes a look at the inner circle of the royals. The program focuses on Queen Elizabeth II, the past

monarchs, and contemporary British royalty, including footage of Princess Diana, Prince William and the other royals.

PAGES 80–81

1. premiere   2. comprehensive
3. ambitious   4. finale
5. installment   6. monarchs
7. E! joined with Ardent Productions, which is owned by Edward Wessex.
8. She is saying that another person is affecting her relationship with Prince Charles. Many people have heard that Prince Charles was supposedly having a relationship with another woman.
9. Answers should include going inside the barracks of the Buckingham Palace guards, visiting the tartan factory, visiting Prince William's school, and showing the Queen's bagpipe player.
10. The reviewer is enthusiastic about the breadth of this program and the unique, insider coverage. The reviewer's enthusiasm indicates that she likes the program.
11. **(1) The program emphasizes the importance of today's royals based on history and humanizes the events in their lives.** This summary tells the main point of the final paragraph—that the program focuses on who the Royal Family is today and humanizes the stories about their lives.
12. **(3) History, Characteristics, and Habits of Siamese Cats** The comprehensive scope of *Royalty A–Z* is made clear in the review. It covers the history of the Royal Family as well as many in-depth details about their lives. This option covers both history and details of Siamese Cats and would therefore be most like *Royalty A–Z*. The other options are not comprehensive enough.
13. **(5) The coverage is an inside look that shows the Buckingham Palace guards as real soldiers.** This covers the main point

of the paragraph. The other options emphasize one particular point in the paragraph, but do not offer a balanced statement of the main idea.

14. Many people have watched miniseries on television, perhaps a miniseries based on a romance novel or a historical event. Some people enjoy watching miniseries, while others find it difficult to remember to watch all the episodes, or lose interest after a couple of episodes.

15. Some people have thought about what it would be like to be a king, queen, prince or princess. There are many privileges such as wealth, travel, and the opportunity to meet interesting people. Difficulties may include the media exposure and having "normal" relationships with people.

LESSON 12

PAGE 82

Some people keep a journal or write stories about their lives.

Many answers are possible, but they might include writing about joyous occasions such as the birth of a child, a wedding, or a trip abroad. Other responses might include more difficult life experiences such as the loss of a loved one or other events that might be soothed through writing. Some people like to keep a record of their family history and events that they can pass on to the next generation.

1. According to the reviewer, most people have had experiences with bad jobs or crazy relatives. However, people may or may not find anything funny about their particular experiences.

2. Answers may vary. One sample answer is: I didn't think it was humorous when it happened, but later I was able to laugh about it. It was Thanksgiving and I had invited my boss to join my family for the holiday. Earlier that week, my son had celebrated his birthday and had been given a gag gift by a friend—a whoopee cushion. Well, my son accidentally left the whoopee cushion on the chair that my boss sat in. It was very embarrassing, but we all laughed about it later.

PAGE 83

1. a   2. a

PAGE 84

1. b

2. Answers should include three of these examples: she had a rainbow of regrettable romantic partners; her dad had a helpless obsession with Thermoses; her grandparents were eccentric; and she'd taken bad vacations.

PAGE 85

1. c

2. Answers should include two of these ideas: Kaplan gets enough just right in her first book; she leaves her readers feeling less alone; and she leaves her readers more willing to laugh about the small stuff.

3. a

PAGES 86–87

1. resonate   2. chronological
3. obsession   4. disclaimer
5. eccentric   6. facets
7. Her publisher urged her to.
8. They are more mature stories that are touching/moving.
9. the essays that aren't necessarily comedic but uncover unique facets of Kaplan's life
10. It's comical and contains a metaphor comparing French truffle pigs to Kaplan's life.
11. **(2) casual** The reviewer uses informal language throughout the review. The review is more of a casual conversation between the reviewer and the reader, rather than a formal, technical piece.
12. **(2) . . . a man with a helpless obsession with gadgets . . .** This statement creates a funny picture of her father and is written

in a humorous way, so it contributes to the informal, humorous tone of the review.

13. **(1) She regrets going out with them.** Since the book is written from Kaplan's point of view, this is the only option that indicates how she felt about her boyfriends. Options 2 and 5 refer to how the boyfriends felt. Options 3 and 4 are not supported by the passage.

14. Answers may vary. One sample answer is: I once read a collection of jokes. Even though some of them were pretty corny, most of the jokes made me laugh out loud.

15. Answers may vary. One sample answer is: I would like to read this book because I've had some similar experiences and would enjoy seeing what the author says about things such as migraine headaches. It'd be nice to get a laugh out of a normally painful experience. I think I can appreciate the more mature essays, too. They may give me something to think about without being too serious.

READING AT WORK

PAGE 89

1. **(4) Spring Meadows will help Carverton build its community center.** Option 4 states the main idea, as demonstrated in the headline of the article. The other options are details that support the main idea of the passage.

2. **(4) Spring Meadows residents will receive a discounted membership.** Option 4 is correct because discounted memberships at the community center may be a powerful selling point for the development. The article does not support option 1. Option 2 is untrue because the Spring Meadows Development Company is building the center. Options 3 and 5 are true but not as important as the discount in membership fees.

3. Answers should include three of these

points: a new community center is being built in Carverton; the community center will house two pools, a fitness center, an indoor track, a gymnasium, meeting rooms, and locker areas; Spring Meadows residents will receive a discounted membership.

UNIT 1 REVIEW

PAGE 91

1. intersected   2. pessimist

3. optimism

4. **(3) his ability to empathize** This is clearly stated in the first paragraph of the review.

5. **(5) There is more rising on "The Rising" than in a month of church.** This is the only option that expresses an opinion or bias; the other options are factual statements.

6. **(5) "The Rising" includes the return of the E Street Band, which should close any gap between Springsteen and his fans.** This answer is the main idea of the third paragraph. The other options express part of the content in the third paragraph but do not summarize the entire content of the paragraph.

PAGE 93

7. h   8. e   9. d   10. b

11. c   12. a   13. f   14. g

15. The word "jam" means a performance or recording session in which musicians play improvised, unrehearsed material.

16. In the reviewer's opinion, the collection is complete and well-documented.

17. "If Brown was, as advertised, 'the hardest working man in show business,' the guys who worked in his backing bands were tied for second."

18. **(1) to give an example of how unusual James Brown is** This option is supported by the first sentence in the paragraph about the sax player: "Brown was always a character." The passage does not support

Answers and Explanations

options 2, 4, and 5. Option 3 is the opposite of what is suggested.

PAGE 95

19. mountains, hills
20. "A beautiful symphony of brotherhood" means a society in which people of all races live in harmony.
21. **(1) hope** This option is correct because the author is talking about a positive idea that he has. He also says that he has hope and faith. Option 2 is wrong because his dream is the opposite of despair. Option 3 does not contain the vitality of a dream. Options 4 and 5 may or may not be included in achieving a dream.
22. **(5) By working together, all people can become free.** This is the general message suggested by Martin Luther King's examples. Options 1 and 2 are too negative to be the theme of this uplifting speech. Options 3 and 4 may be true, but they are not suggested in this passage.
23. **(1) . . . we will be able to work together . . . (2) I have a dream today. (3) This is the faith that I go to the South with.** Option 1 shows that King wants to work with other people, option 2 shows his strong desire for change, and option 3 shows that he is taking action to achieve his dream. Option 4 repeats the words from a song and is not about what King is doing. Option 5 is wrong because it is just a description of the mountains.

PAGES 96–97, MINI-TEST

1. **(2) Andy's education, service, and work experience qualify him for the job.** *(Comprehension: Summarizing)* This is the statement that encompasses all of Andy's qualifications.
2. **(2) competent** *(Analysis: Drawing Conclusions)* This letter is business-like and well-written and portrays Andy as competent, which is his goal—to appear competent to the prospective employer.

3. **(3) customer relations specialist** *(Application: Applying Ideas)* You could apply your understanding of Andy's experience and qualifications to determine that he is best suited for a higher-level job in customer service.
4. **(4) He left certain parts out of the film.** *(Analysis: Making Inferences)* The reviewer uses this characterization as shorthand for his analysis of the relation between the book and the movie.
5. **(1) if more adorable elves were included** *(Synthesis: Interpreting Point of View)* The reviewer isn't fond of "cutesy" techniques or sets that are overly sweet and beautiful, so probably would not enjoy seeing more adorable elves in the film.
6. **(1) upbeat and clever** *(Synthesis: Understanding the Author's Tone)* The reviewer uses many clever phrases such as "hobbit-forming" and "elf shelf" to describe a film he generally has high regard for.

UNIT 2: FICTION

LESSON 13

PAGE 100

Many answers are possible. Some cultures believe in life after death while others don't. Answers may include personal, religious, or cultural beliefs about life after death.

1. This story takes place in the country in the evening.
2. At the time the story takes place, it is noisy, with "a thousand little wind sounds."

PAGE 101

b

PAGE 102

1. He heard the sound of feet on earth and cloth scraping. He saw many things—for example, a black stocking cap, a pea coat, a boot, and a leg.

2. a small girl who is thin, Navajo, frightened, and speaks English

PAGE 103

a

PAGES 104–105

1. hogan   2. gusts
3. plausible   4. tentatively
5. forlorn   6. ponderosas
7. He heard coughing and sniffling; he thought no Navajo would go in a death hogan.
8. Chee was shaking, but the girl was not.
9. She says that she borrowed the horse because she plans to take it back.
10. The hogan belongs to Hosteen Ashie Begay, the girl's grandfather.
11. **(4) Other crimes besides the horse theft may have taken place here.** This option is correct because Chee says he was looking for Gorman last week, wonders where the grandfather is, and remembers a "missing St. Catherine's student." Options 1, 2, 3, and 5 are details rather than the main idea.
12. **(2) He had come to terms with the ghosts of his people.** This option is correct because it describes a spiritual challenge Chee has faced and dealt with successfully. Options 1, 3, 4, and 5 describe his actions—what he does or sees—rather than his character.
13. **(5) Along the ponderosa timber covering the slopes.** This option offers the best picture of the landscape. It tells the reader that the place is hilly, and the hills have pines. Options 1 and 2 describe things Chee feels and hears. Option 3 is not related to the land. Option 4 partly describes the land, but not as much as Option 5.
14. Many answers are possible: find a place for the girl to stay; return the horse to its owner; look for Begay, to ask him questions about Albert Gorman.

15. Many answers are possible. Some students may describe a negative shock, such as surprising a burglar. Others may describe a positive event, such as a surprise birthday party.

LESSON 14

PAGE 106

Many answers are possible. Many people have had frustrating experiences with technology. Others are fascinated by computers, the Internet—even robots—and all other advancements in this age of technology.

1. nervous
2. Yes. In the third paragraph she says, "It's no use getting impatient," which implies that she is patient and Alfred Lanning is not.

PAGE 107

a

PAGE 108

b

PAGE 109

Possible clues are: they can see nothing but stars; no engines or controls are visible; the walls are very thick and might contain the engines.

PAGES 110–111

1. g   2. e   3. c   4. d   5. b
6. f   7. a   8. b   9. a   10. b
11. She doesn't want to upset The Brain and cause it to break communication.
12. The ship appears to be controlled by an outside source. Powell and Donovan do not know how to get control of the ship or bring it back.
13. **(1) The scientists have lost control of their own experiment.** This option is correct because it is the basis for all the events that take place in the story. Option 2 is incorrect because The Brain is quite happy; the people are angry and upset. The passage contains no evidence for

option 3. Option 4 may be true in many cases, but is certainly not true here. Option 5 may be true of The Brain, but it is not the main idea of the story.

14. **(4) "Just interesting," said The Brain, slyly.** The Brain is not responding in a totally honest and cooperative manner. This confirms the scientists' suspicions that the men on the ship are in danger.

15. **(4) . . . he was out of his seat with sudden frenzied energy . . .** Jumping out of one's seat and "frenzied energy" best portray the idea of shock. Option 1 is too calm to portray shock. Option 2 is an unemotional statement of fact. Option 3 is a detail that describes tension rather than shock. Option 5 conveys irritation, but not shock.

16. Any of the three choices is reasonable. Dr. Calvin appears to have more power; she is the one in charge of The Brain. On the other hand, Dr. Calvin may be held responsible for losing control of the experiment. Dr. Lanning may be considered less at fault for the problems with The Brain. Other readers may choose to be a different character altogether— such as The Brain itself!

17. Many answers are possible. Some people believe that thinking robots are impossible. Other people believe that someday robots may be able to think much like humans do.

LESSON 15

PAGE 112

Many answers are possible. People may describe any experience they have had investigating something strange. A sample answer is below.

I was very scared. I was holding my son's baseball bat as I went to the kitchen to investigate the loud noise I had heard. After I discovered that the noise had been caused by my cat knocking a glass off the counter, I felt very silly.

1. The use of the word "they" makes the reader picture something or someone that is scary.

2. He is described as having eyes like a toad and being capable of smiling while breaking a baby's arm. This creates a frightening mood.

PAGE 113

a

PAGE 114

b

PAGE 115

b

PAGES 116–117

1. glimpse   2. methodical
3. pondering   4. hunkered
5. incline   6. cylindrical
7. momentarily   8. synchronized

9. Answers should include two of the following: he got his father's target pistol; he took a piece of ash from the wood pile; he whacked one end into a rough point.

10. He doesn't want to be seen or heard; the twigs on the ground would break and make noise if he stepped on them carelessly.

11. She's sneaking around Straker's house; she's carrying a stake.

12. **(2) She turned around and looked at him. . . .** This is the only sentence that tells what Sue saw; all the other options tell what Mark saw or felt.

13. **(3) . . . she went on up the hill toward the break in the trees.** The setting is outdoors; the other options refer to being indoors or refer to descriptive details—such as a car or a living room—that are not where the action of the story takes place.

14. **(3) prepare somewhat and deal with things as they happened** This option is correct because it shows how Mark would do things. This is reflected in the story in the way that he prepared to go to Straker's

(by taking a pistol and a length of wood) and the way that he dealt with the sudden appearance of a girl (by spontaneously deciding to team up with her).

15. Many answers are possible: Sue might be relieved to have a partner in this adventure; she might be mad because she wanted to handle this herself; or she might not like Mark because he thinks he knows everything.

16. Many answers are possible. Some people like the camaraderie of working with other people. Other people prefer the independence or control they have when working alone.

LESSON 16

PAGE 118

Many answers are possible, but should include a description of what happened at the reunion. Often both happy and sad feelings are involved when such a reunion occurs.

1. There are three people in the conversation: one man and two women.
2. She disapproves of Etta's behavior.

PAGE 120

a and c

PAGE 121

a

PAGES 122–123

1. e   2. f   3. a
4. b   5. c   6. d
7. Ciel has been in San Francisco.
8. Miss Eva was Ciel's grandmother, and she was a good cook who made great angel food cake.
9. She's worried that they won't approve.
10. They approve of him because he is both good to her and good for her. They don't care that he isn't black. These ideas are supported by the way the women volunteer to take part in Ciel's wedding.

11. Many answers are possible. They argue with each other, but they've known each other for years, and they're like family to each other.

12. **(3) at an outdoor neighborhood party** The passage mentions dancing in the street, the outdoor grill and other food, and the number of people present. Etta also refers to the event as a party. Options 1 and 2 are wrong because the passage does not mention reunions or birthdays. Option 4 is wrong because they are in Brewster Place—not San Francisco. The only mention of a wedding refers to the future, so option 5 is wrong.

13. **(1) She had some kind of personal trouble.** This is suggested by Ciel's references to her "scars, " and to getting over all that happened. She got to the ocean because she "just kept going," not because she intended to go there, so option 3 is wrong. The passage does not support options 2, 4, and 5.

14. **(5) Etta likes to go out and party, while Mattie is an at-home type.** The passage clearly portrays Etta as someone who loves to dance and have a good time. Mattie is the one who holds Ciel, dries her tears, and calls her "child." The passage does not support options 1, 2, or 3. Option 4 is the opposite of what the passage suggests.

15. Many answers are possible. Some people see themselves as outgoing and social, like Etta. Other people think of themselves as more quiet and less social, like Mattie.

16. Many answers are possible. Reasons for wanting to stay in the same neighborhood might include the security of being in a familiar place and near family and friends. Reasons for wanting to move might include the joy of experiencing new places and meeting new people.

LESSON 17

PAGE 124

Many answers are possible. Some families have faced war or political upheaval; others have struggled over money. For others, personality differences have led to conflicts.

1. to settle down
2. "the water would be so low that"

PAGE 125

b

PAGE 126

b

PAGE 127

a

PAGES 128–129

1. furrow   2. churned
3. listlessly   4. abode
5. subsided   6. relented
7. He believes that fishing for carp is bad luck, though he doesn't know why.
8. The people ate the carp because there was a forty-year drought, a period with little or no rain. The people's crops died and in order to survive, they caught and ate the carp.
9. One of the gods loved the people very much and argued that they should be saved.
10. **(3) muddied water carried many secrets** This option is correct because a human quality—the ability to carry secrets—is given to water. Option 1 uses figurative language but does not attribute human qualities to something non-human. Option 2 describes the actual behavior of the carp in the water. Options 4 and 5 simply tell what happened to the people in the story.
11. **(1) that the boy thought of his mother while Samuel was talking** This option is correct because the boy did not speak of his mother; he only thought of her. If the story were told from Samuel's point of view, Samuel would not know what the boy was thinking. The other options are all part of the story Samuel tells, so the reader would still know about them.
12. **(2) after the people had been turned into carp** This option is correct because the god chose to be turned into a carp so he could take care of the people. The other options are not supported by the story.
13. Many answers are possible. Some people learn about their culture from family stories; some learn about their culture through reading. Others learn through classes, visiting museums, educational opportunities, or by other methods.
14. Many answers are possible. Some people are more motivated to follow a rule if they know the reason for it. For others, knowing that something is not allowed is enough to motivate them to follow the rule.

LESSON 18

PAGE 130

Many answers are possible. Most people find such experiences upsetting, but some may be fascinated by all the things they can hear.

1. It's a suspenseful, dramatic story.
2. a sign or an indication, an informer; a tattle-tale

PAGE 131

a

PAGE 132

b

PAGE 133

a

PAGES 134–135

1. g   2. j   3. c   4. b   5. d
6. i   7. h   8. a   9. e   10. f

11. the old man's strange-looking eye

12. On the first seven nights, the man's eyes were closed. When the narrator couldn't see the eye, he didn't feel the need to kill the old man.

13. He sensed that the black shadow of death stalked him.

14. **(2) entered the narrator's brain** This option is correct because the word "conceived" restates that the idea entered the narrator's brain. The passage does not support options 1, 4, or 5. Option 3 describes the effect the idea had on the narrator—that it haunted him.

15. **(5) For a whole hour, I did not move a muscle . . .** This sentence adds to the scary feeling of the passage because it emphasizes how sneaky the narrator is and how slowly the time is passing. Options 1 and 2 add little to the mood of fear the author is trying to establish. Option 3 states a fact, and option 4 tells something about the old man, who is not the main subject of the passage.

16. **(1) The sound of the old man's heartbeat will haunt the narrator.** This prediction fits best with the haunted, nervous personality of the narrator, his acute hearing, and the title of the story. Options 2 and 4 are extremely unlikely considering the personality of the narrator. Option 3 cannot be correct because, as he is telling the story, he keeps insisting that he isn't mad. Option 5 is possible, but less likely than option 1, considering the title of the story.

17. Many answers are possible. The narrator is crazy. His reason for killing the old man is not the thinking of a sane man.

18. Many answers are possible. People who like suspense will enjoy many of Poe's stories; people who like more cheerful fiction will probably choose to read other authors.

LESSON 19

PAGE 136

Many answers are possible. Some children and parents believe they differ from each other in significant ways, such as in their ages, education, personalities, or the time period in which each grew up. Other children and parents believe that their family identity is so strong that they do not differ from each other in significant ways. Feelings such as pride, joy, puzzlement, resentment, and many others may be involved.

1. The daughter talks back to her mother.
2. Most people have had this experience and may describe situations from their childhood or with their own children.

PAGE 137

a

PAGE 138

b

PAGE 139

b

PAGES 140–141

1. pursuing
2. opportunities
3. blend
4. fabulous
5. advantage
6. circumstances
7. American circumstances and Chinese character
8. Many answers are possible. She feels her mother might make a mistake without her guidance, or she wants to make sure her mother looks just right for the wedding.
9. Mr. Rory says that Mrs. Jong and Waverly look very much alike. Waverly probably doesn't like this comment because she thinks of her mother as old-fashioned and not stylish. This is not the image Waverly has of herself.
10. **(1) The Chinese are more careful and quiet and observant than Americans.** This is the best option because it's the idea that underlies everything Mrs. Jong

says. Options 2, 3, and 5 are not supported by the passage. Option 4 may be true, but it is not the focus of the passage.

11. **(2) They look directly at each other.** The mother's criticism implies that Americans do the opposite of the Chinese. Option 1 is what she says about Americans. The story does not support options 3, 4, and 5.

12. **(3) . . . her famous Mr. Rory.** This option suggests that the mother doesn't think much of the hairdresser. She is making fun of how well-known he is. Options 1 and 4 reveal what the mother thinks Waverly feels. Option 2 is a comment by Waverly. Option 5 is a judgment unrelated to the daughter's ideas.

13. Many answers are possible. Mrs. Jong's "American" face is like a mask that hides her true feelings; her "Chinese" face shows her true feelings.

14. Many answers are possible. Some people see Americans as superficial in their relationships with one another and therefore not "really looking at one another." Others may consider Americans to be very open, honest, and direct in their relationships.

LESSON 20

PAGE 142

Many answers are possible. Some people have been in dangerous situations, either alone or with others. Descriptions of the situations might include where they occurred, what made them dangerous, and how the situations were resolved.

1. worried, anxious
2. Buck is Thornton's dog—he never takes his eyes off his master.

PAGE 143

a

PAGE 144

a

PAGE 145

b

PAGES 146-147

1. ceased
2. submerged
3. propelled
4. impede
5. veered
6. miscalculated
7. Hans pulled the rope suddenly.
8. Thornton ordered Buck to go back to the bank because Buck was struggling in the water.
9. to allow Buck time to heal
10. **(5) tough** Thornton hangs on and eventually makes it to shore in an area of the river where "no swimmer could live"; he holds onto the slippery rock, and orders Buck to return to shore because it's too dangerous for the dog to try to save him.
11. **(1) They don't give up trying.** These two men and the dog repeatedly attempt to rescue Thornton.
12. **(5) skydiving with his trusted friends** Thornton is not afraid of difficult situations, and his work on the boat implies that he enjoys the outdoors and working with others rather than working alone.
13. Many answers are possible. Some students may describe similar feats of strength. Others might describe more fearful responses.
14. Many answers are possible. Answers should describe what the person did and the problem that resulted.

READING AT WORK

PAGE 149

1. to suggest new books for customers to read; to keep the most popular books in stock
2. Let Me Hear It Again
3. Answers may vary. A sample is below: I enjoy reading horror stories the most. I love they way they grab and play with my emotions. Some parts of the book make

me shiver and shake. A really good horror story can make me so scared that I leave the lights on when I go to bed.

UNIT 2 REVIEW

PAGE 151

1. c   2. a   3. b

4. **(1) proud** This option is supported by Marsha's comments about how beautiful her baby is. Options 2 and 3 reveal the way Victor feels. The story does not support options 4 and 5.

5. **(3) The baby is not normal.** This option is supported by the fact that the baby clearly focuses on Victor's eyes, which is not normal for a newborn. Option 1 is wrong because the passage states that the baby is a newborn. The passage does not support options 2, 4, and 5.

6. **(5) frightening** This option is supported by the last sentence in the passage, ". . ." Victor felt a thrill of fear." Option 2 describes what Victor and Marsha think of the baby, not his eyes. Options 1, 3, and 4 are not supported by the passage.

PAGE 153

7. work   8. hunger, anger
9. cannery
10. **(1) to grow slowly** This option is suggested by the fact that the people's hunger was slowly turning into anger. Option 2 has nothing to do with the passage. The story does not support options 3 and 4. Option 5 is the opposite of what is meant.

11. **(4) uneasy** The migrants are restless, and the author suggests that the situation will soon change for the worse. Options 1 and 2 are too positive for the situation described. The passage does not support options 3 and 5.

12. **(4) They felt desperate.** The two words suggest the extremes of hunger and violence. Options 1 and 3 are the opposite

of what is suggested. The passage does not support options 2 and 5.

PAGE 155

13. perceived   14. lariat
15. yelping   16. trotting
17. **(3) a horse** This is stated directly in the passage. Option 1, a pony, and Option 2, a dog, are both mentioned in the passage, but they are not Baba. Baba is an animal, and not a human as in Options 4 and 5.

18. **(5) because she had been separated from him** You can infer this when Ramona says that they will never be parted. Option 1 is wrong because Alessandro brought her the surprise. Options 2, 3, and 4 are mentioned in the discussion but are not the cause of her happiness.

19. **(4) Alessandro wants to please Ramona.** You know that Alessandro wants to please Ramona because he finds her horse and returns it to her as a surprise; and he expresses joy at returning her lost horse to her. He also says that if she does not want the horse, he will lead the horse back.

PAGES 156–157, MINI-TEST

1. **(1) gloomy** *(Analysis: Determining Mood)* The author begins by describing "one of those cold rainy spells that sometimes occur in summer." She also describes climbing "rickety steps" to a "stuffy, dusty loft." All of these elements set a gloomy mood.

2. **(3) messy and cluttered** *(Comprehension: Summarizing)* The author describes all of the discarded objects that have been treated like junk. This creates a picture of a room that is messy and cluttered.

3. **(5) read it with interest** *(Application: Applying Ideas)* Although the character is bored at the beginning of the passage, he begins to show more interest as he looks through the attic. The last sentence is very shocking. Based on his growing interest

throughout the piece, you can anticipate that he will read the diary.

4. **(4) the sea was completely full of gulls** *(Analysis: Making Inferences)* The entire third paragraph is a description of how the sky above the sea was filled with gulls.

5. **(2) not take him seriously** *(Comprehension: Restating)* Lines 34–39 describe different ways that the police will react to his warning about the gulls—all of which reflect not taking him seriously.

6. **(3) He was afraid of an attack by the gulls.** *(Synthesis: Expanded Synthesis)* Based on Nat's anxiety about the gulls and his unusual actions of boarding up his windows and blocking his chimney, it is likely that he is afraid that this huge hoard of gulls will attack his house.

UNIT 3: DRAMA

LESSON 21

PAGE 160

Many answers are possible. Some people may have attended or given a surprise party; others may have had a party given for them. Some people feel special to have a party given for them; others may feel embarrassed.

1. Meg, Babe, and Lenny
2. Meg and Babe are getting a birthday cake ready to surprise Lenny.

PAGE 161

a

PAGE 162

b

PAGE 163

a and c

PAGES 164–165

1. ravenously
2. glimmer
3. improvising
4. superstition

5. spontaneous
6. Lenny wishes to have a moment with her sisters, just being together and laughing.
7. Babe means that Meg should watch to see if Lenny is coming. She wants to be sure the surprise isn't spoiled.
8. If you tell someone what you wish for when you blow out the candles, the wish won't come true.
9. Students may mention that the celebration was a day late, and that they celebrated at breakfast, an unusual time for a birthday party.
10. **(4) She says that Lenny's wish will come true if she makes it deep enough.** This is a "fact" that Babe makes up to convince Lenny to tell her wish. Options 2 and 5 are facts about Babe that are stated in the story. Options 1 and 3 are opinions that Babe has.
11. **(1) "...we've just got to learn how to get through these real bad days here."** The phrase "real bad days" indicates that the sisters have some problems. The remaining options are lines spoken by the characters, but the words contain no sign of conflict.
12. **(5) All the sisters were having problems.** The first line in the play supports this option. Option 1 is the opposite of what is stated. The passage does not support options 2 and 4. Option 3 is wrong because Lenny loves making birthday wishes.
13. Yes. Lenny wants her sisters to laugh with her. In the last minutes of the play they do. They have gotten to that magical moment.
14. Many answers are possible. Answers should include a wish that was truly meaningful and specific actions taken to help it come true.
15. Many answers are possible. Some students may discuss feeling nervous when speaking in public; others may mention feeling nervous when discussing a conflict or an embarrassing subject.

Answers should describe the situation and the outcome.

LESSON 22

PAGE 166

Many answers are possible. Conflicts about noise, animals, property maintenance, or racial differences are possibilities. Answers should include a reasonable solution to the conflict described.

1. *(He looks at the slip of paper.)*
2. "Mrs. Lena Younger" is written on the paper. Man has to look at the paper where he's written it down because he doesn't know her name.

PAGE 167

a

PAGE 168

1. a and b   2. b

PAGE 169

b

PAGES 170–171

1. affirmation   2. quizzical
3. consulting   4. deplore
5. labored   6. expectantly
7. Beneatha is suspicious. The stage directions say that Beneatha watches the man carefully, responds to him dryly, and is the only one who gets Lindner's two meanings.
8. The Youngers treat Lindner politely, offering him a drink and a comfortable chair.
9. He is probably referring to racial conflicts.
10. Many answers are possible: Lindner is planning to talk about something difficult, and this makes him feel uncomfortable; or Lindner feels uncomfortable because he is talking to people he perceives as different.
11. (3) **suggest in a nice way that they sell the house** This option is supported by

Lindner's awkward way of getting to the idea that there is a problem. He is gentle and hesitant and thinks he is being reasonable. Options 1 and 5 do not fit with Lindner's personality so far. Options 2 and 4 would mean that the association had no problem with African-American families.

12. (4) **Lindner suggests that people should sit down and talk.** This answer is reasonable because people can't understand one another's point of view if they don't discuss it. Options 1 and 2 don't relate to the stated theme. Options 3 and 5 are not ideas mentioned in the story.
13. (1) **The organization looks after upkeep and special projects.** This detail explains how the organization keeps an eye on the people in Clybourne Park by looking after upkeep (maintaining the neighborhood). The special projects involve exactly what Lindner is doing—checking on residents who may be seen as undesirable. The other options are not related to the association.
14. Many answers are possible. Some people would agree that people need to talk about differences and would set up neighborhood meetings to discuss issues. Others would be insulted and possibly choose to evict Lindner instead of talking.
15. Many answers are possible. Some people may have experienced prejudice because of race, age, sex, or disability. Answers should describe the prejudice, including how it was shown and what was done about it.

LESSON 23

PAGE 172

Most people have met someone new and experienced an awkward meeting. Some people may have said things they wish they hadn't said, while others may have been so embarrassed that they couldn't think of anything to say. Some people may have found that it was the person they were meeting that acted awkward or embarrassed.

1. b   2. a

PAGE 173

a   c   d   e

PAGE 174

1. b   2. c

PAGE 175

c

PAGES 176–177

1. indicted   2. spectacular
3. prominent   4. frantic
5. cliché   6. traditional
7. She is the host of a radio talk show on which she apparently gives relationship advice.
8. She doesn't want to be thought of as a run-of-the-mill housewife because she has done more than that with her life.
9. She was bored and wanted to add something interesting to her life.
10. She means that since the soft drink Dr. Pepper uses the title "Dr." even though it is a drink, and not a real medical person, then she can use the title "Dr." too.
11. **(4) does not pay much attention to other people** She did not bother to listen to Mervyn carefully enough when he told her his name.
12. **(1) He would ignore the insult.** In the passage, Mervyn does not appear to be insulted when Gorgeous mildly insults him by saying that if he ever listened to the radio, he would know that everyone calls Dr. Gorgeous. He also isn't insulted and doesn't even correct Gorgeous when she gets his name wrong.
13. **(5) Mervyn tends to be sarcastic.** Mervyn never appears to be terribly enthusiastic about Gorgeous and her fabulous career and life; rather, he comes across as fairly

doubtful about Gorgeous' claims. For example, his statement about the rabbi who was indicted shows that he doesn't share Gorgeous' view of the man, which supports the idea that he doesn't quite believe Gorgeous. However, he never actually says he doesn't believe her. Instead, he makes short statements that seem positive but really show that he is almost mocking her—that is, he is being sarcastic.

14. Answers will vary. Most people have seen or heard a talk show on television or on the radio. Many people enjoy them; others think they are silly or even annoying. There are many types of talk shows—for example, some are for personal advice, while others may be about sports or politics.

15. Answers will vary. Many people will find that Gorgeous comes on rather strong and may dislike this. Others may find her amusing, and still others will appreciate that she is outspoken.

READING AT WORK

PAGE 179

1. **(3) The job of stage manager requires the ability to organize a variety of tasks.** This passage focuses on the range of tasks and skills involved in being a stage manager. The other options are details from the author's experience, but do not encompass the entire passage.

2. **(2) to explain what a stage manager does** The title provides a clue, as does the first paragraph where the author mentions that people ask him what his job entails. The other options are not supported by the article.

3. Answers may vary but should include three of the following tasks: organizes the production of the play, runs the performance, gives cues to actors, finds the furniture and props for the play, manages the budget for the furniture and

props, runs the backstage and onstage areas during the performance, coordinates everything between the director and other staff, and supervises the tearing down of the set at the end of the show.

UNIT 3 REVIEW

PAGE 181

1. They have been trying to pick up radio signals from deep outer space.
2. Friday
3. If they know the future, they will be able to make money by betting on football games or other events. By knowing the scores ahead of time, they can never lose.
4. They are husband and wife; they work together.
5. **(3) were expecting to receive radio signals from outer space** This answer is provided by the narrator's introduction, which describes Adela's and Marcos' work. The passage does not support options 1, 2, and 5. Option 4 is the opposite of what is stated.
6. **(4) do something good** This option is correct because Adela and Marcos might prevent a death if they share the news bulletin. Option 1 is wrong because the information about football scores, not the bridge, could make them money. Option 2 is inconsistent with the goal of scientific work, which is to discover evidence or proof, not to fool people. Option 3 is wrong because only one unsubstantiated broadcast is insufficient as proof. Option 5 is wrong because the broadcast is anything but ordinary.
7. **(4) go to the authorities and try to convince them that the bridge will collapse** Option 1 is incorrect because the discovery is too important to ignore. Option 2 is incorrect because they could make more money if they kept the radio.

The passage does not support option 3. Option 5 may be true in the future, but it is not the next thing they would do.

PAGE 183

8. Lord Caversham thinks Miss Chiltern is pretty and would like his son to propose to her. However, he thinks she may be too good for his son and therefore she'd probably refuse a marriage proposal from him.
9. Lord Goring means that he isn't sure whether he'd have any luck receiving an acceptance from Miss Chiltern if he proposed to her. He's suggesting that it's a toss up and could possibly happen, but it may not.
10. Lord Caversham is somewhat pushy—he probably ignored the servant and went in to see his son anyway. He accuses his son of wasting time and then he bothers his son with questions about proposing to Miss Chiltern.
11. **(4) Men don't deserve good women.** Lord Caversham says that his son doesn't deserve Miss Chiltern, implying that she is too good for him. His son flippantly responds by saying that if men married the women they deserved, they would be in a terrible situation. The clear implication of this is that men aren't good and therefore don't deserve good women.
12. **(5) "Thanks awfully, but I think I'd sooner be engaged before lunch."** Lord Goring doesn't really prefer to be engaged before lunch. He is just bantering, or kidding around, with his father. Obviously he knows that it is ridiculous to talk about whether he wants to be engaged before or after lunch, so he is not being very serious.
13. **(5) comic** Even though the characters are discussing serious issues, they are discussing them in a very humorous and sarcastic way. It is the way the characters say what they say that gives the passage a humorous tone.

1. **(1) She is too old to drive her car safely.** *(Comprehension: Summarizing)* Boolie tells his mother that because she wrecked the car and because she is in her seventies, she shouldn't be allowed to drive a car anymore.

2. **(3) Daisy and Boolie are both stubborn.** *(Analysis: Identifying Conflict)* Daisy refuses to accept that she needs someone to drive her; she believes her son is overreacting. Daisy shows her strong will by saying, "Think what you want. I know the truth," and by insisting this is her business, not her son's. Her son similarly insists that his opinion is the correct one.

3. **(4) frustrated with Daisy** *(Analysis: Drawing Conclusions)* Boolie's frustration with his mother comes out when he says, "Lord Almighty! Don't you see what I'm saying?"

4. **(3) She will dislike him in the beginning.** *(Application: Applying Ideas)* Daisy is so set against getting a driver, insisting that her accident was the fault of the car and not her poor driving, that it is almost certain she will be resentful of her driver in the beginning and will dislike having him.

5. **(4) Daisy doesn't believe her son.** *(Synthesis: Understanding Author's Purpose)* The author has Daisy say that her son is being hateful even though the son is not really acting that way. He does that to make it clear that Daisy does not share the same view of the situation as her son does.

6. **(1) sarcastic** *(Synthesis: Understanding Tone)* Boolie's frustration with his mother increases and he exaggerates the situation to make a point. He says the insurance companies will be lining up to have her as a customer. He doesn't really mean this, but he uses sarcasm to make his point.

7. **(3) argumentative** *(Synthesis: Synthesizing Ideas)* Boolie is frustrated because his mother won't see the reality of the situation, while Daisy refuses to accept that she won't be able to drive, or that the situation is any of Boolie's business. Throughout the passage, Boolie and Daisy argue over how to resolve the situation. This conflict creates an argumentative tone.

8. **(5) resistant to accepting** *(Synthesis: Expanded Synthesis)* Daisy is clearly highly resistant to the idea of having a driver. However, many years later, when she is in a nursing home, she wants to spend time with him and share a piece of pie with him. This shows that she has accepted him and has even come to care for him a great deal.

UNIT 4: POETRY

LESSON 24

PAGE 188

Some people are doing exactly what they expected to be doing with their lives and can recount this. Other people will note that their lives have taken a different course from what they expected. They can discuss what they thought they would be doing with their lives in contrast to what they are doing now.

1. Yes. Lines one through five form the first stanza and there is a break between lines five and six.
2. No. The words at the ends of the lines do not rhyme.

PAGE 189

b

PAGE 190

b

PAGE 191

a and b

PAGES 192–193

1. embrace   2. mantel

3. precious   4. extend
5. awkward   6. countenance
7. smaller, more beautiful, wiser in African ways (the poet uses the spelling *afrikan*), and more confident
8. Both characters have lost their mothers.
9. The boy is looking for a mother's love. The meeting with the woman in the store does not truly comfort him because the woman can fill his need for only a few moments.
10. As a mother herself, the woman understands how much the boy misses a mother's love. She hugs the boy in an attempt to comfort him.
11. (3) **She has tried to be like her mother.** The speaker has dreamed dreams for her mother and has made her mother alive again, both of which suggest she wants to be like her mother. Option 1 is wrong because the speaker admires her mother. Options 2 and 4 are not mentioned in the poem. Although option 5 is probably true, it's not the meaning of the given statement.
12. (3) **The child doesn't understand what happened to his mother.** The main idea of this poem is that the child doesn't know where his mother is. He doesn't understand the concept of death, and that he won't see her again. The other options are less important details.
13. (5) **. . . out of my mother's life into my own . . .** This phrase shows that the speaker wants to stop imitating her mother and start developing her own identity. Options 1, 3, and 4 describe her present life. Option 2 describes the way the speaker has tried to be like her mother.
14. Many answers are possible. Some responses may mention how much the mother loved her son and explain that she is always with him in his heart.
15. Many answers are possible. People may describe specific traits or things they miss doing with the person.

LESSON 25

PAGE 194

There are many important decisions that might be included here, such as decisions about education, work, relationships, marriage, children, finances, travel, or health. What has helped people make these decisions may be external—for example, job loss or encouragement from a family member. Or, decisions might based on internal reasons, such as wanting more challenging work or the desire to have a child. Finances are often a major factor in people's decisions.

1. "wood," "stood," and "could" or "both" and "undergrowth"
2. b

PAGE 195

a and c

PAGE 196

1. b   2. b

PAGE 197

b

PAGES 198–199

1. minuet   2. trodden
3. diverged   4. arrayed
5. fluttered   6. claim
7. He stood and looked down the two roads.
8. The granddaughter found it hard to imagine an old woman who naps every day as a young, pretty girl.
9. The suicide was a surprise because Cory seemed to have everything, with no hint of problems.
10. (2) **just as attractive** This option is supported by the phrases "really about the same," "grassy," and "both that morning equally lay." The poem does not support options 1, 3, and 5. Option 4 is incorrect because the poem is about one path being less traveled than the other.
11. (3) **You can't judge a book by its cover.** The saying means that judgements should

not be based on appearances. The poem does not support options 1, 2, and 4. Option 5 is wrong because the poem does not suggest that Richard Cory was evil or that money had anything to do with his death.

12. **(5) Sometimes you can get more out of life if you do something different and don't just follow the crowd.** The speaker states that the route he took "made all the difference" in his life. Option 2 says the opposite of the stated main idea. Option 3 is incorrect because the speaker is not talking about physical travel. Options 1 and 4 are not mentioned in the poem.

13. Many answers are possible. Some people may be happy with the choice because taking a road less traveled is probably unusual and interesting. Others may think this choice is frightening because they may find themselves alone, without help from others readily available.

14. Many answers are possible. Some people may mention that family, love, or honesty are more important than money. Some reasons for Cory's suicide might be that he was disappointed in love, or that he'd done something very wrong and couldn't live with himself.

LESSON 26

PAGE 200

Many people will say they have been in love. Most will discuss an adult relationship. Some people may choose to discuss their love for their family, children, parents, or even pets. People will mention many types of advice for others who are in love. Advice may range from encouragement for following one's heart to cautioning others about falling in love. Advice may be practical, such as remembering to tell the person every day that you love them or not to forget the person's birthday.

1. commas   2. a

PAGE 201

1. a   2. b

PAGE 202

1. Any two of the following: height, sight, candle-light, Right *or* ways, everyday's, Praise *or* lose, choose

2. b   3. a

PAGE 203

1. b   2. a

PAGE 204–205

1. outright   2. breadth
3. jutted   4. slackened
5. passionate   6. strive
7. Women won't value love if it seems to be a sure thing; they need to think it might fade in order to be interested in the game of love.

8. She loves him day and night. She loves him by day, when the sun is out and by night, when candle-light is used.

9. She feels the distance that is growing between her and the person she loves as an almost forced separation, one that she doesn't want.

10. One speaker thinks it's a bad idea to give all his love; the other speaker is giving all her love.

11. **(5) the sharp edges of the night** Anything sharp is likely to be painful, so this is the most logical response. The other options do not contain images that evoke a feeling of physical pain.

12. **(1) rhyming lines** This is the only option that is a characteristic of the poem. Rhymes appear at the ends of the lines; the first two lines end in rhyme, and each subsequent set of two lines rhymes.

13. **(4) I love you totally and completely.** Each line of this poem expresses another way in which the speaker loves this person. The speaker explains how it feels to love this person, and the depth of her love. The last

lines touch on death and loving this person even after death.

14. Answers will vary. Some people strongly believe that there is a difference based on gender. Others will say that gender is not an issue. Some might say that holding back is advisable because letting the other person know how much you care for them might cause them to back away. Others might state that it's important to let the other person know how much you care for them, and if this causes them to back away, then perhaps it is for the best.

15. Answers will vary. Many people have experienced a difficult ending to a relationship, and in many cases this involves mixed feelings. People may share these experiences to varying degrees, depending on what they are comfortable with. Relationships discussed may include love relationships, friendships, or family relationships. Mixed feelings could include sadness, with a realization that the relationship wasn't healthy.

READING AT WORK

PAGE 207

1. **(4) expose the children to a wide variety of stories, poems, and songs** This option is stated in the final sentence of the first paragraph.

2. **(3) the center wants children to develop a love of reading and literature** This option is stated in the first sentence of the passage.

3. **(5) "The Wild Hog," a poem about a mean hog who kills many men** This option is supported by the second bulleted item on the list.

4. Sample answer:
I always liked "Row, Row, Row Your Boat." Even though it is a silly song, I like how it sounds when people sing it in rounds, with singers starting the song at different times.

UNIT 4 REVIEW

PAGE 209

1. The speaker feels that the pillow is his friend and all that he has in the world.

2. It could smother the speaker if properly applied.

3. **(2) It uses punctuation in a regular way.** The poem is punctuated like prose. For example, there are complete sentences that begin with a capital letter and end with a period.

4. **(2) the fresh coolness of his pillow** The clue to this is the previous phrase, "Your underside is cool."

5. **(3) to show the pillow is indented and to suggest unhappiness** The poet wants the reader to think of more than one meaning here—both the depression, or indentation, in the pillow, and the sense of unhappiness because morning has come and the pillow's (and possibly the speaker's) wrinkles are showing.

6. **(2) The speaker is comforted by and feels less alone because of his pillow.** The topic or subject of this poem is the speaker's relationship with his pillow. The most important point about that subject is that the speaker feels comforted and less lonely with his pillow.

PAGE 211

7. The couple divorced.

8. The speaker talks about how bad the nights were.

9. The speaker has torn them up.

10. **(1) arguing bitterly** This option suggests that the two tried to hurt each other with words in the same way they might hurt each other physically by throwing the furniture. Option 2 is wrong because the couple did not really throw furniture. The poem does not support options 3, 4, and 5.

11. **(3) They lived in different parts of the country.** The poem implies that the two are separated by distance, and states that

they now communicate by a yearly letter. The poem does not support options 1, 2, 4, and 5.

12. **(5) held on tight, and let go** This option states that, although reluctant to do so, the couple eventually parted voluntarily. The other options refer to how the couple acted before the end of the marriage.

PAGES 212–213, MINI-TEST

1. **(5) Children's homes are enjoyably messy. (Comprehension: Summarizing)** The poet uses the words "pleasant rumpledness" to express the opinion that children's homes may be messy, but that this is appealing.

2. **(1) One should enjoy life's simple pleasures. (Analysis: Making Inferences)** The poem suggests that adults are too concerned with appearances and getting things done; they should remove themselves from the busy world around them and appreciate all the little things, the way children do.

3. **(4) Children bring warmth and joy. (Synthesis: Identifying Theme)** Many of the images in the poem suggest that children's lives are filled with joy and warmth, even if the result may be toys strewn in the yard. The poet describes children's yards as places where "ants have more hope" and "squirrels dance as well as hide." They also "glow with the leftovers of their affection."

4. **(1) considerate (Application: Applying Ideas)** The speaker learned from her experience as a child to listen when her father asked her to slow down. She also worries what effect things she is not aware of might have on her child when he or she is grown. This indicates that she learns from mistakes and listens to others, which are characteristics of a considerate boss.

5. **(4) their long, complex past (Analysis: Interpreting Figurative Language)** The poem begins with her memory of being a

child with her father, and ends, years later, when she is an adult with her father. The poem is about the impact of events, even seemingly minor ones, from long ago.

6. **(4) Childhood experiences affect us through life. (Comprehension: Restating the Main Idea)** The speaker discusses the impact of her father's actions when she was a child. Those actions still affect her strongly now. She also worries about what impact her actions and behaviors will have on her own child many years from now.

7. **(4) make a promise to herself to never treat her children the same way (Application: Applying Ideas)** The speaker talks about how what her father did affected her and how she is careful about what she does with her own children. Therefore, if she thought she was being treated unfairly by her parents, she would most likely make sure that she never treated her children in a similar manner.

8. **(2) powerful (Expanded Synthesis)** Her father was strong enough to tow her along, while she hung on to his coattails and then to his hand. She felt helpless. Her mother had the power to create her own world. This shows that she perceived them, at least as a child, as powerful.

POSTTEST

PAGE 217

1. **(3) Helen learns the meaning of abstract ideas such as "love." (Comprehension: Summarizing)** The entire piece is about Helen trying to understand the meaning of the word "love." All of the details in the piece point to the climactic moment when Helen finally comes to an understanding that "love" is an abstract idea. Prior to that she notes that she figured out the meaning of her first abstract term, "think".

2. **(5) Helen is hearing impaired.** *(Analysis: Making Inferences)* Sign language is used by people who have hearing impairments and cannot hear the spoken word, so the fact that Miss Sullivan and Helen use sign language most likely means that Helen is hearing impaired.

3. **(2) She would thoughtfully keep trying until she succeeded.** *(Application: Applying Ideas)* Helen showed her patience with stringing the beads and trying to grasp difficult concepts. She never gave up. It is likely that this same trait would characterize her attempts to learn other things as well.

4. **(2) It showed that Helen was blind and did not see the sun.** *(Synthesis: Understanding the Author's Purpose)* Because Helen describes the sun only in terms of how it feels, it helps the author demonstrate how Helen perceived the world—that is, that she could not see but instead knew things by feel, touch, and smell.

5. **(1) She was a highly skilled teacher.** *(Synthesis: Expanded Synthesis)* Helen has clearly learned a great deal. She can communicate and is thoughtful and calm. To bring a child from out-of-control and uncommunicative to the way Helen is in the passage would take a very skillful, as well as patient and loving, teacher.

PAGE 219

6. **(2) Hope comes back more easily for the young.** *(Comprehension: Restating)* The passage states that hope was returning to Becky and Tom because the nature of hope is to come back to the young—when its "spring" (flexibility) hasn't been lost through age and failure.

7. **(1) They will be more likely to die if they don't keep moving.** *(Analysis: Interpreting Figurative Language)* Prior to this statement, the passage says that the children were trying to ignore the fact that they were becoming more and more tired and to think of sitting down was "dreadful." This shows that they think something bad will happen if they sit down and stop moving. To "invite death" is to ask death to come; to "shorten its pursuit" means that it will not take as long to come.

8. **(3) thank her and follow her plan** *(Application: Applying Ideas)* Tom responds to Becky's crying with kindness and friendship. He does not belittle her or decide to leave her or show frustration. It is likely that he would respond with kindness and friendship to her under almost any circumstances.

9. **(4) I will save this; we may be here a while.** *(Synthesis: Interpreting Point of View)* Tom blows the candle out to preserve it because he doesn't know how long they will be lost. He is trying to be practical in a difficult situation. If he had no hope or if he thought they were about to be rescued, he would probably not worry about saving the candle for later. There is no evidence that he is frightened of the dark, or that darkness comforts Becky.

10. **(2) adventure** *(Synthesis: Expanded Synthesis)* Tom and Becky are clearly in a frightening and adventurous situation—they are lost, it is very dark, and they are trying to save themselves. Traveling down a river on a raft is also adventurous. From this information, we can conclude that Mark Twain wrote adventure novels. Although it is dark in the passage and Becky is frightened, there is no other information that indicates that the passage is from a mystery novel.

PAGE 221

11. **(5) What is right for you isn't right for me, Pop.** *(Comprehension: Restating)* The fact that they are so different is the basis of their argument. Lyons wants to pursue his dream of being a musician, and his father

seems to think that is irresponsible. Lyons doesn't want to punch a time clock; Troy punches a time clock. Lyons doesn't want to work for someone else; Troy feels it's the right thing to do.

12. **(4) Troy had told Lyons he should get a job.** *(Analysis: Interpreting Plot)* The issue seems to have been a sore point between the two men for a while. It is quite likely that Troy has told Lyons previously to give up on being a musician and get a job so he doesn't have to ask for money. The other options don't have any clues in the passage to substantiate them.

13. **(2) He is independent and proud of himself.** *(Analysis: Drawing Conclusions)* Troy is proud he has never had to ask anyone for money. He knows he has to take care of himself and works hard to do so.

14. **(2) They both have strong opinions.** *(Synthesis: Comparing and Contrasting)* Neither man gives an inch. They have very different opinions, and each man believes wholeheartedly that he is right.

15. **(1) Troy will insist that Cory not play football.** *(Synthesis: Expanded Synthesis)* Troy clearly values steady work and income above following a dream. Being a musician is Lyons' dream; playing on the football team seems to be Cory's. Troy does not approve of Lyons' priorities, and probably won't approve of Cory taking a similar path and leaving a job to pursue football.

PAGE 223

16. **(1) The boy is upset about something more than the snowman.** *(Comprehension: Understanding Implied Meaning)* The boy is inside his home alone, crying, and fearful. The snowman hasn't done anything to upset the boy. Most likely something else is causing him to feel sad about everything, including the snowman.

17. **(2) The weather is becoming stormier.** *(Analysis: Determining Cause and Effect)* It is the increasingly stormy weather that is making him cry harder.

18. **(1) The snowman was built by the boy.** *(Analysis: Recognizing Unstated Assumptions)* It is likely that the boy built the snowman since he cares so much about it. The other options are not supported in the poem.

19. **(2) The boy would take it home and clean it.** *(Application: Applying Ideas)* The boy seems to be sensitive and compassionate. It is likely he would feel compassion for an "abandoned" stuffed animal as well.

20. **(4) sad** *(Synthesis: Understanding the Author's Tone)* The fact that the boy is sad and the snowman sheds a tear suggests the sadness in the poem. There are no details to support the other options.

Most of the passages you have read in this book are parts of longer works such as novels, magazine articles, essays, biographies, and plays. If you liked a particular passage, you might want to read the entire work it was taken from. On the following pages is more information about the longer works for most of the passages in this book. Look for these works in your local library.

Anaya, Rudolfo A. *Bless Me, Ultima*. Berkeley: Tonatiuh-Quinto Sol International, 1972, reprinted 1988. An award-winning Hispanic novelist tells the story of a boy growing up in a traditional culture.

Arkins, Diane C. "Back When a Dollar Was a Dollar." *USA Today*, November 2, 1989, p. 10A. A newspaper columnist uses a humorous tone to write about modern economic problems.

Asimov, Isaac. "Escape," in *I, Robot*. Garden City, New York: Doubleday and Co., Inc., 1950. A short story about the role of computers in the future as told by a respected scientist and science-fiction author.

Clifton, Lucille. "the thirty eighth year," in *Women in Literature: Life Stages Through Stories, Poems, and Plays*. Englewood Cliffs, New Jersey: Prentice Hall, Inc., 1988. An African-American woman expresses her feelings about getting older.

Codye, Corinn. *Luis W. Alvarez*. Austin, Texas: Steck-Vaughn Co., 1991. The discoveries of an Hispanic scientist who won the Nobel Prize for physics in 1968 are described in this biography.

Cook, Robin. *Mutation*. New York: G.P. Putnam's Sons, 1989. This novel is a medical thriller about genetic engineering.

Dodge, Mary Mapes. "The Minuet," in *One Hundred and One Famous Poems*, ed. Roy J. Cook. Chicago: The Cable Company, 1928. A poet recalls her grandmother's tales of what it was like to be a young woman in America in the nineteenth century.

Dunbar, Paul. "Sympathy," in *Black Writers of America*. New York: Macmillan and Co., 1972. Dunbar, the son of a slave, reflects on the idea of freedom in a moving poem.

Frost, Robert. "The Road Not Taken," in *An Introduction to Robert Frost*. New York: Holt Rinehart Winston, 1971. A poet considers making an important decision at a crossroads in life.

Hansberry, Lorraine. *A Raisin in the Sun*. New York: Random House, 1958. The experiences of an African-American family living in a predominantly white neighborhood in the 1950s are dramatized in this play.

Henley, Beth. *Crimes of the Heart*. New York: Viking Press, 1982. This play is a comedy in which three sisters work out some of their differences and re-establish their family ties.

Hillerman, Tony. *The Ghostway*. New York: Avon Books, 1984. In one of a series of mystery novels, a well-known fiction author relates the investigations of a Navajo detective.

Ibsen, Henrik. *A Doll's House*, in *Four Great Plays*, translated by R. Farquharson Sharp. New York: Bantam Books, 1959, reprinted 1962. This play, written in the mid-nineteenth century, is a social drama. It tells about the tensions in a marriage and is an early example of a drama dealing with women's rights.

Jackson, Helen Hunt. *Ramona*. Boston: Little, Brown and Company, 1884, reprinted 1939. This novel tells the story of a romance between an Hispanic woman and a Native American man during the time when the West was being settled. It was one of the earliest literary works to examine the mistreatment of Native Americans.

Keller, Helen. *The Story of My Life*. Garden City, New York: Doubleday and Company, Inc., 1954. This autobiography is the inspiring story of a woman who achieved international fame and success in spite of the physical disabilities of being blind and deaf.

King, Martin Luther, Jr. "I Have a Dream," in *The Writer's Craft*, eds. Sheena Gillespie, Robert Singleton, and Robert Becker. Glenview, Illinois: Scott, Foresman and Company, 1986. A leading civil-rights activist made this famous speech during a protest march on Washington, D.C., in 1963.

King, Stephen. *Salem's Lot*. New York: A Signet Book, New American Library, 1975. This novel tells the story of a small town terrorized by vampires. Stephen King is one of the United States' most popular thriller writers.

Lee, C. Y. *The Flower Drum Song*. New York: Grosset and Dunlap, 1957. The conflicts between cultures and generations are played out in this novel about a Chinese-American family.

Mathis, Cleopatra. "Getting Out," in *Sound and Sense*, ed. Laurence Perrine, 7th edition. New York: Harcourt Brace Jovanovich, 1987. The breakup of a marriage is described from a woman's point of view.

Meltzer, Milton. *Langston Hughes: A Biography*. New York: Thomas Y. Crowell Company, 1968. The life story and struggles of the African-American poet Langston Hughes are described in this biography. See also Hughes, Langston.

Moore, Kenny. "A Courageous Stand," in *Sports Illustrated*. Vol. 75:6, August 5, 1991, pp. 62–73. This magazine article recounts a protest against racial discrimination made by two American athletes at the 1968 Olympics.

Naylor, Gloria. *The Women of Brewster Place*. New York: Penguin Books, 1982. This novel follows the lives and complex relationships of several women in an inner-city neighborhood.

Neihardt, John G. *Black Elk Speaks*. Lincoln, Nebraska: The University of Nebraska Press, 1961. A holy man of the Oglala Sioux tells the dramatic true story of his travels in the United States and Europe.

Poe, Edgar Allan. "The Tell-Tale Heart," in *Complete Tales and Poems*. New York: The Modern Library, 1938. One of the earliest mystery and thriller writers sends chills up the reader's spine with this story of murder and obsession.

Reeves, Robyn. *The Tomorrow Radio*, in *On Stage, A Readers' Theater Collection*. Austin, Texas: Steck-Vaughn Co., 1992. In this modern science-fiction drama, two scientists accidently discover a way to know what will happen in the future. The play also shows the difficulty they face convincing other people to believe in their discovery.

Robinson, Edwin A. "Richard Cory," in *Sound and Sense*, ed. Laurence Perrine, 7th edition. New York: Harcourt Brace Jovanovich, 1987. This poem was written by the first winner of the Pulitzer Prize for poetry. The poem suggests that people are not always what they seem to be.

Rooney, Andy. "Street Directions," in *And More by Andy Rooney*. New York: Atheneum, 1982. A TV commentator takes a humorous look at giving, receiving, and trying to follow directions.

Steinbeck, John. *The Grapes of Wrath*. New York: Penguin, 1939, reprinted 1987. The terrible effects of the Great Depression of the 1930s are described in this novel. It is about an Oklahoma farming family who was forced to leave their farm and move to California.

Tan, Amy. "Double Face," in *The Joy Luck Club*. New York: Ivy Books/Ballantine Books, 1989. This collection of connected short stories describes how the conflicts between people of different generations can be complicated by changes in cultural values.

Walker, James. "A Picture on the Mantel," in *Contemporary Poets of America*. Bryn Mawr, Pennsylvania: Dorrance and Company, Inc., 1985. A modern poet tells about the emotions of a little boy whose mother has died.

Woolf, Virginia. "Thoughts on Peace in an Air Raid," in *The Death of a Moth and Other Essays*. New York and London: Harcourt Brace Jovanovich, 1942. An English novelist expresses her opinions on war and peace.

Pages 259–260 constitute an extension of the copyright page.

Grateful acknowledgment is made to the following authors, agents, and publishers for permission to use copyrighted materials. Every effort has been made to trace ownership of all copyrighted material and to secure the necessary permissions to reprint. We express regret in advance for any error or omission. Any oversight will be acknowledged in future printings.

p. 4 — From *Sosa: An Autobiography* by Sammy Sosa. Copyright © 2000 by Sammy Sosa. Reprinted by permission of Warner Books, Inc.

p. 6 — Reprinted by permission of GRM Associates, Inc., Agents for the Ann Elmo Agency, from the book FLOWER DRUM SONG by C.Y. Lee. Copyright © 1960 by C.Y. Lee; copyright renewed 1988 by C.Y. Lee.

p. 8 — Excerpt from Act III of "A Doll's House" by Henrik Ibsen, translated by R. Farquharson Sharp and E. Marks-Aveling from *The Complete Major Prose Plays of Henrik Ibsen*. Reprinted by permission of Everyman Publishers Plc.

pp. 41–43 — From *Langston Hughes: A Biography*. Text copyright © 1997 by Milton Meltzer. Reprinted by permission of The Millbrook Press, Inc. All rights reserved.

pp. 47–49 — From *Luiz W. Alvarez* by Corinn Codye. Copyright © 1991, Steck-Vaughn Company.

pp. 53–55 — Reprinted from *Black Elk Speaks: Being the Life Story of a Holy Man of The Oglala Sioux* as told through John G. Neihardt (Flaming Rainbow) by Nicholas Black Elk by permission of the University of Nebraska Press. Copyright © 1961 by the John G. Neihardt Trust. © 2000 by the University of Nebraska Press.

pp. 59–60 — "Street Directions" reprinted with the permission of Scribner, a Division of Simon & Schuster from *And More by Andy Rooney* by Andrew A. Rooney. Copyright © 1982 Essay Productions, Inc.

p. 61 — Excerpt from "Back When a Dollar Was a Dollar" by Diane C. Arkins from USA Today, November 2, 1989, p. 10A.

pp. 65–67 — Excerpts from "Thoughts on Peace in an Air Raid" in *The Death of the Moth and Other Essays* by Virginia Woolf, copyright 1942 by Harcourt, Inc. and renewed 1970 by Marjorie T. Parsons, Executrix, reprinted by permission of the publisher.

pp. 71–73 — Reprinted courtesy of *Sports Illustrated:* "A Courageous Stand" by Kenny Moore, August 5, 1991. Copyright © 1991, Time Inc. All rights reserved.

pp. 77–79 — Excerpt from "E! Entertainment Television explores 'Royalty A–Z'" by Nancy McAlister, as found in *The Herald News* Television section, August 18–24, 2002. Reprinted by permission of the author.

pp. 83–85 — "Life's Peculiar Events Explain 'Why I'm Like This.' " Copyright 2002, *USA Today*. Reprinted with permission.

p. 90 — Excerpt from "Bruce Rising" in *Time Magazine*, August 5, 2002. Copyright © 2002 TIME Inc. Reprinted by permission.

p. 92 — Review of "Star Time: James Brown" by David Hiltbrand from People Weekly, 6/10/91. David Hiltbrand/ People Weekly, copyright © 1991, Time Inc. Reprinted by permission.

p. 94 — Excerpt from "I Have a Dream" by Martin Luther King, Jr. Reprinted by arrangement with the Estate of Martin Luther King, Jr., c/o Writers House, Inc. as agent for the proprietor, New York, NY. Copyright 1963 by Dr. Martin Luther King, Jr., copyright renewed 1991 by Coretta Scott King.

p. 97 — Movie review of *Lord of the Rings: Fellowship of the Ring*, entitled "It's Hobbit-forming" by Chris Hewitt, from St. Paul Pioneer Press, Dec. 19th, 2001. Reprinted by permission of St. Paul Pioneer Press.

pp. 101–103 — Excerpt from *The Ghostway* by Tony Hillerman. Copyright © 1984 by Tony Hillerman. Reprinted by permission of HarperCollins Publishers, Inc.

pp. 107–109 — From *I, Robot* by Isaac Asimov. Copyright 1950 by Isaac Asimov. Used by permission of Doubleday, a division of Random House, Inc.

adventure story a work of literature in which the characters take risks

advertisement a public notice designed to attract attention or customers

applying ideas taking an idea and using it in another situation

autobiography the true story of a real person's life written by that person

bias a strong preference for a particular point of view

biographer the writer of a biography

biography the true story of a real person's life written by another person

brochure a booklet or pamphlet containing informative or advertising material

cause a person, thing, or event that brings about a result

character a person in a story or a play

classic literature literature that has set a high standard of excellence, remains meaningful, and continues to be read after many years

comedy a play that is meant to be funny

compare to find the ways things are alike

conclusion a judgment or opinion based on facts and details

conflict a struggle or problem between characters or forces

context clues the words and sentences surrounding a word or phrase. The context of a word helps show what that word means.

contrast to find the ways things are different

detail a fact about a person, place, thing, event, or time. Details answer the questions *who, what, when, where, why,* and *how.*

dialogue the conversation between characters

document an official paper used as the basis, proof, or support for something

drama a story written in dialogue and meant to be acted on a stage

the result of a cause

a short piece of nonfiction writing that gives the author's opinion about something

fact a statement that can be proved true

fiction writing that is about people, places, and events invented by the author

figurative language words used in a special way to make a point. Personification is an example.

folk novel an elaborate work of fiction that people tell over and over for generations. Folk novels explain people's beliefs of how things began and include many events, people, and experiences.

folktale a story that people tell over and over for many generations. Folktales often explain how people believe things began.

form a printed document with blank spaces to be filled in with specific information

handbook a concise reference book covering a particular subject

head a headline; an important main caption or title

implied main idea a main idea that is not directly stated but is suggested by the author

inference an idea that the reader figures out based on clues an author presents and what the reader already knows

legal document an official paper based on laws

magazine article an informational piece that appears in a magazine

main idea the most important point in a paragraph or passage

manual a reference book used to give instructions on how to do something or operate something

mood the atmosphere the author creates in a written work

mystery novel a story about solving a puzzle. The main character of a mystery is usually a detective who has to figure out who committed a crime.

narrator the character telling the story

nonfiction writing that is about real people, places, and events

novel a long work of fiction that can include many events, people, and experiences

opinion a judgment or belief

personification a type of figurative language that gives human qualities to something that is not human. Example: The leaves danced in the wind.

persuasive essay an essay that is meant to get the reader to think or act a certain way

play a story that is written in dialogue and is meant to be acted on a stage

plot the series of events that create the action of a story

poet a writer of poetry

poetry literature that uses words in special ways to show feelings and create images. Poetry is usually arranged in short lines.

point of view the way the action is seen by the narrator or author of a story

popular drama recently written plays

popular fiction recently written works including short stories, novels, and plays. Fiction comes from the author's imagination.

popular novel a recently written book about people and events that are not real

popular poetry recently written poetry

popular short story a recently written work of fiction that is shorter than a novel but has a full plot and a single theme

predict to tell what you think will happen in the future

preview to look at something beforehand

purpose the reason something is done

restating to say something again using different words

review a short piece of writing that tells what a writer or critic thinks of a book, movie, TV program, musical performance, or work of art

rhythm the repetition of sounds or phrases that make up the beat of a poem

scan to look at quickly; to browse for specific information

science fiction fictional stories based on the possibilities found in science. Science fiction shows what life and people might be like in another time or place, usually in the future.

sequence the order in which events occur; time order

setting the time and place in which the events of a story take place

short story a work of fiction that is shorter than a novel but has a full plot and a single theme

skim to read something quickly, looking for main ideas and main characters

social drama a play that deals with a major social issue

stage directions the directions in a play that tell the actors where to move on the stage or how to say their lines

stated main idea a statement that clearly tells the most important point of a paragraph or story. To restate a main idea means to put it in different words.

subhead a heading of a part (as in an outline); a caption, title, or heading of less importance than the main heading

summarize to state briefly the most important ideas of a longer piece of writing

summary a short statement of the main idea and most important supporting details of a passage

synonyms words that have the same or nearly the same meaning. Example: *paste* and *glue*

synthesizing putting together several elements to form a whole idea

theme a general truth about life or human nature that is suggested in a work of literature

thriller novel a work of fiction that is meant to scare the reader; also called a horror novel

tone the author's attitude or feeling about a subject

visualize to form a picture in your mind